GENDER IN THIRD WORLD POLITICS

ISSUES IN THIRD WORLD POLITICS

Series Editor: Vicky Randall, Department of Government,
University of Essex.

Current titles:
Heather Deegan: The Middle East and problems of democracy
Jeff Haynes: Religion in Third World politics
Robert Pinkney: Democracy in the Third World
Georgina Waylen: Gender in Third World politics

GENDER IN THIRD WORLD POLITICS

Georgina Waylen

LYNNE
RIENNER
PUBLISHERS

BOULDER

Published in the United States of America in 1996 by
Lynne Rienner Publishers, Inc.
1800 30th Street, Boulder, Colorado

Library of Congress Cataloging-in-Publication Data
Waylen, Georgina.
    Gender in Third World politics / Georgina Waylen.
        p.   cm. — (Issues in Third World politics)
    Includes bibliographical references and index.
    ISBN 1–55587–650–1 (hc: alk. paper). — ISBN 1–55587–633–1 (pbk.:
    alk. paper)
    1. Developing countries—Politics and government.   2. Women in
development.   3. Women in politics—Developing countries.   4. Sex
role—Developing countries.   5. Feminist theory.   I. Title.
II. Series.
JF60W39   1995
320.9172'4'082—dc20   95–48802
                                                                     CIP

Printed and bound in Great Britain

Contents

Series editor's introduction

When I was invited to edit this series, I thought long and hard about what it should be called. I ended up going back to the well-worn phrase 'Third World' but recognizing that this very term raises problems that both this Introduction and the books in the series would need to address. Its advantage is that to most people it signals something fairly clear cut and recognizable. The expression 'Third World' has come to connote the regions and individual countries of Africa, Asia, the Caribbean, Latin America and the Middle East. It is the politics, in the broadest sense, of this part of the world, and of its relationship with the rest of the world, that constitutes the subject matter of this series.

Yet the notion of a single 'Third World' has always been problematic. When it became clear that the nations so designated were not going to follow a third, 'non-aligned', economic and political route between the capitalist West and the communist world, it was argued that they none the less shared a common predicament. Directly or indirectly they suffered the after-effects of colonization and they came late and on disadvantageous terms into the competitive world economy. Even then there was tremendous variety – in culture, experience of colonial rule, forms and levels of economic activity – between and within Third World regions.

Over time this internal differentiation seems to have grown. On the one hand we have the oil-rich states and the Newly Industrializing Countries (NICs), on the other the World Bank has identified a 'Fourth World' of lower income countries like Bangladesh or Tanzania, distinguished from the lower-middle income countries like Mexico and Malaysia. Then from the later 1980s we have witnessed the disintegration of most of the 'Second World' of state socialist societies – where does that leave the First and the Third?

These developments certainly threaten the coherence of the concept of a Third World. They must make us wonder whether the concept is any longer plausible or useful in categorizing what are by now well over 100 countries, containing three-quarters of the world's population. Recently writers both on the Right and on the Left have suggested that the notion of a Third World functions primarily as a myth: for the former it is a projection of the guilt of First World liberals while for the latter it evokes for the West a reassuring image of its own opposite, all that it has succeeded in not becoming.

The arguments are not all one way, however. When Nigel Harris writes about the 'end of the Third World' and its dissolution into one world economic system, he is referring to objective economic trends which still have a long way to go and which are by no means automatically accompanied by a decline in Western economic nationalism or cultural chauvinism. Third World countries do still at least some of the time recognize their common status *vis-à-vis* the developed world and the need to stick together, as was apparent at the Rio Earth Summit in June 1992. The fact that some Third World nations may have 'made it' into the developed world, does not negate the existence of the Third World they have left behind. It does, however, undermine the more deterministic arguments of dependency theorists, who have maintained that it is impossible to break out of economic dependence and underdevelopment. The dissolution of the Second World, it could be argued, leaves the confrontation and contrast between First and Third World starker than ever (this might of course indicate the use of a different nomenclature, such as North and South). On the other hand the countries of the old Second World will not be transformed overnight into members of the First and there is a case for retaining a Second World category to refer to countries only recently emerged from a prolonged period of communist rule.

But my purpose here is not to insist on the continuing usefulness of the notion of a Third World so much as to signal the question as part of the agenda I hope that authors in this series will address. It seems to me that there *are* respects in which most of the countries conventionally included in the Third World do continue to share a common predicament and about which it is up to a point legitimate to generalize. But unless we also explore the differences between them, our powers of political explanation will be limited and it may be that it is these differences which now hold answers to the most important and interesting questions we want to ask.

For a long time, and despite the growing impact of second-wave feminism on the social sciences in general, studies of Third World politics, including, I fear, my own, largely neglected the issue of gender. More recently a considerable literature has emerged providing a gender dimension on particular questions, countries or regions. *Gender in Third World politics* is, however, the first text that brings this discussion together. Georgina Waylen's exploration of this important topic offers an excellent introduction, that combines theoretical perspectives with substantive themes in a clear and convincing synthesis.

Vicky Randall

Abbreviations

AMNLAE	Louisa Amanda Espinoza Association of Nicaraguan Women
AMPRONAC	Association of Women Confronting the National Problem
ANC	African National Congress
AWU	Abeokuta Women's Union
BA	bureaucratic authoritarian
CDS	Sandinista Defence Committee
CEMAs	mothers' centres
CONAPRO	National Confederation of Professional Organizations
CONAVIGUA	National Coordinator of Widows of Guatemala
DAWN	Development Alternatives for a New Era
DFI	direct foreign investment
EOI	export orientated industrialization
EPF	El Poder Feminino
FMC	Federation of Cuban Women
FMS	Federacion de Mujeres Socialistas
FORD	Forum for the Restoration of Democracy
FRELIMO	Front for the Liberation of Mozambique
FSLN	Sandinista Front for National Liberation
GABRIELA	General Assembly Binding Women for Reforms, Integrity, Leadership and Action
GAD	gender and development
GAM	Mutual Support Group
GATT	General Agreement on Tariffs and Trade
GDP	gross domestic product
GNP	gross national product
G77	Group of 77 [Third World states]
IBRD	International Bank for Reconstruction and Development
IDS	Institute of Development Studies
ILO	International Labour Organization

IMF	International Monetary Fund
INC	Indian National Congress
ISI	import substituting industrialization
ITO	international trade organization
KANU	Kenya African National Union
KMT	Kuo Min Tang
LDCs	less developed countries
LLDCs	least developed countries
LMWA	Lagos Market Women's Association
MARS	Women's Self-Defence League
MEMCH	Movimiento Pro-emancipación de la Mujer Chilena
MMD	Movement for Multi-party Democracy
MNCs	multinational corporations
MOMUPO	Movimiento de Mujeres Pobladoras
MPLA	People's Movement for the Liberation of Angola
NAM	non-aligned movement
NGO	non-governmental organization
NICs	newly industrializing countries
NLF	National Liberation Front
OEPs	popular economic organizations
OMA	Organization of Angolan Women
OMM	Organization of Mozambican Women
OPEC	Organization of Petroleum Exporting Countries
pa	per annum
PAIGC	African Party for the Independence of Guinea and Cape Verde
PH	Partido Humanista
PMDB	Party of the Brazilian Democratic Movement
PNC	People's National Congress
PPD	Party for Democracy
PRI	Party of the Institutionalized Revolution
PT	Worker's Party
RENAMO	Mozambique National Resistance
SAP	structural adjustment programme
SERNAM	Servicio Nacional de la Mujer
SEWA	Self-employed Women's Association
SMP	Patriotic Military Service
SNM	National Secretariat for Women
SOW	Subordination of Women
SWAPO	South West Africa People's Organization
TANU	Tanganyika African National Union
UCR	Radical Civic Union
UN	United Nations
UNCTAD	United Nations Commission for Trade and Development
UNIP	United National Independence Party
UNO	United National Opposition

USAID	United States Agency for International Development
WID	women in development
WIN	Women in Nigeria
WIZER	Women in Zambia for Equality and Representation
ZANU	Zimbabwe African National Union
ZAPU	Zimbabwe African People's Union

Acknowledgements

I would like to thank my editor, Vicky Randall for all her help, patience and encouragement and all those friends and colleagues who read part of this book in draft form: they are Paul Cammack, Laura Chrisman, Ann Hughes and Maxine Molyneux, and Scott McCracken who read all of it. The responsibility for the final product, of course, remains mine.

Introduction

This book provides a gendered analysis of both 'high politics' in the Third World and a study of women's grassroots political activities. In so doing, it attempts to bring together what have up until now been relatively separate strands within different literatures. In order to provide a gendered analysis of *both* 'high' and 'low' politics, it utilizes a broad definition of what counts as political. As a result the book provides a detailed analysis of both formal politics in the conventional arena – in all its different forms – ranging from competitive electoral politics to revolutionary governments, military and authoritarian regimes and the politics of transition. In addition it looks at the varying forms taken by the political activities of different groups of women outside the conventional arena, both in terms of their engagement with the state and political parties, and their autonomous activities.

The book does not outline a definitive approach to the study of gender in Third World politics but attempts to provide guidelines. Some of the themes covered will be specific to the Third World, while others will also be relevant to the more general study of gender and politics. The book is based on a number of propositions about the relationship between gender and politics. First, 'politics' does not have the same impact on women as it does on men, and this differential impact needs to be investigated. Second, the political process often alters gender relations, that is relations between men and women, and this needs to be explored. Third, women often participate as political subjects in political activity in different ways to men, which raises questions about the distinctiveness of 'women's political activity' – should it be classified and analysed as a separate entity? Addressing these questions has important implications for the study of politics as it has been conventionally undertaken.

It would seem natural to look to conventional political science literature for guidance in this endeavour, but this literature gives rise to several problems. Compared to some other social sciences such as sociology and anthropology and the humanities such as literary and critical studies, orthodox political science has been slow to incorporate a gendered perspective into its approach (Silverberg 1990). This is, in part, inherent in the nature of the discipline of politics. Its traditional subject matter – 'high politics' (treaties, wars, and power politics) – involves areas typically dominated by men; this is equally true of the institutional politics of parties, executives and legislatures. Nonetheless, political science has traditionally treated these areas as gender neutral. The literature on Third World politics, either seen on its own or as a subset of comparative politics, is no exception to this pattern. Basic texts such as Clapham (1985) either make no mention of gender issues, or where they do as in Cammack *et al.* (1993), it is in the form of a separate chapter leaving the rest of the analysis and argument unscathed. The vast majority of more detailed research is also gender blind. For a book of this kind, much of the mainstream literature can therefore provide background material but little more. However, this book does not emerge from a vacuum, and as such critically utilizes some of the orthodox literature as its starting point. While rejecting some existing frameworks, it does attempt to gender others, an act which in itself I believe forms a profound challenge to those frameworks.

There is also a large and growing body of literature, much of it interdisciplinary, which addresses many issues relevant to the study of gender in Third World politics. This book draws upon that work. Any study involving the analysis of gender must inevitably owe a great debt to feminism in all its many forms. One consequence of the second wave of feminism is that there has been a huge increase in the amount of academic work since the early 1970s devoted to improving both the empirical knowledge of and analytical approaches to women and gender relations in the Third World. Much of this literature comes from disciplines other than political science, such as development studies, sociology, geography and anthropology. This has been accompanied by a wealth of theoretical analyses enquiring more abstractly into the nature of gender from a variety of disciplinary perspectives including critical theory, philosophy and political theory.

Within the discipline of politics, there are now an increasing number of feminist academics trying to change the nature of the discipline from the inside. They have already made significant advances. One key area in the discussions of gender relations and politics has been the public/private split. This notion has both informed orthodox accounts and inspired feminist critiques (Pateman 1983a). Much of this literature has been written in a Western context, and despite its often universalist tone, is about the First World. However, because many of the ideas and concepts have influenced political activity and its analysis in the Third World, it is important to consider them here. Stretching back to contract theorists of the seventeenth and eighteenth centuries and beyond, most of the political theory which underlies Western liberal democracy and liberal democratic theory has its roots in the separation of the public and the private. Beginning with Locke, the private domestic sphere was seen as lying outside the proper realms of investigation and interference by the state or others. The public sphere was seen as the arena where the individual was incorporated as a citizen into the political world. Few links were made between the two spheres, and theoretical attention was focused on the public arena. Domestic life and the private sphere were assumed to be irrelevant to social and political theory. Individual citizens active in the public sphere were implicitly assumed to be male heads of household, and most analyses relegated women to the private sphere, where they were subsumed within a household headed by the individual male. This formulation ignores both the links between the two spheres, and varying role played by the state in constructing the boundary between them.

The assumptions underlying the separation of the public and the private are of huge significance to the study of gender and politics. Political theory, while appearing gender neutral, by maintaining a division between private and political life as central to liberal democracy, maintains a division between men and women, where only men can be abstract individuals (Pateman 1983b, 1989). The political is therefore defined as masculine in a very profound sense which makes it hard to incorporate women on the same terms as men and excludes many of those activities that women are involved in as not political. This is combined with an approach which sets up frameworks and theories which, while appearing gender neutral, work to exclude women. It is not enough then just to get a better understanding of the role of women in formal politics. A wider analysis, using broader definitions of the political, is needed.

With this in mind, this book attempts not just to be an empirical study of one area of the world, but also to further the theoretical debates about how to approach the study of gender and politics. It draws upon a number of the developments in feminist theorizing which have occurred since the 1970s to provide the type of wider analysis that is needed. As we will see in Chapter 1, it builds on the questions and categories introduced by feminist academics in the 1970s, as well as some of the more recent insights which have emerged from the poststructuralist/postmodernist critiques of the 1980s, particularly those surrounding notions of difference and the construction of identity. However, the majority of the bulk of existing literature on gender in the Third World comes from within a liberal or socialist feminist framework, and little has been written so far addressing the questions raised by postmodern approaches. This book is therefore inevitably constrained by the nature of the literature available. For example, as will be apparent in the chapter on revolutions, most of the studies have been written by socialist feminists and therefore focus on certain issues to the exclusion of others.

It would be impossible for a book of this type to be geographically comprehensive in its coverage. As we will see in Chapter 2, the very utility of the term Third World is being increasingly questioned. Despite my own misgivings as to its continued usefulness, I have taken what some might consider to be an overly restricted definition, in that I have excluded from the discussion any sustained analysis of the Middle East. I did this because of a number of factors: the Middle East's particular history of colonialism; the role played by oil; the impact of the Arab–Israeli conflict; and the role of religion – all factors which I believe make an adequate analysis of the Middle East impossible within the structure of this book. The related issue of the nature of Islam and Islamic states and their impact on gender relations, while profoundly important, is also beyond the scope of a book of this type. Fortunately anyone interested in this area will be able to follow the growing literature on the subject.

There is also no sustained discussion of the gendered nature of religious, particularly fundamentalist, movements, in part because the book is structured around the discussion of political formations. The influence of Islamic, Jewish, Hindu and Christian (primarily Protestant) fundamentalism is increasing in many parts of the Third World. The majority of these movements have particular roles for the women involved in them and depend on particular visions of the ideal arrangement of gender relations.

As the Third World is such a large and diverse area, to try and avoid some of the worst excesses of overgeneralization, the book focuses on four political formations: colonialism, revolution, authoritarianism, and democratization. It therefore provides a gendered analysis of some of the standard themes of comparative politics, rather than a study of gender in Third World politics which moves wholly outside these existing frameworks and categories and which might be organized very differently. This focus entails a thematic rather than a country based or regional focus, and different chapters concentrate on one area or on several case studies rather than trying to be comprehensive in their coverage of the Third World in contrast to works such as Nelson and Chowdhury (1994). Chapter 1 uses the theoretical discussion to set up a loose framework with which to examine each formation and Chapter 2 provides background by exploring the nature of the Third World and development. Chapter 3 examines colonialism as one of the key influences which shaped not only gender relations in the contemporary Third World. It concentrates on the African and Indian experience, in part because of its recentness and in part because of the recent growth of a large and innovative literature on gender and colonialism in these regions. Chapters 4, 5 and 6 deal with three of the most significant Third World political formations of the postwar period: revolution, authoritarianism and democratization. The discussion of revolutionary movements ranges widely over the Third World, while the examination of revolutionary regimes focuses on three very different case studies: Cuba, Mozambique and Nicaragua. The analysis of authoritarianism combines a general discussion of one party states and personal dictatorships in the Third World with an in-depth analysis of military regimes in Latin America as the area where the most sustained gendered analyses have occurred. Similarly the discussion of democratization looks at transitions from neo-patrimonial regimes, particularly in Africa, but concentrates on Latin America as the region which at the time of writing, has been the most thoroughly researched. Each chapter follows the same basic structure. After a brief introduction which sets out the topic, sections follow on gender relations in formal politics, the nature of state policies and women's political activities outside the conventional political arena.

1

Analysing gender in the politics of the Third World

Introduction

This chapter will outline some of the issues involved in the analysis of gender in Third World politics. The inadequacy of the conventional politics litera- ture indicates that several things have to be done. First, women have to be put back into the study of formal politics. But gender should not be 'added in' to the analysis of political processes at the expense of other forms of social relations such as class and ethnicity. Second, it is necessary to make clear how ostensibly neutral political processes and concepts such as nationalism, citizen- ship and the state, are fundamentally gendered. Third, it is not enough simply to reintegrate women as actors in the study of conventional politics. Those activities women are typically involved in outside the male dominated institu- tional sphere must also be included in any analyses. This challenge to the conventional construction of the political is crucially important, as without it much of women's political activity can be dismissed or marginalized as it does not fit easily into conventional categories and, as a result, the important role it plays in the political process will be ignored. Before doing this, it is useful to consider the development of gender as an analytic category.

Gender as an analytic category

Feminist academics have debated whether to focus primarily on 'women' or on 'gender'. This debate has encompassed both intellectual and political arguments and raises more complex issues than might at first appear. Those advocating a focus on 'women' have argued that a book about gender will inevitably be predominantly about women, rather than gender as an analytic category, and that a reluctance to make this explicit is due to a desire to sound 'academic', that is more respectable, less political and therefore more acceptable within the academy. There are several strong counter arguments to this position. First, as we will see, there are so many difficulties associated with the use of the term 'woman' that it cannot be used as a catch-all category, disregarding difference in terms of race, class and sexuality, in any simplistic way. Second, focusing on 'women' can result in women being 'added in' without any fundamental transformation of disciplines occurring. Third and most importantly, using the term 'gender' demonstrates the interconnectedness of relations between men and women, which might be lost in a focus on women alone. This book will not just have women as its subject matter, although inevitably this will provide a large focus, but will also analyse the nature of the social relations between men and women.

The term 'gender' has been used widely over the past two decades. Initially it was utilized, particularly by social scientists, to describe a fundamental axis of social differentiation, alongside class and race. Many sociologists and psychologists used gender in a simplistic way almost synonymous with socialization. The construction of gender difference was seen in terms of boys and girls being socialized into different roles. Of particular importance was the notion that gender was a social construct, and therefore observed gender differences were seen as the product of social relations. This problematizing of gender had a huge significance (Flax 1987: 627). Within this framework, many characteristics which had been considered the result of inherent biological differences and as such natural, universal and unchanging, were the product of social relations. If gender differences are historically and culturally specific and what it means to be a man or a women varies over place and time, then the variations need to be investigated and, if desired, political programmes can be instituted to alter gender differences.

The understanding of gender has become more sophisticated and complex. More recently, the influence of other disciplines and deconstructive and psychoanalytic theories has moved the emphasis towards an analysis of the construction of gendered subjectivities. The influence of Freud, Lacan and Derrida has been important as well as French feminists such as Kristeva and Irigaray (Butler 1989). As a result, attention has been focused on the ways in which masculinity and femininity are constructed in the individual subject rather than seeing gender as a set of roles into which people are socialized.

Much of the interest in gender relations is due to feminism. Feminists of all descriptions have characterized gender relations as relations of inequality and subordination. There have, however, been important developments in the ways in which these relations have been theorized and understood. The 1970s was dominated by feminist academics searching for origins of unequal gender relations and trying to find explanations and causes for these relations of subordination (Barrett and Phillips 1992: 2–3). As we will see in succeeding chapters, much of the work on gender in the Third World has been influenced by liberal feminism and socialist feminism, two of the three strands which were important in this period.

It is radical feminism and socialist feminism which formed the two major analytical camps dominant in the 1970s. Both strands believe that societies are fundamentally structured around profound inequalities in gender relations and both use the term 'patriarchy' to describe such systems of male dominance. However they differ as to the causes and solutions. Radical feminists argue that gender divisions are the most profound division within society and that all societies are patriarchal. They believe that men as a group oppress women, and that men benefit from that oppression. Put simply, men are the problem. As a result the radical feminist analysis highlighted certain issues which hitherto had been neglected. They directed attention towards the control exercised by men over women's sexuality, their reproductive capacity and its role in their oppression (Firestone 1970; Brownmiller 1975). In political terms this resulted in campaigns centring around sexual violence and pornography. Radical feminists have been criticized for being essentialist and biologically reductionist; that is, that their approach is rooted in the belief that men are somehow destined to oppress women and that they are unable to provide a non-biological explanation of why this should be the case.

Socialist feminists, while sharing a structural analysis of women's oppression and using the term patriarchy, differ from radical feminists on several important points. They are influenced by Marxism, but believe that it has strong limitations, due primarily to its concentration on class differences, which makes it 'sex-blind' (Hartmann 1981) and therefore unable to provide an adequate analysis of women's subordination. But socialist feminists often use the work of Engels, examining gender relations in the spheres of production that is paid employment, and reproduction that is the reproduction of the labour force in the domestic sphere, and the links between them. Socialist feminists therefore believe that capitalism plays a role in the oppression of women but that this is not the only factor. In capitalist patriarchy, while capitalism did not create women's oppression it has often used and transformed it (Barrett 1981).

Liberal feminism is the third and perhaps the most diverse strand. It is less concerned with finding structural explanations for women's subordination than either socialist or radical feminism. Instead it sees the socialization of men and women into different roles, reinforced by discrimination, prejudice and irrationality, as responsible for women's unequal position in society. The solutions to inequality are changes which will give women a better deal within the existing system such as legal changes and the promotion of equal opportunities, allowing women access to things on the same terms as men. Liberal feminism has been criticized for its overly individualistic approach and its lack of a coherent analysis of women's oppression.

These feminist approaches, dominant in the 1970s, came in for profound criticism in the 1980s. They had often taken for granted the notion of 'woman' as a unitary and ahistorical category. Some had treated women as one homogeneous group, making the assumption that it was both possible and unproblematic to generalize about all women and their interests. This often meant that the experience of white, middle-class and Western women was generalized to black, working-class and Third World women. As part of a sea change in theoretical debates, the different ways in which the category 'woman' has been constructed historically have been explored (Riley 1988). The notion of a 'women's interest' shared by all women regardless of race, class and sexuality became highly contested. It is impossible to say, in any uncomplicated way, that all women are oppressed by all men. As a result the need to forge commonality across difference through alliances and coalitions becomes a key issue within feminism.

This critique had particular implications for analyses of Third World women made by First World feminists and academics (Spivak 1987). First, many analyses were informed by notions, paralleling ideas about the common oppression of women, that 'sisterhood is global', i.e. that there was more uniting women of different races, classes and sexualities than dividing them. This was often expressed in various cross-cultural analyses of patriarchy. Second, when difference was actually acknowledged it was often done by turning all Third World women into a non-Western 'other'. As we will see in Chapter 2, the 'women in development' literature, in particular, is often marked out for displaying these characteristics – treating all Third World women as the same, whether they were, for example, upper-class urban educated professionals or lower-class rural peasant women and advocating general 'solutions' to various perceived problems which affected them from the framework of a universal homogenizing feminism. This had the effect of removing agency from Third World women, by seeing them as objects rather than subjects and as passive victims of barbaric and primitive practices (Lazreg 1988; Mohanty 1988, 1991; Ong 1988).

Three major elements have contributed to the breakdown of this kind of universal theorizing (Barrett and Phillips 1992). First, black women have provided a powerful challenge to much of the work of white feminists, arguing that their analyses were imbued with racist and ethnocentric assumptions, again generalizing the experience of white feminists to black women (Moraga and Anzaldua 1983; hooks 1984). Second, the re-emergence of the 'equality versus difference' debate broke down the confident distinctions between sex as a biological category and gender as a social construct. In some quarters (often women–centred or radical feminist) sexual difference came to be celebrated rather than denied (Scott 1988). Debates moved on to ask how to deal with embodiment, arguing that it is not difference that is the problem, but how it is constructed and dealt with (Bock and James 1992). Third, the feminist challenge to mainstream theorizing has been paralleled by the post-structuralist and postmodern critiques of the universal grand frameworks which characterized enlightenment thought and have heralded the end of the metanarrative (Nicholson 1990). There has been a shift from 'things', that is an emphasis on structures so favoured by a social science approach, to 'words', an emphasis on language and discourse derived from literary and critical theory (Barrett 1992). Form and representation become much more important if language is no longer seen as transparently and directly reflecting 'reality' but as playing a significant role in the construction of that reality.

Interest in notions of identity and the ways in which subjects are constructed has therefore increased. This has been accompanied by the fracturing of the Cartesian unitary human subject and the self so beloved of rationalist enlightenment thought to be replaced by multiple subject identities, notions of difference, plurality and multiplicity. Identity is seen as complex and a combination of different elements such as class, race, gender and sexuality, rather than simply one factor (Butler and Scott 1992). Therefore a plurality of identities exist in the single subject. At the same time, there is also a greater recognition of diversity and difference between women. According to Scott (1992), the task becomes one of seeing how subjects' identities are constructed through 'experience' and discourse without essentializing them. Subject's identities are created through agency, and this agency is 'created through situations and statuses conferred upon them' (Scott 1992: 34). Within this kind of framework, politics becomes a discourse by which people 'determine who they are and who they shall become as social beings' (Schild 1991: 140).

As a consequence of these theoretical developments, the study of gender relations has become complex. Jane Flax (1987: 630) argues that it entails two levels of analysis: gender as a construct or category that helps us make sense out of particular social worlds and histories, and gender as a social relation that enters into and partially constitutes all other social relations and activities. Uniting several analytical strands, the historian Joan Scott (1986) also argues for the adoption of gender as an analytic category. In the past, she claims there has been a tendency for gender to be used either descriptively, as a substitute for women, or causally, in the quest for origins of women's subordination. Scott (1986) too, wants a two part but interrelated definition of gender, which she claims, must remain analytically distinct. First, gender is a constitutive element of social relationships based on perceived differences between the sexes, for example through the representation of cultural symbols and their interpretation; subjective identities and the construction of gender not just in the kinship system but also in the polity and economy. Second, gender is a primary way of signifying relations of power.

It is in her second proposition that gender is a primary way of signifying relationships of power that Scott (1986) believes the theorization of gender can be developed. Clearly influenced by Foucauldian notions of power, gender becomes implicated in the way power is constructed. Power, its construction and legitimation, is obviously crucial to the study of politics. Foucault advocates a radically different way of conceptualizing power to that used by the majority of political scientists. He believes that modern power is 'capillary', in that it is exercised 'strategically' at all levels of society right down to the level of 'micropractices', that is everyday social practices. Foucault is therefore arguing for a 'politics of everyday life' in a way that gives potential for a politics of resistance. This conceptualization of power finds some resonance with those who argue for wider definitions of the political. As part of his interest in the way in which power is exercised, Foucault argues that knowledge and the ability to construct knowledge equals power to define 'subjects' (Fraser 1989; Barrett 1991). Oppositional political activity can therefore play an important role in subverting dominant discourses and representations.

While it has often been obscured and overlooked, the contextually specific ways in which politics constructs gender and gender constructs politics become an important subject of enquiry. Scott (1986) outlines some of the ways in which gender can be used, both explicitly and implicitly, in the study of politics. Gender has been used explicitly in political theory to justify or criticize rulers and to express the relationship between ruler and ruled. Changes in gender relationships can be initiated by views of the needs of the state. According to Scott, these actions can only be understood as part of an analysis of the construction and consolidation of power. Gender has also been used implicitly as a crucial part of the organization of equality or inequality. As we will see in Chapter 3, it formed part of the British project of colonialism where the empire was constructed around a specifically white masculine self.

Where does this leave the study of gender in Third World politics? New developments in feminist theorizing have meant that, if universalistic discourses of patriarchy and women's oppression can no longer be used uncritically by a white Western and predominantly middle-class feminism, new forms of analysis must be found which can accommodate specificity, diversity and heterogeneity. This would make possible an approach which can look at the complexity of gender in the Third World from a perspective of the multiplicity of difference rather than 'otherness'.

Conventional politics

While conventional politics is largely seen as synonymous with electoral politics in the First World, this correlation doesn't hold so clearly in the Third World where authoritarian and military regimes and even the revolutionary overthrow of the state have been more commonplace. But it is now well documented that men and women participate differently in all forms of formal politics in both the First and Third Worlds, whether getting issues on the political agendas, or in policy making and implementation (Ackelsberg 1992). In the past men's political behaviour has been seen as the norm by political scientists, and women's analysed in terms of its deviation from this male norm. As part of this, many myths and stereotypes about women's political participation have grown up, for example that women are passive, apolitical and conservative, which feminist political scientists have endeavoured to dispel. It has been widely observed, that initially on gaining the vote, women don't vote with the same frequency as men in either the developed or developing world. However, this gap closes rapidly and once voting rates are controlled for age, class, education, etc., these differences disappear. It is clear that women's 'tendency to vote less' is not inherent but transient and contingent, for example it declines with increasing urbanization (Randall 1987).

There is, however, a marked tendency for women to participate less than men in formal politics as one ascends higher up the echelons of power (Peterson and Runyan 1993). At the grassroots level women on the whole make up a smaller percentage of the members of political parties than men. In the late 1960s women made up between only 15 and 20 per cent of party members in Chile and Peru. There was no greater number in the socialist bloc; in 1980 women formed only 19 per cent of ordinary Cuban communist party members. Women have often been marginalized in women's sections. Many one party states in the Third World, particularly in Africa, created women's organizations or co-opted already existing ones which became part of the dominant political party. These organizations have been more vehicles for the state to control women's participation, mobilizing them on its own terms and providing the regime with a base, rather than ways for women to gain representation within the system (Staudt 1986: 208). In Zimbabwe, for example, the ZANU women's organization was headed by Sally Mugabe, the president's wife. However, as we will see in Chapter 6, in parts of Latin America, with democratization many women activists have set up more autonomous women's sections in parties of the centre and centre left with distinctly feminist agendas (Waylen 1994).

Inevitably, given the low numbers of women members of political parties, the numbers elected to representative bodies are also low. While women tend to participate in greater numbers in local level politics, the average percentage of women in national legislatures globally in 1987 was 10. This number hides wide diversity. In 1987 the proportion of women legislators in sub-Saharan Africa was approximately 7.5 per cent; Latin America 7 per cent; South Asia 5 per cent and Southeast Asia 12 per cent, but the proportions had increased all regions since 1975 (United Nations 1991: 32). It appears that women fare better in systems with proportional representation.

There tend to be even fewer women found in the executives of governments whether they are authoritarian, elected, state socialist or revolutionary. Often, the very small number of women are appointed to posts which reflect the role that women so often play in the private sphere, e.g. women are often given responsibility for health, education, welfare and women's affairs (where this portfolio exists). In 1987–8 an average of only 3.5 per cent of the world's cabinet ministers were women and 93 countries, including 31 from Africa, 24 from Latin America and the Caribbean and 30 from Asia and the Pacific, had no women ministers at all. Women are largely excluded from key areas such as economic policy, defence and political affairs. Even in the 'social' areas, women formed only 9 per cent of the ministers in Africa and 6 per cent or less in the rest of the Third World (United Nations 1991: 31).

There are several explanations for this pattern of participation in conventional politics. In Africa, the low political representation of women is attributed, amongst other factors, to low levels of literacy and formal sector employment among women and the operation of the legal system, particularly laws concerning property and land (Parpart 1988). Many women are constrained by their roles in the private sphere, which prevent them from participating in the public sphere on the same terms as men and gaining the experience deemed necessary for a career in politics. However, it has been suggested that this affects middle- and upper-class women to a lesser extent in much of the Third World, because they can utilize the labour of female servants to free them from their domestic responsibilities (Richter 1990–1: 530). Shirin Rai (1995) found that in 1994 the majority of the 48 women representatives in the Indian parliament were highly educated and came from high caste and élite backgrounds. Almost universally, middle-class and élite women, because of factors such as economic resources and employment, levels of education and confidence, find it easier than poorer women to participate in the upper echelons of conventional politics. However, it is not only the nature of many women's lives which prevents them from participating, but also the structures of formal politics. This ranges from the timing of meetings, the combative style and machismo (often commented on in left-wing parties), and more widespread discrimination against women, for example in selection procedures, which prevents them from rising in political parties (Caldeira 1986).

One phenomenon which has been noted particularly in Asia and appears to go against these trends, is the relatively high number of women leaders in the Third World, such as Indira Gandhi in India, Benazir Bhutto in Pakistan, Corazon Aquino in the Philippines and Violetta Chamorro in Nicaragua amongst others (Genovese 1993). There are particular explanations for this which do not contradict the basic pattern. Mary Fainsod Katzenstein (1978) has claimed that in India there is a link between the degree to which politics is institutionalized and the participation of women, as the permeability of institutions allows women to achieve political prominence. Also in the Asian context, Linda Richter (1990–1) has argued that, among the factors which enable women to reach leadership positions are élite status, high levels of female participation in the movements struggling for independence, and crucially, links to politically prominent male relatives, often accompanied by their martyrdom, e.g. their assassination. However, Wolkowitz (1987), in her study of women politicians in Andhra Pradesh, argues that it is misleading to place too much emphasis on the significance of the family ties of female politicians.

Richter (1990–1) claims that women leaders suffer important disadvantages over their male counterparts; they do not generally have an institutional base, a regional constituency, an administrative track record or a military niche; they are often seen as temporary leaders, making them vulnerable to coup attempts. Women leaders are sometimes seen as conciliators who can bring the country together after a period of profound conflict and dislocation. Elsa Chaney (1979) has argued that, in Latin America, women in politics have often played the role of the 'supermadre', the mother of the people. The social welfare activities of Eva, the wife of Argentinian president Juan Perón, dispensing help to the poor and sick are often cited as an example of this role.

While women are, on the whole, underrepresented in formal politics, this does not mean of course that the policies made and implemented in the political process do not have a huge impact on the lives of different groups of women and on gender relations in general. When examining policy making and its outcomes, the gendered nature of the state becomes an important focus. There are often large numbers of women employed in state bureau-cracies, but few are found at the top of the state hierarchies in all types of political system whether electoral, authoritarian or state socialist (Staudt 1989a). In the 1980s the highest proportion of female public sector administrative and managerial workers was found in Latin America at 20 per cent, with 13 per cent in Africa and 10 per cent in Asia. While these figures had increased significantly in all areas since 1970, women are found only rarely in positions in central banks, economic ministries or foreign trade (United Nations 1991: 35). The state therefore is a gendered hierarchy, with women having an uneven representation in the bureaucracy (Franzway *et al.* 1989: 30). Some analysts have gone on to focus not simply on the lack of women but also on the embedded masculine style and organization of state bureaucracies, epito-mized for example by the Weberian rational model (Ferguson 1984). It has been suggested, however, that in some Third World states, middle-class educated women are in a good position to play a strategic role in the bureau-cracy (Charlton *et al.* 1989: 13). Indeed Alvarez, after examining Brazil, has suggested that state-led development increases employment opportunities for female professionals and technocrats within the state (Alvarez 1990a: 261).

When examining links between state action and gender relations, policies and their impact can be divided into three major categories (Charlton *et al.* 1989). The first category consists of policies which are aimed particularly at women. These often focus around so-called protective legislation and repro-duction, for example abortion and laws surrounding childbirth such as the provision of maternity leave. A second category is those policies which deal with relations between men and women, particularly property rights, sexual-ity, family relations, areas where power relations between men and women and therefore sets of gender relations are often institutionalized. As we will see in Chapter 3 the laws and regulations surrounding these issues frequently become an area of contestation when attempts are made to alter the existing pattern of power relations, as occurred with the enforcement of colonial rule in Africa when marriage, divorce and women's mobility became highly contested (Channock 1982; Barnes 1992; Manicom 1992).

The third category, general policies, are supposedly gender neutral but have a different impact on men and women. These can be further subdivided into those policy areas linked to the public sphere and somehow seen as 'masculine', such as state-defined politics, war, foreign policy, international trade, resources extraction and long distance communication, and those con-nected with welfare and reproduction. Women have traditionally been ex-cluded from the so-called masculine areas of policy. The most extreme example of this has been war, where women have, until very recently, participated on a very different basis to men. As we will see in Chapter 4, while recent national liberation struggles and revolutionary mobilizations have incorpor-ated women as fighters, this too has often happened in gender specific ways, i.e. the image of the woman fighter as mother with a rifle in one arm and a baby in the other (Reif 1986). Those policy areas more intimately con-nected to the private sphere and reproduction, for example, housing, health and education, fall under the general rubric of welfare and the welfare state. In contrast to the 'masculine' policies of the public sphere, welfare states have, for some time, been the subject of feminist analyses, particularly in the First World, looking at how they were established assuming particular patterns of gender relations or with the effect of creating or maintaining particular gender roles, and emphasizing issues of control and empowerment for women (Wilson 1977).

Even in much of the Third World where welfare states are far less developed and comprehensive, women are, on the whole, in the majority among providers of state welfare services. The state sector provides employment opportunities for different groups of women. Middle-class professional women are more likely to be employed by the state than the private sector, for example as teachers, social workers and nurses in sex-segregated employment (Seager and Olson 1986). Women also form the majority of consumers of welfare services. This is because of the role traditionally ascribed to many women in the domestic sphere as mothers and household managers that it is women within the household who often liaise with welfare services on behalf of other members of the household, for example the young and old. It is women who often make up the majority of the poor and are the major recipients of whatever welfare services exist. Any cuts in welfare services have particular implications for many women, both as providers and consumers of state welfare services, as has been seen in the impact of adjustment policies in the Third World (Afshar and Dennis 1992). Welfare states therefore have a differential impact on particular groups of women such as women in female headed households. Poor women, as the recipients of welfare services whether chosen or imposed, experience the welfare state very differently to the middle-class professional women who are employed to provide these services. This brings us to consider the gendered nature of the state, citizenship and nationalism.

Citizenship, nationalism and the state

These three categories are linked together. Citizenship, for example, is an important way in which the relationship between the individual and the nation state has been theorized. It is not gender neutral. Men and women have been incorporated into citizenship in Western states in very different ways. Initially citizenship was restricted to men (for long periods excluding working-class men and men of different races such as black slaves in the United States, for example) and incorporated them as soldiers and wage earners, that is through activities in the public sphere, and only later women were incorporated, often as mothers, that is through their activities in the private sphere. So despite formal equality as voters, men and women have been differentially incorporated as citizens by the state.

This raises the question of links to the nation and nationalism, as citizens are citizens of a nation state. Clearly in the study of Third World politics, an analysis of nationalism and the processes surrounding the creation of ethnic identities and the nation state is crucial. Nationalism also is not constructed in a gender neutral fashion (Parker *et al.* 1992; McClintock 1993). While recognizing the lack of a unitary category woman, Nira Yuval-Davis and Floya Anthias (1989) have located five major ways in which women have tended to participate in ethnic and national processes and state practices on different terms to men. These are:

1 as biological reproducers of members of ethnic collectivities, as 'mothers of the nation';
2 as reproducers of the boundaries of ethnic/national groups, for example by accepting or refusing sexual intercourse or marriage with prescribed groups of men;
3 as central participants in the ideological reproduction of the collectivity and transmitters of its culture, for example as mothers or teachers;
4 as signifiers of ethnic/national differences – as a focus and symbol in ideological discourses used in the construction, reproduction and transformation of ethnic/national categories, expressed for example in the advertising slogan 'Singapore girl – You're a great way to fly';
5 as participants in national, economic, political and military struggles.
(Yuval-Davis and Anthias 1989: 7)

The control of women and their sexuality is central to these processes. Kandiyoti (1991) has argued that this identification of women as bearers of cultural identity and boundary markers will have a negative effect on their emergence as full-fledged citizens. In the postcolonial context, as we will see in Chapter 3, many nationalist movements and nationalist projects equated the emancipation of women with 'modernity', for example through battles over 'women's souls' (seen in conflicts over education for women) and over women's bodies (exemplified in battles over fertility control). Some successor states have then appeared to reverse reforms, for example women's civil rights, when the previous secularist projects appear to break down (Kandiyoti 1991).

It is clear that a gendered analysis of the nation state is also necessary here. The conventional literature on the state is of little use. Both the more recent work on the state in the First World (including the statist literature inspired in part by Skocpol (1985) and her colleagues) and the now quite large body of work on the Third World has paid very little attention to questions of gender when examining the state. With the exception of the Rothchild and Chazan volume (1988) which focuses on different aspects of societies', including women's, disengagement, from the state in Africa, this omission is the same, regardless of the analytical approach adopted. Alavi's (1972) structuralist approach to the postcolonial state inspired by Marxist and underdevelopment theory is as gender blind as the more recent strong/weak state literature exemplified by Migdal (1988).

At the same time the analysis of the state has not been a priority for feminist academics. Many writers tended to concentrate on either the macro, e.g. overarching theoretical studies analysing the relationship between capitalism and patriarchy seeing the state as a mechanism to reconcile the two systems, or the micro, for example detailed empirical studies, with very little in between (Alvarez 1990a). Others focused on women as the *objects* of state policy, seeing the state as something external and 'out there' which affects women's lives but over which women have very little control. Those who did look at women's struggles with the state often used a 'them and us' framework.

Few feminist analyses have gone beyond seeing the state as either somehow essentially good or essentially bad for women in general. In the First World context, some feminist academics more identified with radical feminism such as Mackinnon (1983) and Ferguson (1984), argued that the state is inherently patriarchal in that it simply reflects society outside the state. Indeed it is an agent of control over women and feminists are well advised to steer clear of any involvement with it, as it will inevitably act to uphold patriarchy. Other feminists writing about the First World and Scandinavia in particular, were more enthusiastic about the potential of the state to further the interests of women in general (Hernes 1987). This enthusiasm resulted in a benign analysis of the welfare state arguing that, because they can get resources from the state, women can escape dependence on individual men.

A new literature on women and the state in the Third World has begun to develop but much of it replicates the general characteristics outlined above (for example Parpart and Staudt 1990). Most studies do not conceptualize the state in a very sophisticated manner and partly as a result of this lack, concentrate on women as the objects of policy (for example Charlton *et al.* 1989). They have replicated the tendency either to see the state as essentially good, that is as potentially a modernizing force which will bring benefits for women, or as essentially bad, inevitably representing men's interests to the detriment of some notion of women's interests (see Kandiyoti 1991 for some discussion of this tendency).

It is too simplistic to portray the state as essentially good or bad. It has no necessary relationship to gender relations, but this is evolving, dialectic and dynamic. 'The state' can rarely if ever be seen as a homogeneous category. It is not a unitary structure but a differentiated set of institutions and agencies, the product of a particular historical and political conjuncture. It is far better to see the state as a site of struggle, not lying outside of society and social processes, but having, on the one hand, a degree of autonomy from these which varies under particular circumstances, and on the other, being permeated by them. Gender (and racial and class) inequalities are therefore buried within the state, but through part of the same dynamic process, gender relations are also partly constituted through the state (Pringle and Watson 1992). The state therefore partly reflects and partly helps to create particular forms of gender relations and gender inequality. State practices construct and legitimate gender divisions and gendered identities are in part constructed by the law and public discourses which emanate from the state (Showstack-Sassoon 1987). Manicom (1992), among others, highlights the gendered nature of these processes in colonial Africa. Manicom (1992: 456) argues that the naming and recording of 'the native' as head of household in the administration of urban townships in southern Africa early in the twentieth century was 'a moment of moral regulation and gendered state formation and an example of the way in which an, apparently neutral, regulatory process inscribed gender and authorized a particular social form. "The Native" as a category of rule was a masculine one.' Manicom (1992: 456) goes on to stress that, as part of the process in which categories are defined within practices of rule, 'state policy and practices are also constructing "women" as objects of rule, reproducing or restructuring normative gender meanings and subordinate social and political identities in the same process'.

Because the relationship between the state and gender relations is not fixed and immutable, battles can be fought out in the arena of the state. Consequently, while the state has for the most part acted to reinforce female subordination, the space can exist within the state to act to change gender relations (Alvarez 1989a; Charlton et al. 1989). At different times and within different regimes, opportunity spaces can be used to alter the existing pattern of gender relations. Women's relationship to the state, particularly its welfare element, can also be seen as a site of contestation which provides the context for mobilization, and the welfare state can function as a locus of resistance. The actions of the state can also become a focus for political activity by groups outside the state, for example poor women campaigning for an extension of services. Alvarez, for example, has argued that the extension of the remit of the state into the realm of the private has the effect of politicizing the private, for example through issues such as abortion, rape and domestic violence. This politicization then gives women's movements a handle to campaign around and influence the political agenda. Shifting the boundary between the public and the private then becomes an important point of influence (Alvarez 1990a).

Different groups of women therefore interact with the state in different ways, and can have some influence over the way in which the state acts. Feminist analyses therefore have advanced from looking at the way the state *treats* women unequally in relation to men, to examining the ways in which particular states act to construct gendered state subjects and the public/private divide in different contexts. As part of the process of engagement with the state, interests and identities can also be constructed. It is therefore important to analyse under what conditions and with what strategies women's movements can influence the state and policy agendas. Debate has centred around whether women's movements should attempt to work with the state and political parties. Australian 'femocrats' argue that it is a potential agent of empowerment and feminist strategies should involve winning gains from the state (Watson 1990). As we will see in Chapter 6, 'state feminism' has emerged as an issue in the context of democratization with the return to civilian governments in some Latin American countries. The point at issue here is whether feminist movements can enter the state and achieve their own agendas or whether incorporation means co-optation (Waylen 1993)? This brings us to look at 'women's political activity'.

Women's political activity

Once the definition of the 'political' is widened, whole new areas of activity, many of them involving women, come under scrutiny. Why do women undertake political activity under certain circumstances, what form does this activity take and how can women's movements be analysed in the Third World context? If identities are complex, comprising multiple intersections of class, race, gender and sexuality, leading individuals to react in different ways at different times, women will act politically, not simply on the basis of gender, but race, class and sexuality as well, in a complex interaction. In the same way as it is difficult to talk of a unitary category 'woman' and women's interests, it is impossible, therefore, to talk of a women's movement. There is not one movement, but a diversity of different movements of which feminist movements are one part. Broad generalizations are therefore not possible.

It is important not to fall into the trap of essentialism by attributing specific qualities to all women. Some scholars, for example, have analysed women's activities in terms of an 'ethic of care' and maternal thinking, arguing, in positive and perhaps rather romantic terms, that women bring to activities in the public sphere supposedly 'female' values of caring, mothering and peacefulness (Gilligan 1983; Ruddick 1989). They have been criticized for both essentialism and universalism: looking at gender to the exclusion of other forms of difference such as race and class, and trying to create grand universal frameworks.

Recently attention has also focused on the form that women's political activities take, including whether women find new ways of 'doing politics' (Waylen 1992a). Using approaches influenced by postmodernism and poststructuralism, political action is seen, in part, as a struggle over dominant meanings, including dominant ideas of woman, and aiming to change those meanings. Foucault has been influential here with the suggestion that knowledge and the ability to construct knowledge equals power. Much greater emphasis is therefore placed on the form of political protests: on their use of the body and symbols and metaphors and how far they subvert dominant discourses of womanhood. One of the most powerful symbolic and subversive acts carried out by women protesting at the disappearance of their relatives, for example in Argentina, has been the takeover of public space not normally seen as part of their domain for their protests. This has been accompanied by other metaphorical and symbolic devices, leading some to highlight the importance of staging and performance in political action, for example, contrary to an essentialist interpretation, that the Madres are 'performing' as mothers (Franco 1994). In Chile women protesting about human rights abuses danced the Cueca, the national dance. It is usually danced by a man and woman, but they danced it alone to powerfully emphasize that their men were missing.

What is needed, therefore, is some exploration of the bases on which women come together as women. This would also focus on, for example, the ways in which women use their socially prescribed roles to act politically, and, without ignoring class and racial identities, explore both the relationship between gendered identities and political activity and the form that this activity takes. Increasingly, the politicization of women's social roles has been analysed, for example the ways in which women have used their roles as mothers or household managers as the basis of protests or to make demands (Kaplan 1982). Most of the activities involve entering the public sphere and either making demands or acting collectively, whether on a national, local or community based level. This kind of action therefore entails the politicization of the private sphere and entry into the public sphere on that basis. The participant's gender therefore becomes a fundamental part of this type of political activity, as the fact of their being women is a central part of the action. This can involve using 'traditional' social roles for oppositional purposes and also challenging and subverting these roles. Often women involved in 'the politics of everyday life' do not see their activities as political (Caldeira 1990). However, in some contexts, for example, under authoritarian rule, such activities are defined by the regime as oppositional, subversive and therefore come to be seen by both protagonists and others as political.

Women's movements are organized in a variety of different ways around a variety of different issues. One fundamental division that can be made is between those activities which defend the status quo, that is try to preserve the existing social order, and those which attempt to change the status quo, that is broadly defined as oppositional.

Activities which seek to defend the status quo have sometimes caused anxiety to feminists. Often this has been framed in the following terms: why should groups of women mobilize in defence of something that is not seen as being in their long term interests (which are defined as some kind of a feminist project of emancipation and liberation) and organize to uphold and continue a system that is seen as oppressing them? In the past, this has been explained as being due to women's naivety, and by political scientists as due to women's inherently reactionary political beliefs. Debates have also centred around how far women have either shown complicity with or been victimized by certain regimes. None of these approaches is terribly helpful. The examples of women mobilized by the Right show that the women involved often found their activities empowering, enabling them to be active and mobilized in the public sphere, often doing things in the name of motherhood and womanhood using very 'unfeminine methods' (Waylen 1992a). Valentine Moghadam (1994: 19), discussing female support for Islamist movements, uses the concept of identity politics arguing that they promise women of different classes security and meaning, offering stability in part through clearly defined sex roles, family life and a religious orientation.

Deniz Kandiyoti (1988) has supplied a potentially useful way of explaining and analysing the apparently contradictory reasons for and strategies behind women's political activities in defence of the status quo, in the form of the patriarchal bargain. According to Kandiyoti (1988: 277), 'different systems may represent different kinds of "patriarchal bargain" for women with different rules of the game and differing strategies for maximising security and optimising their life options'. Kandiyoti believes that this formulation helps to explain why women act in certain ways which may superficially seem to be in conflict with their long term interests. Women pay the price of a particular bargain and in return get a degree of protection. If a particular bargain looks as if it might be breaking down, women may mobilize to hold on to rules which appear to worsen their situation, because it is part of the strategy of maximizing security by gaining and keeping the protection of men. This is likely to occur in the absence of other more empowering alternatives for women. Kandiyoti cites the case of the United States where one response to some men opting out from the breadwinner role has been attempts to bolster the family in order to reinstate the patriarchal bargain in a society which has very little to offer women on their own. Other examples might be female support for arranged marriages and women binding the feet of their daughters. This notion of the patriarchal bargain can provide a framework with which to analyse, for example, the activities of middle-class women on behalf of the Right against Popular Unity in Chile in the face of their elevation of women's 'traditional' roles and the apparent attempts of the Left to undermine them (Waylen 1992a).

The most documented form of activity undertaken by women's movements is oppositional. There is great diversity in those movements and activities which can be seen as oppositional and attempting to alter the status quo. First, there are those activities which attempt to influence the state and political parties, and therefore interact with the conventional political arena. This can be through protest or lobbying, for example the human rights campaigns of the Madres of the Plaza de Mayo. The demands made can either be specifically concerning women, for example abortion, or more general demands relevant to their roles as household managers, for example around food subsidies and prices. Second, there are autonomous activities which don't attempt to pressurize the state, e.g. autonomous women's organizations and community organizations organizing around economic survival.

Important questions therefore arise: first, how can these movements be disaggregated, for example in terms of the sorts of women involved and their aims and objectives; second, what are the links between different types of women's movement, particularly between feminist and other women's movements; and third, what is the relationship of these movements to other oppositional movements.

One widely used way of disaggregating these questions has been to utilize Maxine Molyneux's (1985a) notion of practical and strategic gender interests. According to Molyneux, 'women's interests' do not exist in any general sense, but she argues for a notion of 'gender interests', which can be divided into practical and strategic gender interests.

Practical gender interests arise from actual situations and are formulated by the women in those situations, and will vary from situation to situation. A number of analyses have used this notion to explain female collective action arising in response to an immediate perceived need, e.g. the leading role often played by women in food riots, and the examples of miner's wives mobilizing to defend the jobs and interests of their male partners. Practical gender interests therefore are generally expressed as social and economic demands. These sorts of activities correspond to the category 'the politics of everyday life'. They can take the form of spontaneous protests, the most obvious being food riots of the sort which occurred in many Third World countries in the 1980s, sparked off by the imposition of harsh structural adjustment packages. They can also take the form of more organized campaigns and activities (Radcliffe and Westwood 1993). These are often not exclusively women-only but women frequently make up the majority of the members. Movements organizing around practical gender interests frequently focus around consumption issues, often organizing in a particular location or community. Some activities which can be characterized in this way involve the pressurizing of the state or political parties, for example campaigns in poor areas to get the state, whether on a local or national level, to provide services such as water, electricity and improved health care. Other activities operate more autonomously, often focusing around collective survival strategies, for example communal kitchens providing food on a collective basis, setting up workshops to produce goods for sale as part of income generating schemes such as bakeries, craft workshops, and credit unions like SEWA in India (Everett 1989). Other examples include women's centres which offer crèches, advice and meeting rooms. While these sorts of activities are often based in poor urban areas, there are examples of women's movements operating in rural areas, particularly among peasant and landless women (Fisher 1993: 75–102). The tradition of women's informal or voluntary associations in Africa can be fitted into this category (Wipper 1984).

It is clear from the examples of women organizing to protect the livelihoods of their families that class and gender are closely linked in this case. Many of these movements can be categorized as 'popular' or working-class, although this is not always so; Argentina's housewives' movement can be seen as an exception, it was middle- and lower middle-class based as the middle class had been very badly hit by economic crisis (Fisher 1993: 145–50). This kind of activity typically involves the politicization of women's social roles, as their roles as mothers and household managers form the basis of their political activities and entry into the public sphere. According to Molyneux, movements operating around practical gender interests do not necessarily act to reduce gender inequality, nor are they often intended to.

In contrast, strategic gender interests are those interests which can be derived deductively from an analysis of women's subordination and from the formulation of a more satisfactory set of arrangements (Molyneux 1985a). It is these strategic gender interests which are often called 'feminist' or women's 'real' interests, and, according to Molyneux, require a feminist level of consciousness to struggle for them. Feminist movements can therefore be seen as movements of women coming together autonomously and self-consciously as women, pressing gender based demands. They do not, on the whole, rely on the politicization of women's social roles. Different types of feminist movements have appeared in the Third World as well as in the First World. Some middle-class based feminist movements emerged at the same time as nationalist movements campaigning for independence from colonial powers, for example in India, and middle-class based movements campaigning for female suffrage appeared in Latin America in the early part of the twentieth century (Jayawardena 1986; Miller 1991). A variety of feminist movements have (re)emerged in the last two decades (Saporta *et al.* 1992).

However, there is a need to explore the links between 'feminism' and popular women's movements. Many studies have shown that groups of women involved in campaigns around practical gender interests have become increasingly focused on issues around women's subordination and come to see themselves as increasingly feminist (Fisher 1993: 177–200). They often see this as a form of 'popular feminism', however, that is it is not the same as either feminism from the First World, nor often the feminist movements active within the Third World countries themselves. The difference is often expressed in terms of movements which do not prioritize gender issues over and above the issues which surround class and imperialism. As Mohanty argues, 'feminist movements have been challenged on the grounds of cultural imperialism, and of short-sightedness in defining the meaning of gender in middle-class, white experiences, and in terms of internal racism, classism and homophobia' (Mohanty 1991: 7). Some contemporary feminist movements, for example in many parts of Latin America, are seen by many as predominantly middle-class movements, and for example in Brazil, as predominantly white. A rigid analytical dichotomy between movements active around practical and strategic gender interests is overly simplistic as there is considerable overlap between the two.

Conclusion

It is clear when looking at gender in Third World politics that Third World women do not constitute an 'automatic unitary group', but that the term Third World women can be used as it designates a political constituency (Mohanty 1991: 7). Mohanty believes what constitutes 'Third World women' as an oppositional alliance is a *common context of struggle*. She wants to get away from analyses which see Third World women as victims, focusing instead on a dynamic oppositional agency of women. Mohanty uses Benedict Anderson's notion of 'imagined communities' to move away from essentialist notions of potential alliances, substituting 'imagined communities of women with divergent histories and social locations, woven together by the *political* threads of opposition to forms of domination that are not only pervasive but systemic' (1991: 4). She therefore believes that it is possible to 'retain the idea of multiple fluid structures of domination which intersect to locate women differently at particular historical conjunctures, while at the same time insisting on the dynamic oppositional agency of individuals and their engagement in "daily life"' (1991: 13). The notion of an imagined community of struggle can be extended to Third World oppositional struggles in general. It therefore becomes difficult to see women's oppositional activities as discrete entities somehow separate from other struggles, for example against colonialism, imperialism and for national liberation.

It is important, however, that the analysis of the political activities of women's movements does not occur separately from the analysis of formal politics. The use of wider definitions of the political means that the two must be integrated. In particular, there is a need to explore the interaction between the two in terms of the state and political parties. This will allow for more sophisticated understandings of concepts such as citizenship which play such an important role in the analysis of political processes.

Now that we have examined some of the key issues, such as what is meant by gender, and unpicked some of the concepts involved in a gendered approach to Third World politics, it is possible to outline a loose framework with which to examine key political formations. Combining some of the themes and questions which emerge from the structural analyses of socialist feminists developed in the 1970s together with some of the new insights of the 1980s we will focus on three key areas in each formation. In each case, we must consider first the role played by different groups of women in conventional political arenas. Second, we have to make a gendered analysis of the state and policy making in that context, examining the impact of particular policies in constructing and changing existing patterns of gender relations. Third, it is necessary to examine the political activities undertaken by different groups of women outside of the conventional political arena, and their interaction with the state and the policy making process in each formation.

Before it is possible to focus primarily on the domestic political arena, we must consider what is meant by the term the Third World, look at the position of Third World countries in the international economic and political system and examine the relationship between the national and the international context. This inevitably leads us also to consider the nature of 'development' and the impact of diverse processes of social and economic change on women and gender relations. It is to this topic that we move on to in the next chapter.

2

The Third World
and development

Introduction

In the previous chapter we looked at various ways of thinking about gender relations and how they could be used to examine gender in Third World politics. Now it is necessary to consider the nature of the Third World. This raises several questions: what is meant by the term Third World? Its meaning has been highly contested and more recently its usefulness has been questioned because of the increasing differentiation between Third World countries. Does the category Third World now overgeneralize about and falsely homogenize a culturally, economically and politically diverse group of countries? Generalizations have also been made about the nature of the politics and political systems in the Third World. It is necessary to ask how far this too is legitimate.

We will see that it is impossible to make an assessment of the usefulness of the category Third World without analysing the external influences which flow from the Third World's position in the international system. In political terms this means examining the Third World's role in the international system during and after the Cold War. But it is the position of the Third World in the global economic system which has been the subject of the greatest controversy. Frequently seen as one of exploitation and dependence, it has led to much discussion of what can be done to combat it and about the nature of 'development' in general. These questions have preoccupied politicians and academics alike, looking for both satisfactory analyses and development strategies. As we will see one variant of development theory, modernization has been linked to capitalist-style development, another variant underdevelopment theory has been linked to socialist-leaning strategies and in the 1980s neo–liberalism has been associated with structural adjustment programmes. All these versions of 'development' have particular implications for women. It is the particular implications of 'development' for women and gender relations which we need to consider before being able to examine various political formations in the rest of the book.

The Third World

The term Third World has been used to describe a group of countries which, until recently, were seen to share some common characteristics and a similar position within the international economic and political system. It is generally used to refer to the countries of Latin America, the Caribbean, Africa and Asia. The concept of a Third World emerged after World War II when a large number of countries (mainly in Asia, Africa and the Caribbean) gained their independence from the colonial powers and became more important actors on the international stage. It has had both a political and ideological as well as a predominantly economic usage. By the 1960s and 1970s the category Third World was used to describe those countries which shared certain characteristics: poor, non-industrial, peripheral or marginal to the global system and ex-colonial (Worsley 1979). However increasing differenti-ation among Third World countries, apparent in the 1980s and 1990s, has meant that it is now much harder to use these general descriptions. It is increasingly difficult to classify certain countries such as the newly industri-alizing countries (NICs) like South Korea and Taiwan, which are no longer poor and non-industrial, as Third World.

Other terms have been used to describe those countries generally considered to form the Third World. Economists often favour the phrase less developed countries (LDCs) in contrast to the developed countries of the First World, and more recently they have also begun to use the expression LLDCs, the least developed countries, to refer to the poorest Third World countries. Others, including international relations experts, use the term South, stemming from the geographical split whereby the majority of less developed countries lie in the southern hemisphere and the majority of the developed countries lie in the northern one. In literary and critical studies the category postcolonial has become widely used, although it too has been criticized for being a rather overgeneral catch-all category.

One advantage of using terms such as LDC or South is that they can avoid many of the stereotyped views associated with the term Third World held in the First World. Despite attempts by some First World aid organizations to change dominant representations, media images of the Third World often portray starving people, particularly women and children, as passive victims. These images fit into a general picture of the Third World as poor, unstable, tropical, backward, overpopulated and traditional, reflecting the generalized feelings of superiority in the First World. Indeed the Third World has fre-quently been defined as 'savage', 'barbarian' and 'other', in contrast to the self-styled 'civilized' First World. Setting aside, as far as possible, these very negative constructions associated with the phrase Third World, the term Third World will be used in this book to describe a diverse set of countries in Africa, Latin America and Asia, while trying not to homogenize and overgeneralize their experiences.

The Third World in the international political system

For many the category Third World was defined by decolonization and the Cold War (McGrew 1992). This conflict created a First World – the developed capitalist 'West' led by the USA; and a Second World – the communist 'East' led by the USSR, leaving a Third World of the newly independent states. The USA and USSR established blocs and alliance systems around these divisions and the conflict between them imposed its dynamic on the international political system. For much of the postwar period, North–South relations were marginalized on the global agenda, or manipulated by the superpowers. The Third World only became politically important when it impinged upon or was implicated in the global rivalry of the superpowers, that is when superpower competition extended to the Third World, especially when each tried to prevent the other from extending their influence there. From the 1960s onwards the Third World formed a major arena where superpower rivalry was fought out, with the 1963 Cuban missile crisis providing the most vivid example of this.

Third World countries were forced, often unwillingly, to choose between East and West and their domestic politics were interpreted according to the superpower agenda. Frequently 'national liberation struggles' which had little to do with superpower rivalry, were seen in Cold War terms and turned into proxy battles between the superpowers. As we will see in Chapter 4, this occurred throughout the postwar period, from the Korean War in the 1950s, the Vietnam War in the 1960s, the anti-colonial struggles in Africa such as Angola and Mozambique in the 1970s to Central America in the 1980s. Indeed, the number of Third World revolutionary struggles reached their peak in the 1970s (Halliday 1986: 86). In the six years between 1974 and 1980 14 states were taken over by revolutionary movements in the third wave of Third World revolutions.

Halliday (1986: 41) argues that the Soviets and Americans did not react symmetrically to insurgencies in the Third World. The Americans saw it as their task to prevent the spread of communism in the vulnerable Third World and implemented a two pronged strategy to achieve this. As we will see in Chapter 5 the US gave both political and economic support to pro-Western right-wing dictators such as the Shah of Iran, Marcos in the Philippines, the Duvaliers in Haiti and Somoza in Nicaragua. It also trained and armed the militaries of its allies, often offering support if the military seized power on its own account (Halliday 1986). The US also took overt and covert action against those it believed to be communists. The American reaction to the Cuban revolution can be seen in this way and has led some to argue that it was American antagonism which forced the Cubans into the Soviet camp. This antipathy was expressed in various ways ranging from the Bay of Pigs invasion of 1962 to the economic blockade maintained despite the collapse of the Eastern bloc. Reagan initiated a second Cold War in the 1980s, ending the period of *détente* which had characterized the 1970s after the humiliating American defeat in Vietnam and the failure of Carter's human rights orientated foreign policy. As part of this, Reagan reacted with hostility to the Third World revolutions of the 1970s implementing, for example, an economic blockade on Nicaragua and funding the Contra War.

The Soviet Union, in contrast, saw itself as the ally of Third World liberation struggles and provided some military, economic and diplomatic support to revolutionary movements. This did not mean that all revolutionary movements received aid, or that they all became client movements, as demonstrated by the example of southern Africa in the late 1970s (Potter 1992). Nor did all those states receiving Soviet aid, such as Egypt and India, leave the Western orbit. However, while the USSR did have different motivations to the United States, it also built up a network of client states which it supplied with armaments. As a result there was an important superpower military presence, in the form of both temporary invading forces and the longer term maintenance of alliance systems, in much of the Third World, which contributed to its militarization.

The collapse of the Eastern bloc and the subsequent end of the Cold War has had important political implications for the Third World. The demise of communism has meant that state socialism is no longer a model for the Third World and countries such as Cuba are left without support. The US, while maintaining its antagonism to Cuba, no longer fears the spread of communism in the Third World as it did in the past. As we will see in Chapter 6, this has contributed to the increased emphasis on the promotion of human rights and democracy, now that dictatorships no longer have to be supported as anti-communist bulwarks. In concert with international institutions such as the World Bank, emphasis has shifted, from turning a blind eye to one party states and other undemocratic regimes while supplying armaments to anti-communist allies, towards the promotion of competitive elections and 'good governance' (Leftwich 1993: 606). This change has been seen most clearly in Africa, for example in the pressure put on Kenya and also Zambia. The end of the Cold War has not brought the end of superpower intervention in the Third World. Initially the Gulf War was seen as heralding a period of a more benign 'condominium' of bilateral diplomacy between the superpowers used to resolve conflicts and tensions in the Third World (Halliday 1990). While the Third World may no longer be an arena for rivalry, American intervention in Somalia in 1992 and Haiti in 1994 shows that the Third World is still an arena for political interference by the superpowers, particularly the US.

The discussion so far has made no mention of gender. In part this reflects the disciplines of international politics and international relations. Up until recently, this literature shared many characteristics with that focusing on conventional politics in the domestic arena. Commonly the global political system has been analysed as if gender relations do not exist and, if they do, they certainly do not impinge upon international politics in the public sphere (Peterson 1992; Tickner 1992; Sylvester 1994). This is due in part to the theoretical roots of international relations, relying on political philosophy which itself does not consider gender issues overtly (Grant 1991). This situation is now beginning to change. Feminist academics, often echoing many of Joan Scott's arguments about power and gender, have begun to make more visible the gendered nature of power in the international arena (Enloe 1989; Foot 1990; Sylvester 1990). Enloe (1989: 13) has argued that the introduction of 'masculinity into a discussion of international politics, and thereby making men visible as men, should prompt us to explore differences in the politics of masculinity between countries – and between ethnic groups in the same country'.

Connections are increasingly being made between nationalism, militarism and masculinity within the global system (Enloe 1988; Elshtain 1989). Enloe (1989) has examined some of the issues surrounding foreign bases and foreign troops which are particularly pertinent in the Third World. American troops have been until recently almost exclusively men, and a large component of the 'rest and recreation' industry has been prostitution and other sexual services. It has been estimated that in 1987 20,000 women were entertainment workers in Olongapo City, a town in the Philippines overshadowed by the Subic Bay Naval Base (Enloe 1989: 86). However, Soviet troops for example in Afghanistan, were not associated with the presence of a sex industry in the same way. Sexual tourism more generally is increasingly seen as another gendered link between the First and Third Worlds. First World men travel to Third World countries such as Thailand to procure a variety of sexual services, including child prostitution and child pornography, for which the participating men would be severely sanctioned in their own countries (Enloe 1989: 82). The changing nature of conflict and the demilitarization associated with the end of the Cold War also has implications for gender relations (Enloe 1993). The making of foreign policy, conflict and confrontation such as the Cold War have all to be seen in this gendered light.

The Third World as self-definition

If the Third World was frequently defined in terms of the Cold War, it has also been defined by the Third World itself. The term Third World was used to denote a third way – neither capitalist nor communist – not lying in the middle of these two but creating a distinctive route, linked to non-alignment (Worsley 1979). Included in the category Third World were those poor ex-colonial countries sharing a common colonial heritage who wanted to break away from the colonial past and develop a distinctive identity, free from the domination of the First World. This group first came together at the Bandung Conference held in Indonesia in 1955. Most of the independent countries of Asia and Africa attended this Afro-Asian solidarity conference, while much of Latin America remained closely allied to the United States and members of the Organization of American States (OAS).

'Third Worldism' became increasingly associated with the philosophy of non-alignment which stood initially for peaceful coexistence and anti-colonialism to which was added economic independence from neo-colonialism in 1970 (McGrew 1992). Non-alignment also became an important political movement, translating its radical nationalism to action on the international stage. The first non-aligned conference was held in Belgrade in 1961, and by the sixth conference held in Havana in 1982, there were 92 full members (including three national liberation movements). The non-aligned movement (NAM) also helped the development of the so-called Group of 77 (G77) of Third World states, which increased to 120 states as more gained independence. G77 became a voting bloc in the United Nations (UN) and because of the large number of countries, the Third World could use its majority in the UN General Assembly.

From the early 1960s to the early 1980s, Third World states formed a fairly united group, which helped them become a significant political force internationally, able to force Third World concerns onto the international agenda. The major issues were economic. The NAM aimed not just to counteract superpower domination, but also to alter the global economic system from one which favoured the First World to one which reflected the development priorities of the Third World. New international institutions such as UNCTAD, the United Nations Commission for Trade and Development, set up specifically to improve trade for developing countries, were established in the 1960s.

The NAM achieved its greatest success at setting the international agenda in the 1970s. The era of *détente* meant that the superpowers were more amenable to being pressurized by Third World countries (Ravenhill 1990: 733). The major campaigning issue was the establishment of a new international economic order (NIEO). In 1974 the UN General Assembly agreed a declaration for the NIEO, which, through restructuring, would provide a more equitable position for the Third World in the international economy. This was to be achieved through: the democratization of key international financial institutions such as the World Bank and International Monetary Fund (IMF); commodity agreements, giving better trading terms for Third World primary products; more preferential trading agreements; increased aid and debt relief; and greater control over the activities of multinationals. Ultimately, the campaign failed and its failure is often seen as signalling the end of 'Third Worldism'.

More recently, changes both on the international scene and within the Third World have meant that Third World unity has become more difficult to achieve and led to a questioning of the category Third World itself. Several international changes are often highlighted as contributing to this: first increasing globalization in terms of culture (world music, TV satellite and video, tourism), telecommunications, economics and the increasing importance of global issues such as the environment, migration and refugees and global organizations; second, the rise of the New Right in many parts of the world in the 1980s; and third, the end of the Cold War and superpower rivalry. The political identification shared by Third World countries has been reduced by the greater differentiation that has emerged between them. Third

World political unity became harder to maintain as most Third World countries retained a capitalist economic orientation after independence, and increasingly the non-aligned path came to be seen as unsustainable. As a result the NAM became more associated with left-leaning Third World states such as Cuba, while the majority of countries allied themselves with the West. The rise of Islam as a political force at state level has also increased the political differentiation between Third World states (Ayubi 1991).

The Third World in the international economic system

Increasing differentiation has, if anything, become more marked in economic terms. While some Third World countries, such as the NICs, have experienced high rates of economic growth and industrialization, others such as parts of sub-Saharan Africa have experienced stagnation and economic decline most marked in the 1980s. It is to the crucial question of the Third World's role in the international economic system that we now turn. The nature of this role has been highly contested and has implications for the internal politics of Third World countries.

Any discussion of the economic position of the Third World must begin with its original integration into the international economy. Underdevelopment theory, which became the 'radical orthodoxy' during the 1970s, highlighted the importance of external factors and argued that incorporation into the global economy was fundamentally exploitative for the Third World. Beginning in the colonial period it became a supplier of cheap raw materials and labour to the First World, thereby helping the First World to develop. Indeed, A.G. Frank (1969), examining Latin America, argued that it was through this relationship that surplus was drained from the satellites (the Third World) to the centre/metropoles (First World), preventing development in the satellites or periphery but enhancing it in the metropoles. It was claimed, particularly in the 1970s, that political independence did not bring any profound changes to these economic structures. According to some Third World academics and politicians, such as Julius Nyerere of Tanzania, formal political colonialism was replaced by neo-colonialism. Informal economic imperialism continued to work to the detriment of the Third World through mechanisms such as multinational corporations (MNCs) and international institutions such as the IMF which replaced colonial institutions.

While underdevelopment theory was increasingly criticized in the 1980s by both the Left and the Right for being overly crude, simplistic, deterministic and externally orientated, it still remains important to examine the Third World's economic relations (Warren 1980). The changes which have occurred in the world economy since 1945 have affected countries differentially, further contributing to the breakdown of the category Third World. Changes have affected trade, manufacturing and finance (Brett 1985). The volume of international trade has increased hugely in the postwar period, growing at an annual rate of over 7 per cent between 1948 and 1971 (Joekes 1987: 29). International trade has increased in importance for all except the poorest developing countries. Between 1960 and 1982, the middle income countries increased their exports from 17 to 23 per cent of their total output, while the developed economies increased theirs from 12 to nearly 20 per cent. However, apart from the Asian NICs, the Third World's share of world trade declined from World War II until 1972, and although this was reversed after 1972, the economic gap between the First and the Third World has become, if anything, more marked. At the same time the economic differences between Third World countries themselves have also increased.

At the root of the growth in world trade is a huge expansion of the trade in manufactures, while the trade in commodities has grown only slowly. Until 1973, the First World's exports of manufactures were not only the larger part of world exports but grew faster than those of other regions. Since then, however, it has been manufactures from the developing world which have grown most (Joekes 1987: 37). However, this increase in manufactured trade has been highly concentrated. The countries achieving the fastest growth of manufactures have been the NICs. The four East Asian NICs, South Korea, Hong Kong, Taiwan and Singapore, together account for approximately 33 per cent of Third World manufactured exports (Williams 1994: 17). The share of manufacturing output of the middle income and newcomer economies increased from 19 to 37 per cent of the world's total between 1960 and 1981, while the global share of the low income countries (including China, India and most of sub-Saharan Africa) remained about the same during this period (Harris 1987: 103).

The postwar period has also seen the growth of international capital movements (Spero 1990). Each of the decades saw the appearance of a new source of international financial flows. Initially the United States provided capital for postwar reconstruction through the Marshall Plan; in the 1950s private corporations were the major source of finance in developing countries; official development assistance, primarily from the United States, became important in the 1960s; but in the 1970s private banks became a major channel for international financial flows and private international transfers grew by 20 per cent per year.

In order to trace these developments and their impact on the Third World, it is useful to divide the postwar period, characterized by economic growth until the early 1970s and crisis and instability subsequently, into four subphases (Hewitt 1992). The first phase of postwar restructuring was probably the shortest, lasting from 1945 to the early 1950s. Along with the establishment of the political structures of the UN to regulate the international system, attempts were made at Bretton Woods in July 1944 to set up structures to control the international economy. The aim was to avoid the depression of the interwar years, through the international coordination of finance and trade. However the system never functioned in the ways that some of its founders, such as J.M. Keynes, had wanted (Harris 1988).

The international economic order put into place at Bretton Woods created two regimes – a financial and a trading one (Williams 1994). The financial regime was the stronger of the two and had its institutional expression in the establishment of the International Monetary Fund (IMF) and the International Bank for Reconstruction and Development (IBRD) which became known as the World Bank. The IMF was intended to supply loans to tide countries over short term exchange rate and balance of payments problems, while the World Bank was intended to be a supplier of longer term investment loans. The trade regime which aimed to regulate and free world trade proved more difficult to establish and the initial proposal for an international trade organization (ITO) failed and was only partially replaced by the General Agreement on Tariffs and Trade (GATT) (Gilpin 1987; Gill and Law 1988).

Bretton Woods clearly reflected the interests of the dominant economies. The original negotiations had been bilateral, but it was American not British hegemony which became enshrined in the postwar economic order. This was reflected in the dominance of the dollar as the *de facto* world currency with a system of fixed exchange rates set up around it and the influence of the United States in institutions like the IMF and World Bank. Few Third World countries were present at this stage because, apart from the Latin American states, most were still subsumed under the colonial empires. There was no consensus on commodity agreements, the issue of perhaps greatest importance to the Third World at that time, and GATT, based more on multilateral negotiation, proved much harder to achieve. The postwar economy was therefore not restructured in the interests of the Third World. It was dominated by the First World, particularly the United States, and set up a framework which subsequently had a determining impact on the global economy.

The second phase, the 'golden years' of the 1950s and 1960s were boom years characterized by economic growth and stability for the world economy as a whole. The Third World experienced respectable rates of growth. Between 1965 and 1973 the low income economies grew by an average of 3.6 per cent per annum (pa) and the middle income countries by an average of 4.6 per cent pa, while the countries of East Asia grew by 5.4 per cent (Hewitt 1992). The general climate was one of optimism, and modernization theory, the dominant approach of American social scientists to the Third World at this time, shared this view to some extent. Initially it was believed that the newly independent Third World would develop relatively easily, reaching the desirable goals of modernization and Westernization without too much difficulty (Weiner 1966; Smelser 1968; Bernstein 1979; Higgott 1983; Randall and Theobald 1985). At the same time, however, there was considerable concern at the apparent success of the Soviet Union, and its potential attractiveness as a model for Third World states. This led to anxiety at the dominant role of the state in promoting development, and fears that private enterprise would be undermined (Cammack 1996).

However, three other trends were becoming apparent by the 1960s. First, many Third World countries, dependent on the export of primary products (estimated to form 70–90 per cent of exports from developing countries in the 1950s) were experiencing balance of payment difficulties, made worse by declining terms of trade, estimated to have decreased by 25 per cent between 1951 and 1965 (Hewitt 1992: 225). One solution was to diversify from the production of primary commodities and place greater emphasis on industrialization, forming the second trend. Industrialization increased the disparity between those Third World economies which were doing so successfully and the others. The strategies used varied. The major two were import substituting industrialization (ISI) and export orientated industrialization (EOI). In the postwar period ISI was favoured in Latin America. It involved industrializing behind tariff barriers, erected to protect the 'infant industries', to supply the domestic market initially with consumer goods. But it often resulted in inefficient and uncompetitive industries. The countries of East Asia such as South Korea and Taiwan, having initially industrialized to supply the domestic market, during this period began to export manufactured consumer goods. But when some Latin American countries attempted this shift in the 1970s, they were faced with a much more unfavourable international climate. Third, multinationals were moving into the Third World to establish manufacturing capacity. In the 1960s 70 per cent of the capital flows into the Third World were in the form of direct foreign investment (DFI). In many cases, MNCs were jumping over tariff barriers, so as not to lose internal markets, and in others establishing branch plants to manufacture for export using cheap local labour.

By the end of the 1960s it was becoming clear that industrialization, particularly ISI, was not the answer to all the economic problems of the Third World. Once the so-called easy stage of ISI had been completed, economic stagnation seemed to result. Economies had not achieved the hoped for self-reliance, but in many cases were becoming dominated by MNCs and still dependent on the First World for technology. Balance of payments problems remained and were exacerbated by profit repatriation. In many cases, the promised 'trickle down' of benefits had not materialized and the lot of the poor did not appear to have improved. In Brazil levels of inequality had increased despite an 'economic miracle' between 1967–73 based on industrialization. These factors prompted some Latin American analysts to formulate dependency theory, which while it shares certain similarities with underdevelopment theory, provides a far more sophisticated analysis of the unequal way in which Third World countries were integrated into the global economy and the interaction between this, their internal structures and class relations, but it is conspicuously gender blind (Cardoso and Faletto 1979).

The years 1971–3 brought the end of the long boom and the inauguration of much greater instability in the world economy. Parts of the Bretton Woods system began to unravel. This reflected major upheavals which were occurring in the international economy, in part brought about by the move from US hegemony to multipolar hegemony as Japan and Germany became major economic powers. In addition, First World economic growth had begun to slow down. Partly as a consequence of the large deficits the United States incurred to fund both the Vietnam war and increased social spending at home in the 1960s, it suspended the free convertibility of the dollar to gold at a fixed exchange rate. In combination with the freer movement of capital, a system of floating exchange rates resulted. The breakdown of Bretton

Woods provided further stimulus to the growth of international movements of finance, as private banks became a major channel for international financial flows.

The impact of changes in international financial markets and the economic slowdown was compounded by the 1973 OPEC oil price rises which had a profound impact on the world economy and on the Third World in particular. OPEC, the oil producers cartel, raised the price of oil threefold and the world economy was then faced with recycling the OPEC oil surpluses. The oil producers now had large amounts of extra revenue which their economies could not absorb. Much of this capital was deposited in private banks in Europe and denominated in dollars – in the so-called 'eurodollar' markets. The banks were keen to lend the money on to others, particularly middle income countries in the Third World such as Brazil and Argentina and oil producers such as Mexico and Venezuela, adding to the increase in the level of international financial transactions. The capital was used for a variety of purposes. Some went to finance consumption by the élites, some was used to finance development schemes. At the time the contraction of this debt seemed unproblematic, global interest rates were low and bankers either did not know or care about the ability of the borrowers to repay the loans (Lever and Huhne 1985: Roddick 1988).

At the same time as non-oil producing Third World countries had to pay more for their imported oil, they had to pay more for their manufactured imports. This led to further balance of payments difficulties for many, who also borrowed to finance their deficits, allowing them to continue importing. As a result, Third World borrowing kept the world economy ticking over in the 1970s and prevented the First World suffering a worse recession than it did. Even before these massive debts were contracted in the 1970s, some dependency theorists had advanced the concept of dependent development – that some Third World countries could develop but at the price of technological dependence and indebtedness – with Brazil cited as an archetypal example of a country which industrialized in the late 1960s at the price of indebtedness (Cardoso 1973).

The 1980s have been characterized as 'development in reverse' for much of the Third World. A number of factors contributed to this. The early 1980s saw a change in the dominant ideological climate with the rise to prominence of neo-liberalism and the New Right. Leaders such as the US President Reagan and the British Prime Minister Thatcher and institutions such as the World Bank and the IMF were advocating free market and anti-state policies. In keeping with these ideas, part of the strategy implemented to cope with the economic problems of the early 1980s, in particular rising inflation, was a huge rise in global interest rates.

This rise precipitated the 'debt crisis', which was officially inaugurated in August 1982 when Mexico announced that it could no longer meet its debt servicing requirements. The rise in interest rates meant that repayments for the Third World debt contracted on easy terms in the 1970s went up hugely. Many countries could not meet the increased payments and had to reschedule and borrow more simply to service both their official and unofficial debt, i.e. that contracted with the private banks. The banks, in turn, got scared and where possible stopped lending to the Third World. There were fears for the collapse of the international banking system, and some attempts were made to find solutions but these were primarily piecemeal, often of the 'sticking plaster' variety (Roddick 1988). While many of the middle income Latin American economies were much larger debtors in absolute terms and a greater threat to the international financial system because much of their debt was contracted with the private banks, for many of the African states the relative significance, for example in terms of export revenues and GDP, of their small mainly official debt to their economies was actually much greater. In addition to the rise in interest rates, the global recession had other repercussions on the Third World which exacerbated the impact of the debt crisis. First, the decline in commodity prices continued, particularly for agricultural products so countries were earning less to pay more. Second, there was a decline in direct foreign investment. Third, Third World manufacturers had to face increased protectionism, as more attempts were made to keep Third World manufactured goods out of First World markets.

The diversity between Third World economies increased. With the exception of the East Asian NICs, per capita incomes declined in most Third World countries and levels of poverty increased. Between 1980 and 1986 per capita GNP fell by 1.6 per cent in Latin America and the Caribbean, while in sub-Saharan Africa it declined by 2.8 per cent, wiping out many of the gains made by the poor in the 1950s and 1960s. However, in east Asia (including China) per capita GDP growth averaged 6.6 per cent pa. In contrast to the East Asian NICs who could cover their debt repayments through export revenues, many countries were forced to turn to the IMF for loans. These are subject to strict conditionality. In order to get the IMF seal of approval, often a minimum condition for getting loans from commercial banks as well as the IMF, a structural adjustment programme (SAP) has to be agreed to. This policy package is based on the free market ideas of the New Right. Governments are required to reduce the role of the state, for example through privatization, reduce welfare spending, and free up the economy. This may involve removing distortions to the market by freeing producer prices, removing food subsidies and dismantling state marketing boards in order to encourage agricultural producers. Within this framework, economies should develop according to comparative advantage, specializing in what they are good at producing whether that is mange-tout and carnations for export to the First World, minerals or electronic components. The 1990s have seen continued economic growth in much of Asia and a return to growth in many middle income countries, particularly in Latin America, which have continued to implement liberal economic programmes and experienced an increase in foreign investment. There have been few signs of recovery in Africa.

It is clear from the foregoing discussion that in the postwar period the international system has had a huge impact on Third World states in both economic and political terms. However, as the critics of underdevelopment theory point out, it is crucial not to overemphasize external conditions to the exclusion of internal factors. The ways in which the internal and external interact together in processes of social and economic change in the national context is an important issue in any analysis of Third World politics whether or not it takes gender as its primary focus. The discussion of the role of the Third World in the international system also demonstrates why achieving 'development' has been such an explicit priority for many Third World states since independence, seen by many as a way of breaking out of the poverty and dependence which is considered to be a consequence of the position of the Third World in the international system. Development, too is a highly gendered process and has a very different impact on men and women.

Development

Since the 1960s development has become a catch-all phrase which covers a variety of different processes and activities. It is often seen as synonymous with wider forms of social and economic change, particularly the spread and development of capitalist social relations. Development is also associated more narrowly with the policies and strategies implemented to achieve it. The question of what constitutes development and how to go about achieving it has been hotly debated. Definitions have often polarized between whether economic growth, that is a per capita increase in GDP alone, constitutes development or whether development has a normative content in that it involves an increase in well-being and an improvement in living standards for the majority. Dudley Seers (1979) argued that economic growth was a necessary but not a sufficient condition for development to take place. He stressed the satisfaction of human needs as a key criterion. For this to be achieved, he argued, three conditions had to be fulfilled: people had to be able to buy the physical necessities of life, particularly food; have employment; and there should be equality. A variant of this kind of approach entitled 'basic needs strategies' became popular with multilateral agencies in the mid-1970s, which placed great emphasis on improving health, nutrition and education for the majority of the population.

Many alternative strategies and policy options have been implemented to achieve 'development'. Choices can be made about the balance between industrialization and rural development, the market and the state, and large and small scale projects. There are three main sets of strategies which have resolved the question of these alternatives in different ways. They are 'social-ist' development, capitalist development and the 'third way', neither capitalist not communist. Several Third World countries such as Vietnam, Mozambique and Cuba have, at varying times, followed the 'socialist' models set by the USSR and China. These will be considered in more detail in Chapter 4. A variety of states, from Argentina under General Perón 1946–55 to Jamaica in the 1970s under Michael Manley's PNP, professed to be following a 'third way', associated with the non-aligned movement and the desire for more independent autonomous economies. However, despite an emphasis on planning, an important role for the state and nationalization, it is hard to see this either as a coherent strategy, or as outside a capitalist system. The majority of Third World states have followed variants of capitalist development. Most policy debates have centred on the merits of different strategies within a capitalist framework, with differing emphases on the role of the state and varying types of industrialization such as ISI and EOI.

In addition to the widespread debate which has taken place about strategies, the major theoretical approaches to development have also been analysed (Toye 1987). The three major frameworks which have dominated development thinking have already been described briefly. Modernization theory dominated liberal development thinking in the 1950s and 1960s. Underdevelopment and dependency theory became the radical alternative during the late 1960s and 1970s. The third is neo-liberalism, which while not strictly a variant of development theory, has had a huge impact on both analysis and policy, most marked during the 1980s. While none of these perspectives deal explicitly with gender issues in any great detail, they are all gendered. In contrast, several gendered approaches to development have emerged, in part as critiques of these dominant frameworks. The rest of this chapter will look at the implications of these frameworks and their critiques. While they are often overlapping and difficult to disentangle, it will concentrate in particular on the development of various permutations of the WID (women in development), GAD (gender and development), and empowerment approaches and link them to the policy prescriptions which have emerged from them.

Modernization theory said very little specifically about women. In addition to recognizing that in the transition from 'traditional' to 'modern' societies, some of the traditional values deemed necessary to modern society were maintained by women in the family (such as affectivity), it was believed that modernization would be emancipatory for women, as industrialization, technology and modern values would undermine the patriarchy of traditional society giving women increased access to economic resources (Jaquette 1982). Any failure of this process was seen, not as a failure of modernization, but as a failure of diffusion due to women's relative 'backwardness', caused by the persistence of irrational attitudes and lack of exposure to modern society (Jaquette 1982: 269). The ideas of development planners and their projects reflected these assumptions.

By the late 1960s modernization theory was subject to criticism from many quarters. At this time, there was also a growing perception of a failure of development more generally which combined with the unhappiness of First World women, influenced by the second wave of feminism, about the impact of modernization on women in the Third World. These factors culminated in the emergence of the 'women in development' movement which was inspired by liberal feminism. While WID was in part a response to the inadequacies of the modernization approach, it remained largely within this paradigm. Kabeer (1994) argues that WID retains a universalizing discourse of the individual rational economic agent. Its critique began from the premise that women were not benefiting from modernization and development because of a lack of proper access to a process which was fundamentally a beneficial one (Bourque and Warren 1990: 84). Ester Boserup's work, *Women's Role in Economic Development*, published in 1970, is seen as a landmark in the development of feminist critiques of development policies. It argued that processes of economic modernization marginalized women economically and socially and increased their dependence on men. Boserup undertook a comparative empirical analysis of women's economic role in the developing world and argued, using data primarily drawn from Africa, that in fact new technology in farming actually lowered women's status by reducing their access to productive work, and that during the colonial period and afterwards women were increasingly relegated to the subsistence economy as cash crop production and wage jobs were only made available to men (Boserup 1970).

This kind of approach was utilized in a large number of subsequent studies (Tinker 1976). Many looked at the impact of development planning and projects on women (Rogers 1980). Rogers argued that development planners ignored women's productive activities partly because national accounting ignored much of women's work within the household and subsistence economy, assuming them to be 'housewives', directing technology, credit and other forms of assistance to men. Mainstream development projects therefore largely benefited men, often at the expense of women, displacing women from their traditional productive functions and diminishing the power, status and income they had previously enjoyed (Moser 1991). Where women were included, it was on sex specific terms as housewives, mothers and 'at risk producers' (Kabeer 1994: 5). This has been characterized by Buvinic (1983) as the 'welfare approach' to women and development, which identified women as a vulnerable group, needing help particularly in their reproductive role. The development projects which did cater for women often concentrated on improving women's domestic skills such as childcare and nutrition (Rogers 1980). Where projects addressed women's need to generate income, it was through schemes which fitted in with dominant perceptions of womens' roles such as the production of women's 'traditional' handicrafts catering to insecure markets, often for tourists or export. Women's projects were therefore often ghettoized leaving the majority to cater for men.

The WID critique was translated into policy proposals. The WID group worked to influence USAID policy and in 1973 as a result of lobbying, a congressional amendment mandated US assistance to 'move women into their national economies'. The WID approach was also influential in determining the priorities for the UN Decade for Women (1975–85). The solution to inequality was therefore seen as widening access to factors such as tools, technology and education. Women had to be integrated into development more effectively and not allow it to pass them by. This has been characterized as an 'equity approach' which acknowledged women's productive as well as reproductive role and started from the assumption that economic development strategies had often had a negative effect on women

(Buvinic 1983). It argued, according to Moser (1991), that women had to be brought into the development process through access to employment and the marketplace. It also, very importantly, placed great emphasis on the wider question of equality, and on the need to reduce inequality between men and women. Despite its essentially liberal feminist and reformist bent, wanting to improve women's lot within the existing system, Moser (1993) argues that the equity approach aroused hostility among development agencies and Third World governments.

Towards the end of the 1970s an anti-poverty emphasis emerged as the second WID approach. It was, in part, a toning down of the equity approach which had required agencies to interfere in the relations between men and women (Buvinic 1983). It also coincided with increasing disillusionment with the belief that the benefits of economic growth would trickle down to the poor. This provided the spur both to the ILO to shift its emphasis to employment, focusing on the working poor and the potential of the informal sector, and to the agencies such as the World Bank to redirect their efforts towards the eradication of poverty and redistribution with growth. An important part of this reorientation was the 'basic needs strategy' discussed earlier in the chapter. The new focus on women could be accommodated within the development agencies by linking women to poverty alleviation and basic needs (Kabeer 1994: 7). As part of this new emphasis, low income women could be identified as one important group to be singled out for particular attention, partly because existing projects had ignored their needs and partly because of the important role women generally play in fulfilling basic needs within the household. The anti-poverty approach therefore stressed income generating projects for poor women, often ignoring their reproductive roles and their interconnection with productive roles and without the emphasis on increasing women's autonomy that the equity approach had implied.

Disillusionment with modernization theory also provided an important impetus to the development of underdevelopment theory, discussed above. As part of this, the liberal analyses of women's roles in modernization and economic development provoked critiques from feminist academics writing from a dependency or a global economy perspective (Beneria and Sen 1981). Writers in this school differed fundamentally with the WID critics on a number of important issues. They argued first that the process of modernization and the spread of capitalism was not an inherently beneficial one, but on the contrary, involved widespread exploitation, and within this, the exploitation of women took on particular forms. Second, analysts believed that the individual focus of the liberal perspective lacked a coherent theoretical explanation of the bases of women's subordination, relying on 'irrational' prejudice and sex role stereotypes, reducing the accuracy of their analyses and the effectiveness of their policy prescriptions (Beneria and Sen 1981; Kabeer 1994).

Analyses within this framework, often by socialist feminists influenced by structuralist perspectives including Marxist analyses of capitalism and imperialism, tended to place greater emphasis on analysing the wider global processes of accumulation involved in the spread of capitalist social relations and their impact on gender relations, as well as looking at the impact of particular policies and projects (Young *et al.* 1981). Beneria and Sen conclude in a much quoted passage:

> Contrary to Boserup's implications, the problem for women is not only the lack of participation in this process [of modernization] as equal partners with men; it is a system [of international capital accumulation] that generates and intensifies inequalities, making use of existing gender hierarchies to place women in subordinate positions at each different level of interaction between class and gender. This is not to deny the possibility that capitalist development might break down certain social rigidities oppressive to women. But these liberating tendencies are accompanied by new forms of subordination.
>
> (1981: 290)

These studies performed a twofold task: they incorporated a much needed gender perspective to the analyses of dependency, underdevelopment and the new international division of labour. They also developed much more complex and sophisticated theoretical frameworks, often utilizing ideas developed by socialist feminists for the analysis of gender relations in the First World, expounded in the previous chapter, to analyse gender and development. The emphasis of analysis therefore shifted towards the study of gender relations rather than simply concentrating on women.

A more thorough-going examination of the roots of women's subordination became important, and this was done through an analysis of the global workings of capitalism in combination with patriarchy. For example processes linking different parts of the global economy like migration and tourism were examined in gendered terms (Mies 1986). Despite criticisms of overgeneralization made of writers such as Mies, there was acknowledgement of the need for both specificity and of macrostructural analyses of gender relations within the workings of international capital. Different levels of analysis were used, requiring an examination of the role played by the sexual division of labour and the links between the spheres of production and reproduction in the subordination of women (Edholm *et al.* 1977). Concepts of reproduction and domestic labour were seen to take on particular meanings in a Third World context where the household is often a productive as well as reproductive unit and peasant households and poor households in urban areas are often producing for subsistence and the market. As a result greater emphasis was placed on the household, the role of gender relations within it and the links between the household as an economic unit and the global economy (Mies 1982).

This approach has become known as gender and development (GAD) and its emergence has been associated with the Subordination of Women (SOW) workshop at the Institute of Development Studies (IDS), Sussex in September 1978. It has been influential within academic development discourse and a number of important studies have been produced within this framework.

However, it has had less impact on development agencies and planners, a consequence of its emphasis on fundamental social transformation combined with a lack of concrete policy prescriptions which can be implemented on a small scale. Given that GAD has a greater influence on analysis, it is useful to have a look at some of the main areas which have been examined using this framework.

Studies have analysed the impact of the spread of capitalist social relations, focusing on production and reproduction and the links between them in both agricultural and industrial spheres from the colonial period onwards. They have traced the changes in class and gender relations and the household in agricultural production (Deere 1977; Beneria 1982). Some analyses have demonstrated that the rather rigid distinction made by Boserup (1970) in Africa between subsistence and cash crop farming as female and male systems respectively was too crude and simplistic (Whitehead 1990). The Green Revolution in India provided an example of the way in which the introduction of new techniques, such as high yield seeds and fertilizers, altered the class position of different peasant households and the amount of productive labour undertaken by different groups of women both as unpaid labour within the household and as paid labour outside of it (Agarwal 1984, 1986). Linking the rural and urban, Kate Young (1978, 1982) traced the social and economic processes by which women were displaced from the land in Oaxaca in Mexico and therefore made up most of the migrants to the cities, a phenomenon common in many other parts of Latin America, but very different to the African experience where migration has been more of a male phenomenon.

The gendered nature of much industrial production in the Third World has also been highlighted. Women's labour has played a crucial role in the new international division of labour and the global accumulation of capital. Women's participation in the industrial labour force in developing countries has risen faster than men's, increasing from 21 per cent in 1960 to 26.5 per cent in 1980, while the overall share of women in the labour force remained constant at around 32 per cent (Joekes 1987: 80). In some developing countries, for example, Hong Kong, South Korea, Taiwan, Thailand and the Philippines, women form more than 40 per cent of the industrial labour force, and in Hong Kong and Taiwan it is around 50 per cent – higher than in any First World country. It has been widely commented that women's labour has played a particularly significant part in the EOI strategies of the NICs, often concentrated in the light consumer goods and electronics industries. Park (1993: 132) has argued that women's participation was crucial to the success of manufacturing industry, the 'engine' of South Korea's economic development. These 'female manufacturing industries' accounted for 70 per cent of total national export earnings in 1975, and 80 per cent of the women in the manufacturing sector produced export orientated products in the 1970s.

MNCs have also demonstrated a propensity to employ female labour to complete the most labour intensive parts of manufacturing processes, which are often located in free trade zones in developing countries and most marked in the electronics and textile industries (Mitter 1986). MNCs utilize existing gender relations to their advantage to employ female labour, capitalizing on particular notions of skill and the lower wages paid to women, as well as transforming systems of outworking and household production (Elson and Pearson 1981). It must be remembered that while the export orientated industrial production of the NICs has become increasingly important to the global economy, the absolute number of women factory workers employed as a proportion of the total female workforce in the Third World is still small. Indeed, the use of female industrial labour has not been so marked in those areas implementing ISI except in the light consumer industries such as textiles and footwear. Other commonly promoted domestic industries such as steel production and car manufacturing have not typically utilized women's labour.

The third framework, neo-liberalism and the policy prescriptions which accompany it, while not strictly a corpus of development theory, has eclipsed both modernization and underdevelopment theory and dominated development thinking since the early 1980s. Milton Friedman and Friedrich Hayek provide the theoretical basis for many of these ideas, emphasizing the unfettered working of the free market to promote economic growth. While appearing gender neutral, the theories have implicit within them an assumption of certain gender relations and particular roles for women (Waylen 1986; Elson 1991). While talking of gender free individuals as the basic unit of analysis, the assumption is that women are subsumed within the household providing important reproductive services, leaving men to be the individuals and head of households who enter the free market and the public sphere. The implementation of free market policies and structural adjustment, the major policy prescription flowing from this kind of analysis, has been widely promoted by international institutions such as the World Bank and IMF.

Structural adjustment programmes have particular implications for different groups of women (Afshar and Dennis 1992). Privatization of state enterprises and the reduction in the size of state bureaucracies often mean a reduction in employment opportunities for many, particularly middle-class professional women who often form a large proportion of the teachers, social workers and nurses. The inability of governments to increase welfare spending and indeed the pressure to cut it has implications for women as both providers and consumers of state services such as health and social services, resulting in the expenditure of greater time and effort to replace them. At the same time, increased unemployment and the introduction of measures such as the removal of food subsidies means that women in poor households have to adopt survival strategies which involve greater income generation often through participation in the informal sector, again resulting in the expenditure of greater time and effort (Elson 1992). The contradictory impact of neo-liberal policies, while increasing the burdens on particularly poor women in the household, means that many women are forced to increase their income generating activities as part of household survival strategies, at the same time as women's employment is increased, particularly in the service sector, as part of the restructuring of the economy. In Chile in the 1980s, jobs taken predominantly by women were created in the financial and retail sectors and also in the export agriculture sector (Waylen 1992a). Adjustment, critics therefore argue, is premised on utilizing the elasticity of women's unpaid labour within the household to improve 'economic efficiency' by pushing reproductive activities back into the household, where women's labour is uncounted and unremunerated, so that the costs do not appear in economic calculations (Palmer 1992; Stewart 1992).

The widespread implementation of SAPs by Third World governments at the behest of international institutions has coincided with the predominance of the third variant of WID, identified by Moser (1991: 103) as the 'efficiency approach'. As a consequence, attention has shifted towards development, ensuring that it is made more efficient and effective through women's economic contribution. Kabeer (1994) argues that there is now a new equation: women + production = efficiency. It has been suggested that after two decades of claims that development plans and projects would not succeed unless women's potential and actual productive roles were recognized, parts of a feminist agenda have been absorbed into development thinking. However this has happened in an instrumentalist manner, that is the improvement of women's lives is seen as a mechanism to achieve other development goals, such as population control rather than as a valuable end in itself.

The 1980s also saw the emergence of a new set of critiques of much of the existing literature and policies and projects. Although overlapping and intersecting, three different bodies can be identified. The first critique derives from the work of Third World feminists such as DAWN (Development Alternatives for a New Era), a network of activists, researchers and policymakers formed in India in 1984 (Sen and Grown 1987). The second, still in its infancy, has been labelled a postmodern feminist critique of women and development theory and practice, and despite its very different approach, draws much of its inspiration from the work of DAWN (Parpart 1993). The third consists of mainly First World feminist academics wanting to improve development analysis and policy.

Echoing many of the themes elaborated in the previous chapter, all three groups have criticized much of the WID (and early GAD) literature on several counts. First for the ways in which it homogenizes women, seeing them as a single unitary category ignoring difference. Second, it assumes that women are passive recipients of development policies and projects, that is that Third World women are seen as the passive objects of policy, not agents of change in their own right (Mohanty 1988). Third, as a corollary of this, many of the policy prescriptions and projects are seen as primarily top-down ones imposed from above. More generally much of the literature is seen as ethnocentric, avoiding thorny questions of the understanding and exercise of power and failing to address how knowledge and hierarchies of knowledge are constructed within development discourse.

Lim's (1990) critique of those analyses emanating from an underdevelopment/global economy perspective is representative of the criticisms of a wide range of WID and GAD work. She (1990: 101) argues much of it presented a 'widely accepted stereotype of poverty-stricken Third World women suffering low wages, wretched working conditions, and ruthless exploitation by multinationals', particularly in export processing free trade zones. Lim argues that a more complex and sophisticated analysis is necessary which shows that there is considerable diversity both among women workers in export factories in terms of their social origins, education, age and marital status and in terms of the pay, conditions and status accruing to those jobs. She (1990: 109) claims that the wages earned by women in export factories are generally higher than those in alternative employment which might be available to those women. What is needed, according to Lim, is a more dynamic historical approach, particularly important given the huge changes which have occurred since the 1970s. An analysis of the role of race and racism is also missing from much of this work, as for example there is no recognition that the images of women workers in export processing as passive and 'nimble fingered' involve the overt utilization of racist images of the 'exotic oriental female'.

New directions have emerged therefore in both analysis and policy. The need for greater specificity and sensitivity in terms of approach and methodology is stressed (Elson 1991; Ostergaard 1992). New areas and forms of analysis are being explored. The household, both rural and urban, has become an important focus as its internal dynamics have a huge impact on gender relations, highlighting the need to disaggregate household relations in terms of the resource allocation within it (Young 1992; Kabeer 1994). The notion of 'cooperative conflict' has been utilized to do this (Sen 1990; Elson 1993). Feminist academics are also trying to make sure that gendered analyses are incorporated into all areas. The environment provides one example. The causes and impact of the degradation of the environment can only be understood in gendered terms, as for example, it is generally women within the household who have the major responsibility for collecting water and fuel and any policies implemented to try and reduce environmental damage, such as through the introduction of more fuel efficient cooking methods, have to take different women's needs into account if they are to succeed (Jackson 1993). Stemming from criticisms of structural adjustment, there have been more general calls for gender equity in all development policy and planning (Elson 1992; Palmer 1992).

The critiques of WID and GAD have helped the emergence of a new focus on 'empowerment'. This brings questions of power and politics, widely defined, to the top of the agenda. In a rejection of the top-down imposition of many development schemes the focus has shifted towards bottom-up development. This entails a vibrant civil society created through grassroots collective organizing. Acknowledging difference between women, this also necessitates greater consideration of the construction of identities and interests and highlights the need for alliances between different groups of women. Many of the women's activities described in the last chapter fit into this model of development as 'empowerment'. This approach, while increasingly advocated by First World feminists, is more identified with Third World feminists than First World development practitioners, while governments and international agencies often only adopt 'empowerment' instrumentally as a means to achieve other goals. DAWN (Sen and Grown 1987) have laid out not only their gendered analyses of the wider processes of development and social change, but also put forward ideas for both long term structural change aimed at the elimination of inequality based on class, gender and race, that is around strategic gender interests, and for more short term strategies for grassroots development initiatives which would empower individual women and organizations.

Conclusion

In this chapter we have discussed the meaning of the term Third World and concluded that while it is still useful, it has to be employed very carefully trying not to homogenize and overgeneralize the experience of very different regions and countries. We also examined the nature of the Third World in both economic and political terms, focusing particularly on the ways it has been incorporated into the international system. This inevitably led to a discussion of development: what it is; how to achieve it; and how it is gendered. After examining the major approaches to gender and development and ending with a model of development as 'empowerment', we have concluded the preliminary discussions which provide the backdrop to the rest of the book. It is now possible to put forward a gendered analysis of the internal dynamics of Third World politics through an examination of four different political formations: colonialism, revolution, authoritarianism and democratization.

3

Colonialism

Introduction

Colonialism has often been seen as a quintessentially masculine project, consisting of white men subjugating and civilizing 'natives', also male. The reality of course was different. European women were the 'inferior sex' within the 'superior race' and colonized women played a crucial role within the whole project. This racial dimension was central to colonialism as issues of race and difference became sharply focused. Different groups of women were located in very different positions within the colonial hierarchy, not only according to their class position but also importantly which racial grouping they were deemed to belong to. European women had an entirely different experience of colonialism to women of the colonized peoples.

According to Etienne and Leacock (1980: 17) two incompatible and simplistic (yet familiar) views of women and colonization used to dominate analyses of the impact of colonialism on the colonized. On the one hand, colonization was seen as bringing modernization and therefore as beneficial to women, and on the other, colonized women were seen as its passive victims. In a similar vein, Mohanty and Mohanty (1990: 19) argue that dominant models saw colonialism as an encounter between tradition and modernity. However, it is important to see the colonized not simply as objects of colonial policy but as agents in their own right. As we will see much 'tradition' was actually invented during the colonial period by the colonial state acting together with indigenous rulers (Ranger 1983). It is therefore necessary to consider the collusion between the colonial state and traditional patriarchal forms (Mohanty and Mohanty 1990: 19). Simplistic analyses are not possible as the relationship between gender and colonialism is in fact complex and contradictory.

There is now a large and innovative literature on many aspects of gender and colonialism particularly emphasizing political economy and cultural history.

Much of this work such as Sangari and Vaid (1990) has pioneered the use of new approaches in the study of history more generally, looking at the construction of knowledge and power through colonial discourse. This chapter focuses first on the impact of colonialism on gender relations and women in particular; second on the ways in which the processes inherent within colonialism were gendered and third on the roles played by different women in supporting and resisting colonialism. It will look at some of the attempts to use particular forms of gender relations and also at attempts to alter gender relations in order to create and maintain colonial structures.

An examination of a historical phenomenon like colonialism forms an important part of a study of gender and Third World politics. The nature of the colonial experience has been hotly debated. Of particular relevance to this book is the controversy over the role of colonialism in the making of the contemporary Third World, its connection to the spread of capitalist economic relations and whether a 'colonial legacy' still exists. Underdevelopment and dependency theorists have long seen the incorporation of the Third World into the global economic system as exploitative and colonialism as an important early mechanism through which this occurred. Modernization theorists have tended to have a more benign view of the colonial experience, seeing it as one way in which the 'modern' did meet the 'traditional'. Most are agreed, however, that colonization played a profound social, political and economic role in the creation of what is now considered to be the Third World and that some knowledge of it is necessary for an understanding of its contemporary politics. This argument can be extended to gender relations. No understanding of contemporary gender relations in the Third World can be complete without some analysis and discussion of the colonial period.

The scope and range of the colonial experience is enormous. Fieldhouse (1981) defines the wider phenomenon of imperialism in a broad and minimalist way as the domination of one society by another. Colonialism involves the formal political control of one society by another. This occurred on a huge scale. The colonization of what is now the Third World by the First World was a dynamic and changing process lasting for over 500 years. Some analysts have divided the colonial experience into the 'old' and 'new' empires (Bernstein and Crow 1988). The old empires began with the Spanish and Portuguese conquest of Latin America and parts of the Caribbean from the late fifteenth and sixteenth centuries. They were followed in the seventeenth and eighteenth centuries by other European countries, particularly the English and the Dutch, who moved into the Caribbean and later the East Indies. The old empires had some particular characteristics. The Spanish and Portuguese empires were initially based on pillage and plunder and organized on an almost feudal basis with the monarchs at their head. In the seventeenth and eighteenth centuries merchants and trade tended to play the leading role in the Dutch and English colonies, and the informal trading networks, in existence as part of the period of mercantile accumulation, preceded the development of capitalism. The slave trade which forcibly moved so many Africans to the 'new world' and the creation of the plantation economies of much of the

Americas are two lasting consequences of this period of imperialism (Barratt Brown 1963).

The nineteenth century saw a move away from relationships primarily conducted through trade towards a huge increase in the extent of formal colonialism with the development of the new empires (Wolf 1982). Indeed European imperialism in Asia and Africa reached its height between the last quarter of the nineteenth century to World War II. This chapter will focus on this period and the experience of Africa (and to some extent India) for a number of reasons. First, there is a larger literature on the African (and Indian) experience. Second, these analyses tend to focus on the more contemporary period and therefore are of more immediate relevance to this book. There is a body of work on the colonial period in Latin America and the Caribbean but it looks primarily at the sixteenth, seventeenth and eighteenth centuries, focusing in the Caribbean case primarily on the experience of slavery (Nash 1980; Reddock 1985; Beckles 1989; Bush 1990).

Historians differ in their analyses of why the extension of formal colonialism took place in Africa in the nineteenth century. Some argue that the motives for the scramble for Africa were strategic and political while others claim that they were primarily economic, as this phase of imperialist expansion is inextricably linked to the development of capitalism (Rodney 1972). The colonizing countries were concerned to secure sources of those raw materials, such as cotton, palm oil, rubber and jute, which were essential for the new industrial processes and to ensure markets for the finished manufactured products. This era of colonialism brought profound changes, many linked to the spread of capitalism, such as the creation and extension of export economies, monocultures and the development of markets and class structures.

Lonsdale and Berman (1979) have argued that during this period colonialism had two contradictory impulses and aims: capital accumulation and social control. The needs of capital accumulation meant altering social and economic structures if colonies were to be minimally self-financing to pay for their own administration, if not profitable in the broader sense. At the same time, attempts to maintain social control meant trying to limit social dislocation as much as possible. The contradictory processes of capital accumulation and social control had a profound impact on gender relations. Changes in structure and nature of production and accumulation such as in landholding and the organization of labour affected relations between men and women. In addition the attempts at social control were often enforced in gendered terms through controls over women's mobility and sexuality, and the regulation of relations between men and women through marriage and adultery laws.

In the face of colonialism's contradictory impulses and aims, the legitimation of their rule was a major problem for all colonial powers. The maintenance and implementation of colonialism entirely through force would have been an impossible undertaking in terms of both human and financial resources. Other means had to be found to achieve this. The construction of knowledge was one way through which the institution of colonial rule could be legitimated to both colonizers and colonized. Colonialism was justified through an ideology of racial superiority epitomized by the 'civilizing mission', disguised according to Strobel (1991: xiii) in patriarchal and paternalistic language which identified the imperial power as the 'mother country', placing the colonies as her immature children. A colonial discourse emerged in which the 'natives' were constructed as other and inferior, and the Orient as exotic and irrational compared to the rational West (Said 1978). Therefore the West constructed a systematic knowledge of its colonial subjects in all parts of the world which enabled it to regulate them more efficiently (Said 1978; Bhabha 1993).

Colonial discourse was also highly gendered. De Groot (1989) has highlighted how the Orient and its accompanying imagery was seen as female. As Veena Das (1986) and others have pointed out, 'the knowledge about women was organised and interpreted in a manner permitting such claims of legitimacy to be defended'. British attitudes towards sati (the Hindu practice of widow burning) in India in the early nineteenth century are cited as one area where the construction of knowledge became important and a wide ranging debate on sati has ensued (Loomba 1993). Das (1986: 67) argues that sati came to occupy a prominent place in British administrative and missionary discourse because 'the rite of sati was considered objective evidence for the barbarity of the Hindus and could be assimilated to the category of violent crime which needed the firm hand of the British to suppress it. This launched the civilising mission of the British rule.' Lata Mani (1987) also analyses how the official discourse on sati was produced, and argues that, contrary to the popular perception that British concern was to protect the interests of Hindu women, women were not the objects of the discourse, nor were they its subjects as they were not seen as agents; indeed the women themselves were quickly marginal to the debate. Instead women were 'the ground of the discourse on sati' about what constituted authentic cultural tradition and the debate was framed within a series of constraints created 'by the requirements of an expanding colonial power in need of systematic and unambiguous modes of governance, of law, for instance out of a particular view of Indian society' (Mani 1987: 123).

Regulation through legal channels therefore became a central mechanism of control. The process and importance of creating bodies of law in Africa will be explored below through analysing the ways in which customary law was justified in terms of 'tradition' and used by both colonial and indigenous male authorities to their own advantage. Both colonial authority and racial distinctions, fundamental to the colonial project, were therefore very profoundly structured in gendered terms.

It is hard to generalize about the nature of colonialism because of the huge diversity of experience. Colonialism did not take place on a *tabula rasa*, but the nature of colonial rule was affected by the pre-existing social, economic and political structures. The exact nature of the colonial experience therefore varied according to the particular interaction between the colonizer and the society being colonized. The impact of colonialism on gender relations was varying and contradictory. Some have argued that it was entirely negative, only acting to increase women's subordination. However this view is overly simplistic as some of the changes brought by colonialism did allow some space for some women to resist, use and challenge both new and existing patterns of gender relations. In order to examine this complex experience, we need to start with a discussion of the varying characteristics of certain pre-colonial African societies, as the colonial experience cannot be understood without this background. We shall proceed using an adapted version of the framework elaborated in the first chapter and explore some of the myriad ways in which pre-existing gender relations interacted with the new forms of social, economic and political organization introduced by the colonizers to produce new patterns. First we will look at the political organization of colonialism which is closest to the category of 'conventional politics', then we shall move on to examine the impact of colonial policy on gender relations, both in terms of more general policies and those aimed particularly at women, before turning to examine different forms of women's political activity, particularly in resisting colonialism and in nationalist struggles. We will concentrate primarily on the British colonial experience in Africa and India, in part because the British had the largest colonial empire and also because it has been the most thoroughly researched in the English language.

Pre-colonial societies

Pre-colonial societies did not conform to modernization theorists' under-standing of 'traditional' societies. Many studies of pre-colonial African societies, despite the problems in analysing both pre-colonial and colonial periods because knowledge is so dependent on mediation by colonial texts and sources, have described societies which were dynamic and developing (Rodney 1972). Prior to the advent of formal colonialism, many societies, for example in West Africa, had extensive contact with Europe, often through trading relation-ships. Societies all over Africa exhibited a huge diversity and variety in social, political and economic organization and gender relations and were not static and unchanging. They ranged from subsistence producing societies of East Africa to surplus producing societies in West Africa, which, while peasant-based, were frequently sophisticated hierarchical kingdoms and empires. The majority of African societies were patrilineal rather than matrilineal, that is rights and inheritance passed through the male rather than the female line. In patrilineal societies women were expected to move to their husband's village and were allowed fewer legal rights, giving them less economic secur-ity, for example in terms of access to land and use rights over it (Henn 1984).

While gender relations in pre-colonial African society were not character-ized by equality, however judged, they often entailed greater *inter*dependence than 'modern' societies, with men and women having different but, in many ways, complementary roles. Women often had a degree of autonomy and control over their lives with high levels of solidarity along the lines of gender as much social stratification was based on gender (Staudt 1986). Much of this autonomy stemmed from the access to and control over economic resources which many women exercised in different forms, although this was on unequal terms to men. In the agricultural sphere land was often held in common and women often had use rights over it. However in patrilineal societies access was indirect through men and ultimately insecure as rights were granted by husbands and therefore somewhat precarious, dependent on women becoming and remaining wives. Women often carried out the majority of agricultural work and had responsibility for subsistence production to feed their children, while men performed only a limited number of tasks such as land clearing and preparation. Women often had budgetary independence within the household as they did not see themselves providing unpaid family labour as part of the same economic unit as their husbands, but would often charge men for the use of their labour. In addition to their roles in the agricultural sphere, women, particularly in West Africa, often played important roles in trade both of agricultural and other commodities such as cloth. Women were both market traders and organizers of local and long range trading networks, for example the Ga market women of Accra in Ghana (Robertson 1976).

Etienne's study (1980) of the Baule in what is now the Ivory Coast is an often quoted example of the interdependence and reciprocity which existed in the relations between men and women. For the Baule, the two major items produced, vital to subsistence, were yams and cloth. Those who were considered to have initiated production and taken responsibility for it controlled the product and its distribution. While yams and cloth required the labour of both men and women at different stages, men initiated the production of yams and therefore controlled their distribution and women initiated the production of cloth and therefore took responsibility for it. Men 'owned' the yams because they cleared and prepared the ground; women would then tend the plants, intercropping cotton between them. The cotton was then handed over to their husbands to weave before being returned to the women to distribute. According to Etienne (1980: 221), the control a woman had over cloth 'inevitably gave her power and autonomy both in the conjugal relationship and in Baule society in general'. However, possibilities existed within the production process for men to reduce the control that women had over it.

The economic status enjoyed by women which came through their role in production often brought with it certain political rights, particularly in those societies which permitted women to accumulate wealth (Johnson 1986). Jean O'Barr (1984: 143) claims that, despite huge variations between African societies, in most agricultural communities, whether matrilineal or patrilineal,

women usually (1) had political control over some area of activity, be it farming, marketing, trading or household and family affairs; (2) had political institutions (usually councils) to decide how to rule their own affairs or to influence the affairs of men; and (3) were not subject to general control by men as much as they were autonomous in their own areas of responsibility.

This was often expressed through various women's groups and networks organized around kinship, age, culture and production. While never acting on equal terms with men, women often had well-defined political roles and structures which allowed them a certain degree of power and control within society. Rarely women could become chiefs in their own right, for example among the Mende and Serbo of Sierra Leone, or, as in the matrilineal Akan of southern Ghana, the 'queen mother' could play something of a role as kingmaker.

Judith Van Allen (1972) has analysed the female networks of political organization and solidarity among the Igbo of southern Nigeria. The women had their own structures of power which dealt with issues which concerned them, including the regulation of markets. These structures were headed by a female official, the omu, who had her own council of elders paralleling that of the male official, the obi. Meetings named mikiri were held where women could resolve issues arising from their roles particularly as traders, but also as farmers, wives and mothers. Women could also resort to taking sanctions both on other women and on men to resolve individual or collective grievances. 'Making war on' or 'sitting on a man' – surrounding his hut and protesting at his behaviour – was recognized by men as a legitimate and effective course of action for women to take, as was the strike – refusing to cook meals and provide other services for men (Van Allen 1972). Kemene Okonjo (1976) has named this arrangement where women and men each had separate structures to control their affairs a 'dual sex system'.

While it is impossible to generalize about all pre-colonial societies, it is possible to argue that, while gender relations were not generally characterized by equality and an absence of male dominance, women often had a degree of autonomy and control over their lives. The colonizers brought with them different cultural constructions of gender – those of nineteenth-century Europe – which, to a greater or lesser degree, they tried to impose on the societies they took over. As we will see, the varying nature of gender relations in different pre-colonial societies had an important impact in determining what the outcome of the interaction between the colonized and the colonizer would be.

The colonial period

'Conventional politics' had a very narrow and restricted meaning in the colonial context. Colonies were administered bureaucratically, and, as they were not run on a liberal democratic model, competitive electoral politics did not function. Except at the lower levels, the colonized, particularly colonized women, were excluded from the running of the colonies. There were few, if any, channels of representation for the majority of the colonized populations. In some of the Caribbean colonies such as Jamaica, there was a limited franchise for election to the legislative council which had some powers to intervene in the running of the colony. The only other exceptions were the settler colonies such as Kenya where the white settlers were allowed some jurisdiction over what happened, which was more similar to dominions such as Canada, Australia and New Zealand.

Colonial administration was essentially bureaucratic, hierarchical and authoritarian. The higher levels of the administration were carried out by a small number of officials sent out from the mother country and headed by a governor responsible to a colonial office at home. Until quite late in the history of colonialism, colonial administration was a very male affair. Although some women had begun to be employed, often at very junior levels either at times of labour shortage during and after the Second World War or in the colonial welfare services, colonial officials were almost always men.

Wherever possible the British favoured combining these administrative structures with 'indirect rule' at the lower levels, that is using and adapting pre-existing structures of authority as this provided a cheap means of maintaining colonial rule. In India, both direct and indirect rule were used in the form of 'British India' and the Princely States respectively; in much of Africa, indirect rule was used as widely as possible. Indirect rulers were primarily responsible for levying colonial taxes and administering law and order, often in the form of native courts. When establishing indirect rule, colonial officials disregarded the dual sex system where it existed, thereby often destroying it and reducing the political influence of women. Among the Igbo for example the male obi was turned into a salaried official, while the female omu was ignored (Okonjo 1976). As we shall see, indirect rule often involved some degree of collusion between the colonial state and indigenous male structures of authority where their interests coincided. As Grier (1992: 325) argues, 'the policy of indirect rule reinforced the legal and coercive powers of chiefs and male elders over their historic dependents and of males over females'.

Despite indirect rule, the major division within colonies remained that between the colonized and colonizer. As such it is legitimate to examine the activities of all Europeans, not simply colonial officials, as they, men and women alike, all played a part in the wider relations of domination. Stoler (1989: 635) argues that colonialism was based on two important but false premises: first that the Europeans formed 'an easily identifiable and discrete biological and social entity; a "natural" community of common class interests, racial attributes, political affinities and superior culture'. Second, related to this, that 'the boundaries separating colonizer from the colonized were thus self-evident and easily drawn'. Categories of 'white' and 'native' therefore had to be constructed, people designated as 'white' or 'native' and the boundaries between them maintained through various mechanisms. In addition to the construction of spatial boundaries through separate areas designated for 'whites' and 'non-whites', this required 'regulating the sexual, conjugal and domestic life of both Europeans in the colonies and their colonized subjects' (Stoler

1989: 635). The colonial project was therefore partly implemented and regulated through the control of sexual morality.

Initially many of the colonial powers forbade European women from going to the colonies and the early phase of the establishment of colonial rule was carried out largely without their presence. However, by the nineteenth century, a small number of white women were present. Prior to their arrival, concubinage had been widely tolerated (Hyam 1990). At a time when the presence of white women was forbidden and married officials, particularly at lower levels, were not given employment, liaisons between male colonial officials and colonized women were seen to have a stabilizing effect on political order and to be good for the health of the officials. However, any resulting children caused potential problems by blurring the boundaries between the colonized and colonizer. By 1860 concubinage was frowned upon in India and the issue came to a head in the British Empire in general in 1909 and led to a number of circulars forbidding liaisons with indigenous women (Strobel 1991: 4).

Rather than attributing a large number of changes to the arrival of European women in the colonies, we should see their arrival as part of a restructuring of the colonial project (Stoler 1989). European women were positioned as the bearers of a redefined colonial morality which formed part of the sharpening of racial boundaries (Stoler 1989: 640). White women were seen to require different and superior amenities leading to the embourgeoisification of many colonial communities and women became responsible for 'maintaining standards', for example ensuring that the rituals associated with middle- and upper-class life at home were carried out. The presence and protection of European women was often used as a justification for the clarification of racial lines and the strict control of the colonized, particularly colonized men. While the sexual abuse of black women by white men was not classified as rape, the fear of the 'black peril' (the supposed danger of sexual assault of white women by black men due to their uncontrolled lust for white women) swept through Papua New Guinea, Rhodesia and Kenya in the 1920s and 1930s, resulting in 1926 in the imposition of the death penalty in Kenya for black men who raped white women.

The majority of European women who went to the colonies did so in their capacity as wives, either of colonial officials, men employed by trading or mining companies or settlers such as farmers (Kirkwood 1984). While colonial wives had no official role and they certainly were not paid (nor were they meant to undertake paid employment), it was assumed that they would fulfil certain functions for their husbands. Wives had the responsibility of managing the household, dealing with servants (very often male), entertaining, carrying out 'good works' and the more nebulous function of 'maintaining standards' (Brownfoot 1984). It was felt that the presence of women would help to preserve the requisite moral strictures and a certain way of life, that of the upper middle classes (Gartrell 1984). Life for many European women was very circumscribed, not extending beyond tea parties, bridge and the club, with very little contact with the colonized people except servants.

Wives were also subject to the rigid hierarchies that their husbands were part of. At social functions, such as dinner parties, wives of colonial officials were seated according to their husband's rank (Callaway 1987). This has led some to argue that colonial wives, particularly of officials, had an 'incorporated' status as their position and identity derived entirely from their husband and his position in the hierarchy (Callan 1984). While many wives were almost invisible, however, they played a vitally important role.

It would be a mistake to overhomogenize this picture. It is important to remember that there were tensions between different agents of colonialism: the officials, traders and missionaries and they did not form a monolithic group (Cooper and Stoler 1989). While the dominant stereotype of European women assumed that they were the most reactionary and racist part of the imperial project, and that, while marginal actors, their arrival was responsible for the growing rift between the colonizer and colonized, more recent feminist work has argued for a more complex and sophisticated picture which highlights both European women's complicity and their resistance (Strobel 1991: 1; Chaudhuri and Strobel 1992; Ramusack 1992; Sinha 1992). New analyses, for example, have shown how, in the nineteenth century, women activists in the 'mother country' campaigned on behalf of Empire, and British feminists working to save 'downtrodden' colonized women from 'barbarism', shared and bolstered the imperial assumptions common at the time (Burton 1992; Callaway and Helly 1992). In addition a small number of European women went to the colonies as workers such as nurses and missionaries, often in an attempt to escape some of the restrictions placed on single women in Europe (Birkett 1992). In the later phases of colonialism the notion of the 'incorporated wife' should also not be applied too rigidly. Karen Tranberg Hansen (1992), in her study of Northern Rhodesia (now Zambia) after World War II, argues that the 'incorporated' status of all wives assumes too great a class homogeneity between European women, and that certain opportunities for women to create an identity for themselves through voluntary work and paid employment did exist.

The impact of colonial policies

Colonialism brought important changes, profoundly altering political, social and economic systems. These changes were gendered in crucial ways and men and women were affected very differently. To return to Lonsdale and Berman's formulation (1979) outlined at the beginning of this chapter, colonial states had to pursue two contradictory objectives at the same time: to ensure capital accumulation while at the same time maintaining social control. We will look first at the impact that different methods of achieving capital accumulation had on gender relations before turning to examine strategies for social control.

Colonial strategies for capital accumulation were inextricably linked to the spread of capitalist social relations. These linked processes fundamentally altered the nature of production, altering the balance between production and reproduction and according to Lovett (1990: 26) 'reshaping and reorientating a variety of divergent precapitalist systems of production and social organization in order to generate both cash crops for export and labor for mines, plantations and settler estates'. Many colonial policies, such as the imposition of taxation on households, necessitating a cash income, were organized to facilitate the creation of a male, often migrant, wage labour force and encourage the production of agricultural products such as cocoa, peanuts, cotton and coffee for sale (Staudt 1989b: 75). As a result, processes of proletarianization and urbanization accompanied these developments.

These changes had a huge impact on gender relations. Many commentators agree that the development of export orientated colonial economies contributed to a reduction in the status of women, as their access to economic resources such as land and labour power decreased while most women's workloads increased (Henn 1984; Parpart 1988). Agricultural production was altered in ways which worked to break down the economic interdependence which had existed between men and women in the pre-colonial period. Men were targeted as part of the transition to cash crop agriculture, and within this group men at the top of the social hierarchy were favoured. According to Henn (1984: 11), the 'traditional powers of patriarchs and chiefs were reconstituted, as colonial states attempted to strengthen the power of those househeads and chiefs who could "produce" what the colonial powers wanted: export crops, taxes and laborers'. Efforts of the colonial state to encourage cash crop production were therefore channelled through men. Access to agricultural extension services such as training in new technologies and credit were offered by colonial officials to men, often aided by missions and sometimes settlers. According to Lovett (1990: 37), 'meetings with chiefs and influential elders were arranged by colonial officials to urge the adoption of export cash crops and to distribute the necessary seeds, at times free of charge'. This set a pattern whereby certain men could supervise cash crop production and control its proceeds. Men often withdrew from their roles in subsistence agriculture, resulting in increased workloads for women producing food crops. At the same time, women came under pressure to help in the production of colonial export crops but without rights to share in the resources generated in the process.

A number of studies have examined the effects of colonialism on gender relations in agricultural production. Etienne (1980: 225) in her examination of the Baule discussed above, describes how 'several precise changes introduced in different economic sectors were to converge and complement each other in breaking down the pre-colonial production–distribution relationship, divesting women of their control over an essential and valuable product'. First, colonization brought the opportuniy for male weavers to purchase factory-made thread, reducing their dependence on women's production. This trend was reinforced by the import of manufactured cloth and as a result of these changes women lost control over cloth production. Second, the colonial administration wanted to increase the cash crop production of cotton and policies were implemented to encourage this. Technical expertise and other extension services were directed towards men, and this was combined with taxation policies which necessitated men acquiring a cash income (as men became responsible for their wives' headtax). Unsurprisingly cash crop cotton became a man's domain. Women continued to be active in agricultural production, but because they did not control the cash crops, they were dependent on men for any reward. As a result, the interdependent relationship between men and women characteristic of the pre-colonial period broke down and women became labourers on the men's fields (Etienne 1980).

Grier (1992) details how the transition to cash crop agriculture affected women involved in the peasant production of cocoa in colonial Ghana. She argues that female labour played an important role in almost every aspect of cocoa production and that, in the new export based economy important in the last decade of the nineteenth century, the exploitation of women's labour power was intensified. In a new version of a pre-colonial practice of pawning, women were often used as security for loans for male kin who needed capital to pay debts or buy land, as porters to carry the cocoa and as family labour on cocoa and food farms. A few women played a role as cocoa traders and farmers in their own right (Grier 1992). In a trend which, as we will see, was repeated over much of colonial Africa, the courts played a key role in reinforcing these changes, particularly the increasing pressure to control women's labour power which was expressed through, for example, the reinforcement of controls on women through marriage. Chiefs, with the sanction of colonial officials, could attempt to rewrite the law to protect their interests, for example through a redefinition of pawning. The courts therefore became a place where women tried to resist these changes and struggles over the law became an important point where gender conflicts were mediated and fought out.

In addition to increasing pressures to control women's labour power, colonialism also brought changes in land tenure. The widespread and increasing limits on women's access to property, particularly access to land, has been noted by scholars examining different parts of Africa. Colonial policies favoured an individualization of property rights and it was generally men who gained land titles, while women lost their rights to customary land. Lovett (1990: 39) argues that by the 1930s the value of land as property had risen because of the expansion in cash crop production combined with developing land shortages. This resulted in the increasing fragility of women's access rights to land in the period after World War II. This tendency was consolidated in the 1950s when state-initiated land reform programmes invested land titles in men in the vast majority of cases. Okeyo (1980) has traced this process of the individualization of land tenure and a reduction of women's land rights during the colonial period for the Luo in west Kenya, arguing that the land reform programme implemented after independence had its origins in the colonial period.

In some places the change in land tenure took the form of land alienation. In parts of East Africa land was alienated for the use of white settlers and Africans were confined to native reserves. This intensified the development of a migratory labour system. The European farms and plantations, as well as large scale construction works and other enterprises, needed waged workers. Colonial policies were designed to encourage men to leave the reserves to work for European enterprises. Wages were often very low. Hay describes the methods used by colonial administrators in Kenya, in the face of reluctance on the part of many men, to force labour out of the reserves both through taxation and by fining or even dismissing chiefs who did not supply them with sufficient young men (Hay 1976). There are fewer examples of women entering waged work, but Presley (1986) describes the poor conditions, such as low wages and abuse, that women forced to work in the Kenyan coffee plantations at times of labour shortage were subjected to.

The wages paid to male workers were generally too low to support whole households. They were therefore subsidized by women's unpaid labour in the rural areas, supplying food and other goods and services from the peasant household and keeping the household going, caring for and supporting children. After World War II, there was a clearly established pattern in some regions of leaving wives and children on the land both to subsidize migrant wages and to protect male rights to the land (Hay 1982). The absence of men from rural areas increased the workload of women and children, altering the sexual division of labour. The long term absence of many husbands meant that many women in Kenya played important roles as *de facto* farm managers (Hay 1982: 120). Hay argues that Luo women responded to the withdrawal of male labour, the need to maintain a certain level of food production, declining soil fertility, increased pressure of taxes and the fragmentation of landholdings through economic innovation, particularly in terms of agricultural crops and techniques, allowing them to spend more time trading (Hay 1976). Henn (1984: 15), however, argues that a common result of the absence of males was a gradual decline in rural family welfare as the burdens increased on those left behind.

This pattern of the development of a migratory labour system was replicated over much of southern Africa (Walker 1990). Waged employment in the mines and urban areas was generally confined to men while women were expected to remain in rural areas. Waged work in urban areas was seen by the colonial authorities as a temporary rather than a permanent feature, because ultimately Africans were to remain tied to the rural economy as it was envisaged that the continent would not become industrialized or urbanized. As residence rights were only granted to those with waged employment, only men could legitimately be in urban areas. Women, when tolerated, were assumed to be the dependants of men. However, despite attempts made by the authorities to restrict the activities of women in mine compounds and urban areas, by the 1930s these were seen by many as 'loci of economic opportunity and independence' to which many women migrated (Lovett 1990: 32).

Parpart (1986) has made a study of women in the mining communities of the copperbelt of Northern Rhodesia (now Zambia). She argues that while the colonial authorities together with chiefs tried to control the movement of women into the copperbelt in the 1930s, the mining companies wanted a stable labour force and increasingly realized that the presence of women bought greater stability and higher productivity. While the companies refused to repatriate women, they did agree to supervise traditional control over marriages in the compounds and began to demand that African employees produce marriage certificates before allowing them married accommodation. Prior to this the companies had tolerated informal mine marriages, deemed to exist for example when a women had lived with and cooked meals for a worker for one week. Barnes has noted that similar arrangements existed in urban areas of Southern Rhodesia (now Zimbabwe) in the 1920s (Barnes 1992: 598). These arrangements were extremely fluid, allowing women greater autonomy to contract marriages with whom they wished and to leave unsatisfactory arrangements. Indeed Parpart (1986: 154) claims that changing partners was a major source of upward mobility for women. For married women, access to economic resources via their husbands' wages was very uncertain as men controlled their own earnings. While waged work was not available to them, many women did engage in income generating activities on their own account. Beer brewing, initially legal but subsequently outlawed, was a quick and relatively profitable way of earning money. Women grew food in gardens they planted and sold the excess production for cash. Some women, often single, engaged in prostitution, while others combined selling sexual services with domestic ones. Lovett (1990: 31) claims that one way in which 'steady relationships' were promoted was to deny economic opportunities to unmarried women, for example by denying access to single women to company land for gardening.

Similar patterns were seen in urban areas. Waged labour opportunities were only available to men who, if they possessed a certain level of Western education could become clerks in the colonial administration and European firms, and otherwise could gain employment as manual labourers or servants as men formed the majority of domestic workers in Africa during the colonial period. As there were few employment opportunities for women in the formal sector, the women who did defy colonial restrictions and move to urban areas had to support themselves through informal sector activities which were often illegal. The selling of goods and services was the main avenue available. In West Africa some women's trading networks, such as that of the Ga women in Accra, expanded (Parpart 1988). Beer brewing and selling and prostitution were two important means of generating an income in urban areas. As beer brewing and selling became increasingly undertaken by the colonial state as a means of raising revenue it was forbidden, thereby depriving women of their livelihood. Prostitution, while illegal, was tolerated under certain circumstances, as it was seen as providing a useful service. Barnes (1992: 599) claims that until the late 1920s, colonial officials ignored prostitutes in Salisbury because they were seen as a safeguard for white women. However, Lovett (1990) argues that the colonial state in Nairobi would only tolerate certain kinds of prostitutes. Women who functioned as long term migrants sending income back to their families in the rural areas were allowed to operate while the state moved against those who were accumulating wealth in urban areas, often in the form of lodging houses for migrant workers. The constraints on women in urban areas meant that they were unable to consolidate their positions as entrepreneurs and the majority remained petty traders on the margins of the colonial economy. Several commentators have seen the restrictions placed in the 1930s both on the African ownership of urban property and on women's trading as evidence that the colonial authorities wished to prevent the consolidation of an African urban petty bourgeoisie (Parpart 1988).

The social and economic changes brought about through the colonial imperative of capital accumulation therefore had a contradictory impact on women. Many women found that their position worsened, for example because their control over economic resources such as land was reduced, or their overall workload was increased perhaps because of the absence of male relatives. However other women used some of the changes to provide opportunities to resist patriarchal controls, for example to escape from arranged marriages or the increased burdens in rural areas. The increased movement of women from rural to urban or mining areas is one important example of women defining new lives for themselves (Barnes 1992: 587).

As we have already seen, in the face of social and economic change, new mechanisms of social control, for example over mobility, were used to try and maintain social order. By the mid-colonial period of the 1920s and 1930s the impact of the huge social and economic changes brought by colonial rule on gender relations had resulted in a widespread perception of crisis on the part of both colonial officials and male elders. This was particularly evidenced by a breakdown of controls over women, expressed as the threat of the disintegration of traditional forms of marriage and rising incidence of adultery and 'sexual indiscipline'. In the early colonial period, some individual women had used the opportunities briefly provided by the British to bring lawsuits and the courts were swamped, for example by women seeking divorce (Staudt 1989b: 79). Booth (1992) details examples of young Swazi women using the colonial courts to bring charges of assault and occasionally rape against Swazi men and Allman (1991) cites the cases of a fleeing slave wife and a woman attempting to collect adultery damages in colonial Asante as examples of the efforts of some women to take direct advantage of the legal uncertainties of British colonial rule. By the mid-colonial period, these changes were seen as a threat to social stability by colonial officials and as a threat to their patriarchal power by African leaders. Channock (1985: 189–90) details three sets of factors which contributed to this view in Central Africa. First he highlights the strain put on marriages by labour migration; second the movement of women into urban areas away from the disciplinary control of families; and third the increasing importance of property transactions in marriage, often in the form of bridewealth, in the new cash economies.

The result, particularly evident in the 1930s, was a widespread backlash which attempted to reassert male control over women through an alliance between African male leaders and British colonial officials. This backlash took the form of the imposition of increased controls over women's mobility and labour power often expressed in terms of regulations over marriage. Roberts (1987) has described how, in the context of the peasant production of cocoa, the state intervened in Sefwi Wiawso (Ghana) to guarantee the allocation of women's labour through marriage. Channock (1985) argues that the regulation of marriage was therefore moved from the private to the public sphere as the regulation of marriage, divorce and adultery in both rural and urban areas became highly contested and attempts were made to situate women more firmly in marriage.

The site where many of these struggles were conducted was through the institution of customary law and the native courts. Channock (1982: 56) argues very forcefully that customary legal systems, far from being systems of African law which survived through the colonial period, were in fact 'created by the political economy of colonial capitalism'. According to Channock, women, men and elders all sought to take advantage of the openings brought by colonialism and use the authority of the colonial state, but 'it was men who had the greater success because the remedies they put forward to combat their losing control were fed into the colonial court system and emerged as applicable customary law' (1982: 57). The colonial state codified 'traditional' strictures into laws after male representatives from African communities put forward a version of African customary law to colonial officials which operated to their advantage by overplaying their power. Customary law was therefore created by colonial officials and the male indigenous hierarchy, justified as traditional and used by both as a way of increasing control over women.

Channock (1985: 210) claims that there was a basic ambiguity in the demands for greater controls made by the African élite and attempts of officials to regulate the social effects of economic change, in that 'they were trying to establish a mode of control of women and marriage suited to the new conditions but they sought to do this by an apparent strengthening of rural "customs" and authority'. Barnes (1992: 588) goes further and argues that state policies with regard to women's mobility in Southern Rhodesia were contradictory. On the one hand, colonial authorities, supported by rural elders, tried to restrict the mobility of women and punish those who did move, but at the same time, state policies tacitly encouraged women who travelled around the colony. These contradictions meant that policies had become unworkable by the mid-1930s.

In addition to attempts to regulate women and gender relations through controls over marriage, women's sexuality and mobility, women were also affected by other state policies. While never a high priority in the early years, in the later colonial period there was an increasing emphasis on colonial welfare provision, particularly after the passing of the British Colonial Development and Welfare Act in 1940. Until then much of the health and educational services which did exist had been provided by missionaries. A mission education for girls tended to stress the development of qualities which would make them good wives and mothers and emphasized morality and Christian values (Staudt 1989b: 76). While girls received education focused around the domestic, boys in addition to receiving the skills necessary for employment in European enterprises, for example as clerks, received more technically and agriculturally based instruction.

This tendency towards the emphasis of the domestic for girls has been noted in many European colonies in Africa (and in the Caribbean) and continued once the state became more involved in the provision of education (Hunt 1990). As late as 1942 in British West Africa of the 11,500 children enrolled in the 43 recognized secondary schools only 1500 were girls (Johnson 1986: 240). Much of the domestic education provided for girls was seen as particularly relevant for the future wives of the emerging African male élite. Geiger (1987) has described the efforts of the colonial state in Tanganyika after World War II to use women's organizations to promote domestic training for urban middle-class women on the 'foyer' model of Elizabethville described by Hunt (1990). The limitations on the education available to girls also acted to limit the possibilities for waged employment for women in the formal economy (Parpart 1988). Even where women did gain a Western education, the main occupation open to them was teaching, a restriction which led Nigerian women to fight for employment in the civil service (Johnson 1986).

As we have seen, women's experiences of changes in marriage, customary law and waged work were different to men's. These processes were evolving and dynamic and the results were complex. Individual women were not passive in the face of changes and could in some cases try to use the complex interplay of different factors to their own advantage (Etienne and Leacock 1980: 21). However, by the 1930s, this had often provoked increased attempts to control women by both colonial authorities and African male leaders in concert (Parpart 1988). In addition to these individual responses, many women also responded collectively to colonialism, to be considered in the final section of this chapter.

Women's collective organizing under colonialism

While colonial administrators and official records often ignored or misunderstood women's collective organizing, there are many examples of women acting together during the colonial period. With the advent of colonial rule women lost much of the power they had in the pre-colonial period, and their indigenous political authority became invisible. O'Barr (1984: 144) claims that colonial powers did not try to manipulate female leaders as they were not even aware of their existence. Many of the 'voluntary associations' in which women came together to promote their economic and social interests continued to operate. Often women relied on informal women's groups, based around family or ethnic affiliation and operating on mutual reciprocity to provide welfare and, increasingly, income generating activities (Nzomo 1993). Indeed, Staudt (1989b: 81) has argued that many women initially rejected and/or withdrew from the state and the redefined political order during the early period of colonial rule.

Women not only came together to promote their interests more effectively outside of the state but, particularly in the later phases of colonialism, acted to protect themselves against the encroachments of colonial rule. Parpart (1988: 213) argues that there is clear evidence that the 'most dramatic female opposition to colonial authority was carried out by women where the status differentials of men and women were small enough that it was not unthinkable for women to challenge male authority', and allied to this, women with an independent economic base were often the most successful at challenging colonialism. Johnson's examination (1982) of three women's organizations highlights the importance of several factors in women's organizing: the interaction between pre-colonial patterns of organizing and new forms which emerged under colonial rule; the impact of increasing social differentiation which meant that certain groups of women had a different relation to the state; and the relationship of women's organizing with the emerging nationalist movements.

Women frequently used whatever status they had previously had by protesting with 'traditional female methods'. There are three well-documented instances where women resisted the threat of the imposition of taxes and changes to their control of land and farming practices in this way. The 'Women's War' in southern Nigeria is perhaps the best known example of a women's anti-colonial action which demonstrates both the use of traditional forms of protest and the obliviousness of both colonial officials and other contemporary analysts to the meaning and significance of what became known to the British as the 'Aba Riots' (Van Allen 1976). In 1929, following a decade where British authorities introduced indirect rule and increased controls over cash crop production, the Igbo women believed that they were about to be taxed, despite assurances to the contrary, as households and property were being recounted and officials had lied about taxation in the past. Rumours spread quickly through the women's communication networks and mikiri meetings took place in market squares. These worries combined with resentment at the arbitrary acts of warrant chiefs who abused their power, for example by helping themselves to women's produce and by not taking account of women's rights to refuse a particular suitor in marriage. The disquiet culminated in women taking customary action in the form of the Women's War. Large numbers of women, wearing loincloths and carrying palm-wrapped sticks, gathered outside the district offices in Owerri and Calabar provinces, 'sat on' the warrant chiefs and burnt their buildings. At the same time women in many areas attempted to get rid of the native administration. At the height of the disturbances, thousands of women were involved over an area of 6000 square miles. The British authorities failed to realize that the women were using recognized channels for expressing discontent and reacted harshly to what they considered to be riots of 'frenzied mobs' and over 50 women were killed by troops (Van Allen 1972, 1976).

O'Barr (1984: 145–6) has examined the participation of women in the general tax riots in Pare province in Tanzania in the 1940s. The protests were precipitated by the decision of the district council composed of male chiefs advised by a district officer to impose a graduated income tax on top of the poll tax already levied. Thousands of men marched to the district headquarters claiming that they would remain there until the tax was abolished. After several months, women were mobilized as well. Female relatives of the protestors marched 25 miles to the district headquarters and demanded that either the district officer should settle the dispute, enabling the men to return home, or that he should impregnate all of them, since he had forced their husbands to abandon their wives and disrupted normal life. In the face of crowds of angry women the council relented and introduced a different form of assessment and the next year the graduated tax was dropped. O'Barr (1984) has argued that this was the first active role for many Pare women in modern politics, and that their involvement was essentially a conservative reaction. They wanted order in their life to be restored and the dispute settled.

The Kom women of the Bamenda province in the former British Cameroons also used a traditional mechanism and transformed it into a mechanism of contemporary political power (O'Barr 1984: 46). Among the Kom, women used the anlu, a form of punishment similar to 'sitting on a man', to punish a man who had committed certain offences by surrounding his compound, dressed in vines, dancing and singing defamatory songs (Wipper 1984: 71). In 1957 women formed an organization to use the anlu against the colonial government over grievances centring around a lack of control over their farming activities, particularly rumours that their land would be sold. Within a year practically all Kom women had joined, and they had taken authority from the district councils in mass meetings. Six thousand women were mobilized when the premier visited to assure them that there was no truth to the rumours. The initial involvement of women was crucial in mobilizing wider opposition within the community, even though after gaining some concessions women began to drop out of the anlu organization (O'Barr 1984).

New women's organizations also emerged as colonial rule began to cause important social, economic and political changes. In the Kenyan case, it has been argued that women's organizing entered a new phase in the later colonial period as it became more formalized and more differentiated by class as élite, even white women, played an important leadership role, exemplified in the establishment of the women's organization Maendeleo ya Wanawake in 1952 (Nasimiyu 1993). Because of the lack of opportunities for formal sector employment, women did not often participate in organizations as wage workers, but there is evidence that some of the few employed women did organize collectively. Presley, for example, has documented the strikes undertaken by Kikuyu women working on Kenyan coffee plantations from the 1930s to the 1960s (Presley 1986). Johnson (1982, 1986) has studied the anti-colonial activities undertaken by three women's organizations formed in southwestern Nigeria. The Lagos Market Women's Association (LMWA) which emerged in the 1920s was the first Lagos-wide mass-based market women's organization and the greatest area of contention between it and the colonial authorities proved to be attempts to tax women and enforce government pricing in markets, particularly during World War II. As a result of its activities the LMWA received concessions over both taxation and price controls (Johnson 1986: 246). At this time the Nigerian Women's Party was formed by new Christian élite women who had been educated by colonialism. It campaigned for women's education, employment and the enfranchisement of women and attempted to influence both the colonial government structures and Nigerian political groups organized by male leaders. It had mixed results in its attempt to make alliances with the market women, however. The most successful organization according to Johnson was the Abeokuta Women's Union (AWU) which effectively combined both an élite and a mass membership. In the late 1940s it forced the Alake of Abeokuta, a traditional ruler who was abusing his power under the indirect rule system, out of office in 1949. AWU membership reached between 80,000 to 100,000 and it changed its name to the Nigerian Women's Union. In the 1950s many of its members became involved in the more generalized struggle for independence.

In the late phase of colonialism, nationalist movements were the major form of collective organizing. The changes brought by colonialism had created the conditions for their emergence. In the early phases they were often movements of the newly emerged middle class and élites, led by Western educated professionals frustrated by the inequities and racism of the colonial system which blocked their advancement within it. Indian nationalism became a mass movement in the 1920s and 1930s, while in the British colonies of Africa and the Caribbean nationalism did not become a mass movement until after World War II moving from demands for greater self-government to full independence. In Africa the nature of these nationalist struggles changed over time. The earliest relatively non-violent movements emerged in West Africa in the 1950s and were followed by similar movements in Central and East Africa. In British colonies in Africa and the Caribbean many of the more moderate movements negotiated a transition to independence whereby control was handed to groups who were largely prepared to maintain the existing system and therefore had the approval of the ex-colonists (Leys 1975). Other countries, such as Portugal, refused to grant independence to their colonies for as long as they could, and in other colonies and dominions such as Rhodesia and South Africa, settler groups declared independence and denied rights to all their citizens. More violent struggles took place where either settlers or colonizers were determined to keep control, for instance in Kenya, Algeria, Mozambique and Angola.

In the struggles of the 1970s, movements became radicalized, influenced by both the Chinese and particularly the Vietnamese experiences, and adopted guerrilla warfare and more overtly socialist ideologies of national liberation. Both because they were aiming for a more profound transformation of society than simply independence, and the ways in which struggles were waged means that these movements are better considered as revolutionary and will therefore be considered in the next chapter on revolutions and revolutionary movements.

When considering the relationship between gender and nationalism, three major questions emerge. First, what roles were played by different groups of women in these various nationalist movements? Second, how were these movements gendered and what particular constructions of masculinity and femininity did they use as part of their projects? Third, what was the relationship between feminist movements and nationalism? In her study of the emergence of movements for women's rights in a number of countries of Asia and the Middle East in the late nineteenth and early twentieth centuries, Kumari Jayawardena (1986) argues that movements for women's emancipation came out of the same conditions which spawned nationalist movements and had important links with those struggles. Feminism, she argues, was not therefore imposed from the outside, as has so often been claimed.

We can examine the role of women in the nationalist movement in India to illustrate these themes. Both the 'women's question' and the nationalist movement, which became important in the late nineteenth century, had their origins in the social reform movement of earlier in the century (Sen 1993). The social reform movement emphasized the need for the abolition of sati, polygamy and the provision of better education for women. Indeed the improvement of the position and status of women was seen as a crucial part of the creation of a more modernized India. The construction of the 'new woman' became an important part of nationalist discourse. She was to be created through education but remain the guardian of the spiritual domain, playing a traditional role within the home. Central to these ideas was an association of notions of appropriate femininity and motherhood with the 'new woman' in contrast to the 'common woman' (Thapar 1993: 83). Nationalist discourse did not reject modernity but was selective in its espousal, arguing that 'there would have to be a marked *difference* in the degree and manner of westernization of women, as distinct from men, in the modern world of the nation' (Chatterjee 1990: 233). Women were therefore to play particular roles within the nationalist movement. The domestic was demarcated as an arena of nationalist resistance which involved the 'positing of an idealised opposition between public and private', firmly locating women in the private sphere rearing healthy citizens (Sen 1993: 233). However, while the ideology of domesticity and notions of 'enlightened motherhood' were particularly associated with middle-class women, by the 1920s and 1930s these ideas were increasingly directed towards poor women (Sen 1993: 235).

Women also participated actively in the nationalist movement in the public sphere. While in the late nineteenth century, some educated middle-class women had been members of the Indian National Congress (INC), the main nationalist party, the numbers of women participating in the nationalist struggle increased when it became a mass movement in the early twentieth century. Many women joined in the increasingly militant campaigns such as the boycott of British goods. Male leaders like Gandhi realized that the struggle would be aided by the active participation of women. While remaining a 'traditionalist' in the domestic sphere, he argued that women were ideally suited to the non-violent campaign of civil disobedience. Women could participate from their homes by spinning and weaving khadi as part of the boycott of foreign cloth. But the construct of the 'new woman' was also modified to allow women to take to the streets (Thapar 1993: 87). Many women took part in mass action such as the picketing of foreign shops and the breaking of the Salt Laws, marching to the sea to make salt. Of the 80,000 people arrested during the Salt Satyagraha, 17,000 were women (Jayawardena 1986: 100). Women also played a role in some of the more radical national- ist and communist movements. The left-leaning Women's Self-Defence League (MARS) had 43,000 members at the time of its second conference in 1943.

At the same time a number of women's organizations, such as the Women's Indian Association created in 1917 and the All-India Women's Conference set up in 1927, were formed and influenced by theosophists from Britain such as Annie Besant and Margaret Cousins (Jayawardena 1986: 93–4). Liddle and Joshi (1986: 21) claim that these various women's organizations, com- prising mainly middle-class urban women, constituted a women's movement. Liddle (1992) has argued that after the civil disobedience campaign an alliance was formed between the women's movement and the nationalist movement. However the INC was divided over 'women's issues'. The divisions in Congress over 'the woman question' became more exposed as the issues challenged men's role in the private sphere. While there was almost total support for female suffrage, which could show the INC as more socially advanced than the British, there was mixed support for the inclusion of a sex equality clause in the constitution, and bitter opposition to the reform of the Hindu code which, for example, regulated marriage and the family. Liddle (1992) argues that including some 'women's issues' on the nationalist plat- form diffused some of the opposition to them, but it also meant that the demands had to be posed within the framework of the nationalist struggle.

While the part played by women within the African and Caribbean nationalist movements has been less well documented and researched than the Indian case, some similar trends can be discerned. Women participated actively in a number of movements but the nature of that participation varied. There is a long history of women's resistance to colonialism in the Caribbean. Nanny, a Jamaican national hero, led the Maroons in their battles against the British in the eighteenth century. Slave women employed a variety of techniques, including a refusal to have children (Bush-Slimani 1993). In the early twentieth century women were involved in the growing trade union activities and strikes (Reddock 1993). Women seem to have been particularly active in nationalist struggles in West Africa. Some of the women's organizations described above such as the Lagos market women were im- portant actors and supporters of political parties in the largely electorally based campaigns in Nigeria. Their role in the 1945 general strike increased their importance and they became active in the endorsing and financing of candidates (O'Barr 1984; Johnson 1986). Denzer (1976) describes a similar pattern of women's involvement in the Gold Coast (Ghana), Senegal, and the Ivory Coast. Women played active roles including as fighters during the Mau Mau Rebellion in Kenya (Presley 1992).

Women were also active members of the nationalist political parties. Many nationalist parties such as UNIP in Zambia formed women's sections. Geiger (1987) documents this process in an East African context, describing the role of primarily Muslim urban women living in Dar es Salaam in the formation of the Tanganyika African National Union (TANU) and its women's section. The women's organizations were affected by the dynamics of the nationalist parties. Peake (1993) describes the establishment of the Women's Progressive Organization in Guyana in 1953 which itself split when the People's Progressive Party divided on racial lines in 1955, resulting in the establishment of another organization, the Women's Revolutionary Socialist Movement, the women's arm of the breakaway People's National Congress. At the same time, many broader women's organizations lost influence because their membership became diffused in the nationalist struggle. While women activists were absorbed into the nationalist parties they were not rewarded with high office or influence when the parties gained power, despite both a recognition of the importance of having women involved, and a number of women standing for leadership positions (Johnson 1986: 248). In Chapter 5 we will see how this trend was consolidated in the emerging one party states. Commentators are therefore agreed that despite playing an active role within nationalist movements this was not translated into power and influence for women in post-independence politics (Johnson 1982; O'Barr 1984; Parpart 1988; Staudt 1989b).

Conclusion

We have seen how colonialism profoundly altered gender relations and that these changes have had a lasting impact. However, the impact of colonialism was not straightforward but complex and contradictory. Different women played different roles and were affected in different ways. On the one hand, many women suffered increased burdens as a result of the changes which were part of colonial rule and colonial (and 'traditional') authorities attempted to maintain control through restrictions on women, their mobility and sexuality. On the other hand, the colonial state was also a site of gender struggle and some women attempted to use the limited spaces which had opened up to their advantage. When examining women's collective organizing, we saw how a number of different ways of analysing those activities have been employed, ranging from seeing some of these actions as varying forms of resistance, as conservative reactions or as defending or promoting particular interests. One further potentially important way of examining these issues which has become increasingly important, for example in the discussion of sati, is through an examination of the construction of women's identities and subjectivities (Loomba 1993). This method of examination could be used, for example, in the analysis of women defining new lives for themselves through mobility. We can now move on to examine some of the more radical of the national liberation struggles and revolution.

4

Revolution and national liberation struggles

Introduction

Social revolutions, according to Theda Skocpol (1979: 4), are 'rapid, basic transformations of a society's state and class structures; and they are accompanied and in part carried through by class-based revolts from below'. This notion of important structural change sets revolutions apart from rebellions and other violent overthrows of government and the state. With the Russian Revolution as the notable exception, most twentieth-century revolutions have taken place in the Third World. This chapter will examine some of these attempts to effect far reaching social, political and economic changes in the nature of society through the actions of movements operating from below. It will focus first on the varying roles played by women in different revolutionary settings, examining how this changed over the postwar period and second on the impact that the changes implemented by revolutionary regimes have had on gender relations.

In any study of revolution, an examination of the external context is crucial. First, external help often allows rulers to survive without an internal base. The United States, for example, supported authoritarian rulers during the Cold War as part of its anti-communist strategy. However, if external support wavers (as happened when President Carter prioritized human rights in the late 1970s), personalistic regimes, such as existed in Nicaragua and Iran, can be removed through mass uprisings which include a wide cross-section of the population rather than just sectional interests such as class or ethnic groups. Second, the relationship of Third World revolutionary movements to socialism and communism, both in terms of ideology and support and opposition from outside, is an important dimension of the external context. As we saw in Chapter 2, one consequence of the Cold War was that Third World liberation movements could expect support, such as training and the provision of arms, from the Soviet Union and its allies. They could also expect hostility from the United States and its allies both during the revolutionary struggle and subsequently. Where revolutionary forces gained control of the state, a commitment to social justice and national liberation was often interpreted as communism. As we will see, this opposition seriously limited the ability of many revolutionary governments fully to implement their programmes and has sometimes been blamed for their demise. While the end of the Cold War has not brought an end to United States' hostility to states which still profess to be communist, the collapse of the Soviet Union and the Eastern bloc means that states like Cuba can no longer get practical help from the former Soviet Union. Two of the most important recent guerrilla movements have not adhered to orthodox communist ideologies associated with the old Soviet bloc. Sendero Luminoso (the Shining Path) which reached the height of its activity in Peru in the late 1980s, follows an idiosyncratic Andean version of Maoism. The Zapatistas who emerged on the international stage in Chiapas, a state in southern Mexico on New Year's Day 1994 have been dubbed 'postmodern' because of their tactics, strategy and aims, which do *not* include taking control of the state (Burbach 1994).

There is now a huge orthodox literature on Third World revolutions, much of it influenced by the experience of the 'great revolutions' of France, Russia and China. Analysts have been preoccupied by several questions: Why do revolutions occur? Which groups in society are potentially the most revolutionary (a question which often focuses on different segments of the peasantry)? What role is played by various groups in creating the revolutionary situation? And what is the most effective way to achieve an overthrow of the state (Dix 1984)? The last two questions of agency have preoccupied those analysts, such as Amilcar Cabral and Ernesto 'Che' Guevara, who, as practitioners, were concerned to discover how revolutions could be created. Others have concentrated on the structural conditions. State-centred approaches, for example, have considered the types of regimes and governments most vulnerable to revolutionary takeover, arguing that closed and exclusionary authoritarian regimes with little internal support are the weakest in this respect (Goodwin and Skocpol 1989).

While orthodox definitions of revolution make no specific mention of changes in gender relations, this chapter will consider revolutions which had, as part of their more general programme to change society, an express commitment to alter gender relations and to reduce inequality between men and women. While the nature and strength of this commitment varied between different movements and over time, Maxine Molyneux (1981) has argued that there is sufficient similarity between the analysis and policies of many revolutionary regimes that the various examples can be examined together. One reason for this similarity is that many governments were profoundly influenced by the socialist analysis of the 'woman question', which will be described below.

As indicated in the last chapter, the tactics and ideological content of the aims of some national liberation struggles fighting to throw off colonial domination will also be considered here. Many had fully developed programmes that went beyond the seizing of state power. As Stephanie Urdang (1984a: 157) argues when discussing African movements,

> particularly important is the insistence that their fight stretches beyond victory on the battlefield to the more fundamental question of establishing a new and just society in each of their countries, one that brings the end to all forms of exploitation. Within this context liberation movements have all – in varying degrees – emphasized the liberation of women.

Two types of movements and 'revolutions' fall outside the remit of this chapter. 'Revolutions from above', such as occurred in Ethiopia, will be excluded because these did not involve significant grassroots movements. The Iranian Revolution is also excluded, as the ideological content of its programme of social, economic and political change had very different implications for gender relations to the majority of revolutions. Increasing equality between men and women was not one of its aims.

Women in revolutionary movements

The participation of women in revolutionary movements grew during the twentieth century and their significance was increasingly recognized by both observers and participants alike. The history of women's involvement in revolutionary activity in the twentieth century begins with few women being organized or organizing themselves in any sustained way in revolutionary movements in the first half of the century and culminates in much more active roles played by women in revolutionary movements of the 1970s.

While the women textile workers' strike on International Women's Day triggered the Russian Revolution, organized women did not play much of a role in the events of 1917. They were viewed by the Bolsheviks – despite their commitment to women's equality – as the most backward section of the working class. The Mexican Revolution of 1910 is seen to have had an important impact on women, but little is known, except anecdotally, about the importance of women soldiers in the battles, or about their role in maintaining armies and treating the wounded. Work on these themes has started but has tended to concentrate on tracing the figure of the female soldier (Ramos 1994). The roles played by women in the early nationalist movements' campaigns against colonial rule have been described in the previous chapter.

The emphasis of many early revolutionary movements was more on bringing equality for women through the revolution rather than the need for women to play a large and organized role in the struggle to bring about revolution. Mao wrote in the 1920s that the fourth rope binding Chinese, particularly peasant, women was the authority of men. The struggle to untie this was seen as directly connected to the struggle to undo the other three: state authority, clan authority and religious authority. The women's organizations formed at the beginning of the Long March in 1934–5 had the task of organizing and educating women, drawing them into revolutionary activity, for example through making supplies for the Eighth Route Army. While relatively large numbers were drawn into the mass organizations, the numbers of women actually involved in the fighting and as communist cadres was relatively low (Chinchilla 1977: 91).

This pattern of women's relatively low involvement was replicated during the Cuban Revolution, arguably one of the most important Third World revolutions this century, not least because of its durability in the face of implacable hostility from the United States. Women did not participate greatly in the armed struggle launched in 1952. Two women, Haydee Santamaria and Melba Hernandez took part in the attack on the Moncada barracks in 1953, but both were involved in the creation of the initial 26th of July Movement (Miller 1991: 140–1). Only three women, including Haydee Santamaria, appear to have been actively involved in the guerrilla struggle in the Sierra Maestra, and all were linked to male leaders (Jaquette 1973). Later, however, a Red Army battalion was formed and it has been estimated that by December 1958 one in 20 of the Fidelista troops was a woman (Reif 1986: 155). Despite this participation, no concerted attempts were made to recruit and mobilize women until after the 1959 Revolution and the women involved played largely support and relief roles as messengers, scouts and nurses rather than as combatants.

Many guerrilla struggles of the 1960s were influenced both by the Cuban Revolution and also by the Vietnamese and Chinese experiences of guerrilla warfare and the work of writers and activists such as Franz Fanon. The protracted guerrilla struggles fought in China and Vietnam were a major influence on many of these revolutionary movements. In 1945 Vietnamese communist guerrillas launched an anti-colonial struggle under the leadership of Ho Chi Minh and fought an ultimately successful war against French and subsequently American imperialism to reunite North and South Vietnam. Their defeat of the most powerful nation in the world led to the withdrawal of American troops and the end of the war in 1975. The National Liberation Front (NLF) was active on three fronts: the political struggle within the population; the armed struggle; and 'persuasion' work within enemy ranks. The armed forces themselves took several forms. In addition to the liberation army proper, self-defence units operated locally and regional troops were active within defined geographical areas. The political infrastructure set up within the population was also crucial. The NLF never moved into a village without the political base having already been prepared. Once this happened, land reform was implemented, debts abolished and the village elected its own council (Chaliand 1977: 94–8).

Women played a significant part as fighters in both the liberation army and also in the local people's militias, which were crucial in the liberated areas when many men had left to fight elsewhere (Bergman 1974). Some women also played important leadership roles, particularly General Nguyen Thi Dinh. But women, including General Dinh, also played an important symbolic role.

According to Christine Pelzer White (1989: 179–80), women symbolized the potential of apparently weak and powerless people to fight back. She cites the famous example of the photo showing a small Vietnamese woman pointing a rifle at a huge but subjugated US pilot which was used on a North Vietnamese postage stamp as well as American anti-war posters.

The belief had become widespread among both analysts and activists that, as the small urban proletariat had become a 'labour aristocracy' with little revolutionary potential, the peasantry was the revolutionary class in the Third World. Regis Debray and Che Guevara, building on both these ideas and the experience of the Cuban Revolution, developed 'foco theory' which was used, ultimately unsuccessfully, in Latin America throughout the 1960s (Chaliand 1977). Within this formulation, a group of committed revolutionaries could launch a guerrilla struggle in an isolated and defensible area away from major cities and through their example, create a revolutionary situation which would then spread even to places where, to begin with, there had been little popular support. Guevara argued that in rural areas guerrillas could defeat a regular army and that they need not wait for the objective conditions to be right since, through its creation, the focal point of the insurrection would create them (Chaliand 1977: 43). Women were given a particular role in *Guerrilla Warfare* (1963), Guevara's most famous exposition of these ideas. While discrimination against women was recognized by Guevara and the part that women could play in the development of the revolutionary process was seen as one of 'extraordinary importance', much of the actual discussion of women put them into gender typical roles as teachers, nurses and support for the male guerrillas. In an often quoted passage, Guevara states that 'the woman can also perform her habitual tasks of peacetime; it is very pleasing to a soldier subjected to the extremely hard conditions of this life to be able to look forward to a seasoned meal which tastes of something' (quoted in Miller 1991: 146). While a number of often educated urban middle-class women took part in the guerrilla movements of the 1960s, there is no evidence of mass participation.

The death of Guevara in Bolivia in 1967 and the failure of Latin American rural guerrilla movements prompted a reassessment of the *foco* strategy. The results of this rethinking provided part of the impetus for the increased participation of women in many of the revolutionary movements of the 1970s in Latin America. There was a change of emphasis towards urban guerrilla movements by revolutionaries (Jaquette 1973). Urban guerrilla groups were active in Brazil, Argentina and Uruguay. Some of these, like the Tupamaros in Uruguay, had high levels of female participation, estimated at 25 per cent. These mainly middle-class women recruits played active combat roles in commando groups. Several explanations have been put forward for women's increased participation in activities such as kidnappings and robberies. First, pragmatically, women aroused less suspicion than men. Second, including women was seen as part of the greater emphasis placed on gaining popular support and participation from the local community. Third, the influence of a feminist agenda meant that issues surrounding discrimination against women were highlighted in the Tupamaros programme and activities (Reif 1986).

Some of these trends were reflected in the activities and strategies of other revolutionary movements active in the 1960s and 1970s. In stark contrast to the relatively short guerrilla struggle waged prior to the accession to power of Fidel Castro and the 26th of July Movement in Cuba, most of these movements fought protracted campaigns which needed a different approach. This, combined with the failure of 'foquismo' and the decimation of urban guerrilla movements in Latin America by the military backlash, reinforced the necessity of significant and sustained popular support in the face of repression by the army and the state. The notion of a prolonged people's war, involving the gradual organization of all the mass sectors under a variety of organizational forms, was adopted. Gaining the support of large numbers of women who would become both activists, playing combat and other roles, and sympathizers within the civilian population providing support and often shelter, became an essential part of the strategy of these movements. Many guerrilla movements in Africa such as ZANU and ZAPU in Rhodesia, FRELIMO in Mozambique, PAIGC in Guinea Bissau, the MPLA in Angola and movements in Central America such as the FSLN in Nicaragua, began their long drawn-out campaigns in the 1960s.

Many national liberation movements of the 1970s also stressed their commitment as part of avowedly socialist programmes to an agenda for women's emancipation influenced by feminism as well as the socialist analysis of the 'woman question'. The second wave of feminism brought greater interest in and awareness of gender issues and the implications of this for the class struggle, reopening discussion of the often problematic relationship between class and gender. The FRELIMO leader Samora Machel argued at the founding conference of the Organization of Mozambican Women (OMM) that

the main objective of the revolution is to destroy the system of exploitation and build a new society which releases the potential of human beings, reconciling them with labour and with nature, this is the context within which the question of women's emancipation arises.

(quoted in Urdang 1984b: 9)

In 1973 Machel stated that 'generally speaking women are the most oppressed, humiliated and exploited beings in society'. However, according to Machel, 'the liberation of women is not an act of charity, the result of humanitarian or compassionate attitude. The liberation of women is a fundamental necessity for the revolution, the guarantee of its continuity and a precondition for its victory' (quoted in Urdang 1984b: 9). The liberation of women would be achieved, not just as a consequence of the revolution, but through the efforts of women struggling to bring it about. This new emphasis was partly a result of pressure from feminists within revolutionary movements. But, as we will see later, the relationship of many revolutionary movements with 'Western feminism' was an ambivalent one.

The development of strategies aimed at gaining maximum popular support combined with the ideological content of many of the movements' doctrines which stressed the centrality of the liberation of women, resulted in their extensive mobilization in both military and political roles in the struggles of the 1960s and 1970s. In the Portuguese colony of Guinea Bissau the PAIGC, under the leadership of Amilcar Cabral, decided that the country would have to be liberated through armed struggle, but for three years they conducted extensive political mobilization, particularly in rural areas, to gain mass participation before they launched the war in January 1963 (Urdang 1979: 64–7). According to Urdang (1979: 198) the mobilization of women was always central to this mass participation. Women acted both as political organizers and as essential support workers such as cooks for the guerrillas. However the number of women military cadres was low because the PAIGC made less attempt to train women as fighters than FRELIMO as there were more men available. While women trained and fought as guerrillas, when the units were reorganized into a national army, they were not encouraged to play combat roles anymore. By contrast far more women received military training from FRELIMO in Mozambique. In 1966 the FRELIMO central committee decided that women should be encouraged to participate more actively in the liberation struggle at all levels. Women began to receive political and military training and, reflecting the radicalization of FRELIMO, women's detachments were formed in 1967, three years after the armed struggle had begun. However this was achieved in the face of strong resistance by some men and the women's detachment remained small (Urdang 1984a). Few women progressed to the top of the FRELIMO leadership and women tended to play a greater role in the militias which defended the liberated zones rather than fighting at the front (Kruks and Wisner 1989: 154).

The emphasis on political mobilization went hand in hand with the central role played by the party and its organizations. FRELIMO and the PAIGC saw themselves bringing about a transition to socialism. As part of this, parties like FRELIMO and the MPLA set up special women's organizations like the OMM and the OMA (the Organization of Angolan Women) to coordinate the mobilization of women. The implementation of changes in the liberated zones accompanied this intensive political work. As precursors to the new society to be created once independence was achieved, the liberated zones put into practice policies contained in the parties' programmes. These policies included encouraging women's participation in the new political structures. In Guinea at least two women had to be elected to the five member village councils which were set up when a zone was liberated. Women were elected to the justice tribunals overseeing the new order in Angola. Women were also encouraged to take on new roles as health workers and teachers and in production itself. In terms of relations between men and women, attempts were made to abolish customs and practices seen as outdated and oppressive to women. In both Mozambique and Guinea Bissau practices such as bride-price, arranged marriages and polygamy were discouraged. Francisca Pereira, one of the top women in the PAIGC argued that as a result, 'Women realised that this was a great opportunity for their liberation. They knew the attitude of the party, and understood that, for the first time in the history of their country, they would be able to count on political institutions to safe-guard their interests' (Urdang 1979: 123–4).

The Nicaraguan Revolution took place in 1979 when the FSLN over-threw the American-backed dictator Anastasio Somoza. Nicaragua provides a huge contrast to the Cuban Revolution of 20 years earlier in terms of the increasing participation of women. The FSLN made a positive commitment to women's emancipation in its Programme of 1969. The socialist leaning but pluralist FSLN achieved victory in a two-phase process. In the period up to 1978 a revolutionary vanguard waged a guerrilla war, after which mass up-risings took over. By 1979, the FSLN had a high female membership; most estimate that between 20 and 30 per cent of the fighting force, as well as some of its leading commanders were women, epitomized by Dora Maria Tellez, Commander Two in the assault on Somoza's palace in 1978 (Harris 1983). Women had been actively recruited by the Association of Women Confronting the National Problem (AMPRONAC), the women's organiza-tion founded in 1977 by FSLN cadres and other members of the opposition, but AMPRONAC became increasingly a Sandinista organization. Members active in their roles as mothers of children in Somoza's prisons played an important role in publicizing the human rights abuses perpetrated by Somoza's National Guard (Chinchilla 1990: 375). AMPRONAC was committed to both women's equality and overthrowing the Somoza regime and had 8000 members at its height in 1979. While its support was initially from middle-class women, it broadened out to include poor women, support that reflected a genuinely popular revolution with support from almost all sectors of society (Chuckryk 1989a; Molyneux 1989).

In the 1980s similar high levels of participation were seen in the Eritrean liberation movement. In 1979 women formed 13 per cent of the fighters and a decade later this had increased to 23 per cent of the frontline fighters and a third of the army. Fighters were banned from marrying before 1976, after which marriage was allowed under certain conditions, for example that they were free choice unions (Silkin 1983). Women were also organized polit-ically and training, educational and work programmes for women were organized in liberated areas (National Union of Eritrean Women 1983; Wheel-wright 1993). Some of the more recent guerrilla movements seem more ambivalent towards gender issues and feminism. The Peruvian Sendero Luminoso, while including a relatively large number of women in their ranks, is hostile to 'Western' feminism to the extent of killing a feminist mayor in a district of Lima (Vargas 1992).

Postrevolutionary regimes

Despite the increasing mobilization of women in revolutionary struggles and the expressed commitment of many revolutionary movements to women's emancipation, there has been widespread disillusionment as the gains made during the liberation struggle were not consolidated in many postrevolutionary contexts. One former OMM provincial representative in Mozambique expressed some generalized concerns when she said that,

> During the war FRELIMO said 'Women have always suffered. We must fight for women's emancipation, women too must be liberated'. But it seems that all that mobilization was just to fight the Portuguese, for now it has all gone. During the war women's problems were discussed but now nobody talks about that kind of thing.
>
> (quoted in Arnfred 1988: 7)

Clearly the dire material circumstances, not to mention the opposition of the United States and its proxies, the hostile actions which ranged from economic blockades to both overt and covert military action, drastically limited the freedom of manoeuvre of many revolutionary governments, and reduced their ability to implement measures designed to improve the position of women.

However, it is also important to consider how far the policies and underlying assumptions of revolutionary governments themselves also contributed to the mixed results for women. The question of why the promise of revolutionary mobilization has so often not been fulfilled has preoccupied many analysts. Socialist feminists, interested in the often contradictory relationship between socialism and feminism, have contributed most to the debates. Much of the literature on this subject therefore has a particular analytical slant and was written before the collapse of the communist model of development. It emerged from the theoretical debates of the 1970s described in Chapter 1 and remained largely unaffected by the development of the 1980s, such as the growing influence of postmodernism, poststructuralism and notions of difference. As such, most of the literature pays very little attention to discursive ideas and their role in the analysis of gender relations.

Maxine Molyneux (1981), examining the experience of socialist societies and their impact on women, argues that, despite important and very obvious differences between First and Third World states, that is Third World countries had the impact of imperialism to contend with and were far less advanced in their transition to capitalism, there is a striking degree of uniformity between First and Third World revolutionary development. In addition to the explicit commitment to improve the position of women, she argues that they share broad similarities in policy in terms of what was seen to be required to promote rapid economic development and accelerate social change. They all attempted to bring about a comparatively rapid transformation of the pre-revolutionary order by dismantling and reforming social relations, ideologies, legal, political and religious systems. They also, according to Molyneux, implemented similar kinds of economic policies, with a leading role for the state, nationalization of the commanding heights of the economy, collectivization of agriculture and an increase in the welfarist role of the state.

Molyneux (1981) also points out that there is a great similarity in what core assumptions should inform socialist policies on the 'woman question' based in part on a similar theoretical approach to gender relations. This, she claims, is a selective canonization of some of the observations of Marx, Engels and Lenin which were put together to produce an apparently coherent theory. Within this framework, women would be emancipated through the removal of class relations (and institutions like private property) and through being in productive employment, that is paid employment outside the household (Molyneux 1981). Following the restructuring of FRELIMO's policies towards women according to the classical Marxist theories of women's emancipation in 1976, Machel said in 1979 that 'the antagonistic contradiction is not found between men and women, but rather between women and the social order, between all exploited women and men and the social order' (Arnfred 1988: 7). As a result of this formulation of women's oppression and the measures needed to combat it, an autonomous women's movement was not seen to be necessary under socialism. Indeed, feminism was often seen as a bourgeois diversion distracting from the class struggle. Because there was no struggle between men and women, women's demands were dismissed by the OMM in 1979 as the radicalism of the petty bourgeoisie (Arnfred 1988: 11).

Most socialist states have implemented variants of policies based on this formulation of the 'woman question'. However Molyneux (1985b) argues that, on the whole, the commitment of socialist states to women's emancipation has been subject to three qualifications. First, sexual equality is not a priority; the main concerns are economic development and social stability and equality is realized only in so far as it contributes to or at least does not detract from other priorities. Second, the concept of sexual equality is based on the notion of male and female roles being symmetrical and complementary rather than undifferentiated. Third, 'emancipation' was often seen as emancipation from the constraints of a traditional social order rather than having a broader meaning (Molyneux 1985b: 51).

Many of the contradictions within the policies of revolutionary regimes towards women result from their stress on involvement in production as the key to women's emancipation at the same time as a certain role is assumed for women in the private sphere. Socialist feminist critics have argued that important flaws in this formulation of how to achieve women's emancipation have resulted in shared contradictions when policies based on this analysis are put into practice. These similar results stem from an inadequate explanation of why women are oppressed as women and no understanding of the benefits that men as men get from women's oppression.

Women, despite their common representation in revolutionary iconography with a gun in one arm and a baby in the other, were still seen primarily as mothers. Socialist states kept a biologically reductionist view of women as naturally suited to 'motherhood'. While efforts were made to change women's roles so that they could both continue as mothers and became waged employees as well, very little was done to change men's roles within the domestic sphere or to get them to undertake 'women's' jobs. Attempts that were made to socialize domestic labour and childcare, for example through laundries, canteens and nurseries, did not extend very far and individual solutions, such as the Cuban Family Code of 1975, were largely relied upon. Indeed while the Family Code gave men and women equal rights and re-sponsibilities within the family, it was never seriously implemented. Third World socialist states saw the heterosexual monogamous nuclear family created through marriage as the basic unit of society, with a conventional divi-sion of labour between men and women within it (Molyneux 1985b). The dominance of these ideas resulted in very little discussion of sexuality, sexual violence, or relations between men and women as there was little notion of women's oppression as stemming from men as a group or patriarchy. Women therefore were to be drawn into the productive sphere while at the same time retaining their responsibility for the domestic sphere, resulting in the 'double burden'. One of the only significant differences between this vision and the dominant one in capitalist states was that both partners were to be in paid employment.

In order to see what happened when policies based on these ideas were put into practice, we will examine the role of women in conventional polit-ics, the impact of general policies on gender relations and of policies directed at women, before looking at women's autonomous activity in three case studies: Cuba, Mozambique and Nicaragua. These have been chosen because they span more than 30 years and are different in important ways. Their experience ranges from the more rigid orthodoxy of the Cuban Revolution, which came to power without any clear policies to change the position of women except that women would achieve equality through the revolution, to the revolutionary anti-colonial struggle in Mozambique, and the greater pluralism and increased receptivity to feminism of the Nicaraguan Revolu-tion 20 years later. They also exhibit differences in other areas. Until recently the state had control of all economic activity in Cuba, while the FSLN maintained a mixed economy. However, external constraints have been important in all three cases. FRELIMO's attempts to create a new society in Mozambique were effectively ended in the mid-1980s by the devastation caused by the activities of the South African backed Renamo guerrillas. In Nicaragua, the Contra War launched from neighbouring countries by US backed ex-Somocistas drained the country's resources throughout the 1980s until the election of the opposition UNO coalition headed by Violetta Chamorro, widow of a prominent opposition politician killed by Somoza in 1978. Cuba is currently in a special period of economic hardship following the collapse of the Eastern bloc and the continued economic blockade by the United States.

Conventional politics

The two important issues to consider when examining women and conven-tional politics are: first the role of women within the formal political struc-tures and second the influence and activities of those women's organizations which have been closely tied to the ruling organizations. Most revolutionary regimes give the revolutionary party a leading role in the political system and the state and all have been accused, both internally and nationally, of a lack of democracy. The extent to which political pluralism has been tolerated has varied. While Cuba had still not allowed political opposition to function in 1995, the FSLN handed over political power to an opposition coalition following the 1990 elections and, after a long war, FRELIMO has contested elections with the opposition grouping Renamo.

In Cuba, after what appeared to be a primarily nationalist revolution, Castro declared the country communist in 1961. The 26th of July Movement took the lead as the Cuban Communist Party, and other political parties were not permitted to operate. From early on, women did not participate in the political system on the same terms as men. For example they formed only 10 per cent of Communist Party membership in 1967, a figure which rose to 15 per cent in 1974 (Stubbs 1994: 196). This situation was vividly highlighted by the 1974 experiment with people's power. When electors voted for assembly members in a pilot project in Matanzas in 1974 only 7 per cent of the nominated candidates and 3 per cent of those elected were women (Randall 1992: 143). An investigation into the causes of women's absence identified women's role in the domestic sphere as a major impediment to their political participation.

Subsequently efforts were made to increase the number of women involved in politics at all levels. Women's membership in the party rose to 19 per cent in 1980 and reached 22 per cent in 1984. At the local level some encouraging results were achieved as 50 per cent of the leadership of local committees for the defence of the revolution by 1980 and 46 per cent of local union committees were women in 1984 (Larguia and Dumoulin 1985: 360). At the national level the situation was less encouraging, particularly at the higher levels. While women made up 22 per cent of the delegates elected to the National Congress, the Central Committee elected by the Party Congress of 1980 was made up of only 12.9 per cent of women, and women were still only 12 per cent of the Central Committee in 1991 (Randall 1992: 152). In 1983 only one of the 32 ministers was a woman (Padulla and Smith 1985: 89).

In Mozambique, FRELIMO's accession to power brought changes to the party. In 1976 FRELIMO transformed itself from a broad front into a vanguard party in the Marxist–Leninist model. Many of FRELIMO's policies over the subsequent years were concerned with exerting control over the people and constructing the new state (Arnfred 1988: 13). By the time that FRELIMO tried to create party cells throughout the country in 1978, attempts were also being made to increase the low participation of women, particularly at the higher levels. In 1977 while women were 28.3 per cent of the deputies elected to the local assemblies and 23.8 per cent of those elected to the district assemblies, only 12.2 per cent of the regional delegates elected to FRELIMO's Third Congress in 1977 were women. Higher up only 7.5 per cent of the Central Committee were women (five out of a total of 67) and between 1977 and 1983 there was only one woman minister, who had responsibility for education and culture (Urdang 1984b: 13). However, Urdang believes that the progress made in increasing the participation of women in the six years after independence was not discouraging when compared to the levels of women in political positions in other African states.

While more pluralist in its leanings than the Cuban Communist Party or FRELIMO, the FSLN became the leading party in government in Nicaragua. The Statute of Rights and Guarantees of Nicaraguans of September 1979 repeated the commitment to women's emancipation made in the 1969 Programme and proclaimed the full equality of men and women and committed the state to 'removing all obstacles' to achieving that equality (Molyneux 1985c: 146). Equal rights for men and women were again enshrined in the 1987 Constitution. The FSLN had a slightly better record than some other revolutionary governments in ensuring women were represented in the government. In 1984 women were said to make up 22 per cent of the total membership of the FSLN, having fallen from a height of 38 per cent in 1979, but rising slightly to 24.3 per cent in 1987. Approximately 15 per cent of the members of the National Assembly elected in 1984 were women, including its vice president. It was claimed officially that women formed 37 per cent of the leadership cadre in 1984. While there were no women in the nine person National Directorate which formed the nucleus of the leadership, three women became ministers between 1979 and 1985 as well as others filling top positions such as Vice President of the Council of State.

The FSLN was not only the party of government but also an organization concerned to encourage political mobilization and education. Much of this took place in the mass organizations which formed the intermediaries between the FSLN leadership and the people. Some members of the mass organizations were also members of the FSLN. Women made up half the membership of the youth organization, the neighbourhood CDSs, the Sandinista Defence Committees and the militias whose importance grew as the Contra War intensified. Campaigns were also waged to increase women's low levels of membership in the trade unions and the association of agricultural workers.

Many revolutionary regimes saw women's organizations as an important way in which women could be integrated into the revolution. Autonomous women's movements were discouraged, if not prevented, and the already existing organizations were absorbed into the official women's organization. Great stress was then laid both on mobilizing women in defence of the revolution and transmitting the ideas of the dominant party through these organizations. As we will see, in many instances women's organizations came to be seen as representing the interests of the ruling party to women rather than representing women within the government. As such they lost support and floundered as they became increasingly discredited at the grassroots level. However attempts to remedy these problems were constrained by many factors and achieved mixed results.

The Federation of Cuban Women (FMC) was founded on 23 August 1960 on the initiative of Fidel Castro through the amalgamation of several pre-existing organizations. Vilma Espin who headed the organization was a revolutionary and the wife of Fidel's brother Raul. She did not see the FMC as a feminist organization but a feminine one which 'could defend, support and fight for the revolution' (quoted in Azicri 1987: 364). The membership of the FMC has grown steadily since 1960. It reached nearly 2.25 million in 1978, including more than 50 per cent of Cuban women over 14 years old and rose to 3.2 million in 1990, encompassing 80 per cent of the female population.

Jean Stubbs (1994: 194) argues that the activities of the organization have gone through 'two broadly overlapping but sequential phases: the "mobilizing for revolution" and "revolution within the revolution"'. In the first phase, the FMC used its national organizational network to aid literacy, education and training campaigns and continued working to increase women's employment, that is getting more women into production (Larguia and Dumoulin 1985: 347–8). However, in 1974 at the beginning of the second phase, Espin argued that the 'total incorporation of women in the political, social and economic life of the country in conditions of equality has not been achieved in its entirety' (quoted in Stubbs 1994: 196). Over the next decade the FMC put greater efforts into campaigning to increase women's political advancement and increase male responsibilities within the household, epitomized in the Family Code of 1975.

Criticisms have been levelled at the FMC both in terms of its representativeness and lack of power and influence. It has had only infrequent national conferences; up to 1991 there had only been five, in 1962, 1974, 1980, 1985 and 1990. Vilma Espin, its first director, rarely spoke on women's issues and was not always a member of the inner circle of the Central Committee (Padula and Smith 1985: 87–8). Others have argued that the FMC became increasingly out of touch with younger women, for example through its avoidance of difficult issues in its publication, such as changing sexual mores, preferring instead to stick to recipes and household care (Azicri 1987: 368). Some changes in the FMC's priorities have been visible more recently but Stubbs (1994: 197) claims that in 1990 discussion was stymied at the Congress when the FMC leadership shifted from an 'exciting gender agenda to one of defense and production for reasons of national expediency'.

The Organization of Mozambican Women was established in 1973 by FRELIMO two years prior to independence, in 1975, to increase the involvement of women in the national liberation struggle. When FRELIMO became a vanguard party open only to militants in 1975, the OMM became one of the 'mass democratic organizations' through which the population could be incorporated into politics (Kruks and Wisner 1989: 150). In 1975, at its second conference, the OMM put forward a conventional socialist analysis of the 'woman question'. The OMM was not meant to be an autonomous organization but was 'supposed to provide a channel for informing women of FRELIMO's policies and involving women in carrying them out' (Kruks and Wisner 1989: 155). It too was involved in literacy, vaccination, and anti-bride price campaigns in addition to measures aimed at getting more women into production and political activity. The OMM was criticized for

doing less and less to represent women in the policy making process, inter-
vening and initiating very little (Urdang 1989: 26). In part this can be
attributed to FRELIMO's underlying analysis, the top-down nature of the
political structures and to the replacement of many rural OMM activists who
had in-depth knowledge of the situation of rural women with (often better
educated) urban women (Arnfred 1988: 13).

However, in 1984 there was a return to women as the subjects of their
own emancipation. An extraordinary conference of the OMM was held in
that year after a lively and intense debate. This debate took place when
brigades were sent out throughout the country holding over 2000 meetings
with women and collecting information which was then relayed back to
Maputo. Urdang (1989) believes this was both encouraging and discouraging,
as the potential national movement which had been created as issues were
thrashed out was squashed at the conference where the FRELIMO leadership
dominated. By this time the needs of the war were also having to take
precedence over almost everything else. Some conference resolutions reflected both the domination of the war and the belief that women's struggle
can only be part of the more general struggle to liberation, not waged in its
own right (Urdang 1989: 213–18).

APRONAC, the Nicaraguan women's organization founded in 1977
changed its name after the revolution in 1979 to AMNLAE (the Louisa
Amanda Espinosa Association of Nicaraguan Women) to commemorate the
first woman to die in fighting Somoza's forces. Several of the contradictions
which permeated FSLN policies towards women were reflected in the fate
of AMNLAE. The FSLN was more sympathetic to feminism than many
other revolutionary movements, as evidenced by the law passed in 1979 pro-
hibiting the use of women's bodies in advertising (Chuckryk 1991: 146). At
the same time, the FSLN retained 'traditional' attitudes and policies towards
women, such as the elevation of motherhood and restricted reproductive
rights in terms of access to contraception and abortion. These contradictions
were reflected in some of their proclamations (Chuchryk 1991: 155). In
common with many women's organizations, AMNLAE was closely tied to
the revolutionary organization but overall had more of a role in campaigning
and policy initiation than the FMC and OMM. While AMNLAE was essentially an FSLN organization with its top members also FSLN cadres, and has
been called the women's section of the FSLN, there was an ambiguity in its
role, particularly over how 'feminist' it was to be (Collinson 1990: 139).

Over the 1980s AMNLAE's character changed to become a more overtly
feminist organization by the end of the decade. In part this change was a
response to criticism from both the grassroots and militants. Initially AMNLAE
followed an 'integrationist' policy – trying to integrate women into the
revolutionary process. The main aim in 1979, according to a member of its
National Executive, was 'to maintain the mobilisation of women around the
defence and consolidation of the revolution' (quoted in Deighton et al. 1983:
43). In the first three years after the revolution it concentrated on promoting
legislative reform which would benefit women, such as family reform, national

reconstruction, and involving women in health and education campaigns and in production. Despite a reorganization in 1981, changing it from a direct membership organization like other mass organizations to 'political–ideological social movement', AMNLAE lacked focus in the early 1980s in part because of a lack of clarity about its role. This combined with the needs of the war effort meant that AMNLAE lost touch with its original base.

By 1985 AMNLAE's membership and popularity had declined, in a context where popular support was crucial. In response to this, a re-evaluation of the organization took place. Open assemblies were organized all over the country prior to AMNLAE's second national congress to find out what women wanted from it. The leadership was surprised at the level of criticism of the organization, which focused on AMNLAE's failure to deal with issues around reproduction and sexuality, particularly abortion, and violence against women (Chinchilla 1994: 182–3). Some AMNLAE activists wanted it to take a more 'feminist' line, arguing that integrating women into the revolution was not enough. Their critique was echoed by women active in other mass organizations, in particular the Association of Agricultural Workers (Chinchilla 1990: 384).

These processes led to further changes: a reorganization with a new leadership and a limited radicalization occurred as it took up issues such as rape and domestic violence more forcibly. It also resulted in a shift in the overall public stance of the FSLN towards women (Molyneux 1988: 122). In 1987 the FSLN issued a statement on women (the Proclama) which declared that women suffered specific exploitation and that dealing with this could not be left until after the war, nor was it just the responsibility of AMNLAE but of the whole FSLN. It also highlighted issues such as domestic violence and machismo (Collinson 1990: 145). While still criticized for its lack of a thorough-going feminist analysis, the changes of 1987 have also been heralded as marking the birth of the Nicaraguan feminist movement which mushroomed after the defeat of the FSLN and will be considered below.

Therefore despite efforts made to increase their political participation, women have not figured in postrevolutionary political institutions in the same numbers as men. They have not been equally represented in policy making positions at the higher echelons such as in party Central Committees. This situation mirrors that within competitive electoral systems. At the same time, women's organizations initially have often played more of a role in transmitting the ideas of the party than representing women and this has frequently led to increasing contradictions in their position. In all three cases, these problems led to some attempts to shift their position from one of mobilizing for the revolution towards also mobilizing on behalf of women themselves.

State policy

All revolutionary regimes implemented policies to effect a transformation of the existing system. This process often necessitated the large scale destruction of the old order before the construction of the new one could take place. The changes implemented in these two phases have particular implications for gender relations and the private sphere.

Governments laid great emphasis, particularly initially, on increasing the well-being of all the population in terms of health, education and welfare and took measures to achieve these aims. Health services were improved. Special emphasis was laid on primary health care, particularly establishing services in rural areas. In Nicaragua, health campaigns, for example to promote vaccinations, were launched soon after the revolution. Seventy-five per cent of the health brigades were women and improvements were soon effected in maternal and child health (Collinson 1990: 95–103). Cuba, Mozambique and Nicaragua embarked on mass literacy campaigns very soon after their revolutions. In Cuba and Nicaragua, where female illiteracy rates were higher than the general figures of 23.6 per cent and 53 per cent of the population respectively, these took the form of literacy crusades in which (often urban middle-class) women formed a majority of the brigadistas and (often poor rural) women many of the beneficiaries. In Mozambique, where illiteracy levels were near 90 per cent, one-off solutions were not possible and sustained campaigns were launched every year after 1978. While women were especially encouraged to participate, they also experienced problems, particularly due to a lack of time because of their other responsibilities (Urdang 1989: 229–31). Improvements in education and training also occurred at primary, secondary and tertiary levels. In Cuba, rural women were trained in sewing at Ann Betancourt schools and by the early 1980s almost half of university students were women, with an emphasis on women studying technical and scientific subjects. Women, particularly poor women, benefited enormously from all these measures, although they often were not specifically directed at women. Indeed it is no coincidence that in both Nicaragua and Mozambique counter-revolutionaries targeted health centres, schools and other forms of welfare provision in their destabilization campaigns.

All revolutionary regimes also stressed the need to provide employment which included encouraging women's entry to paid employment. This policy fitted in both with the theoretical assumptions about the emancipatory effects of waged labour held by many socialist regimes and the developmentalist aims of the socialist state with its emphasis on increased levels of production. However, in contrast to the Soviet Union, there was no labour shortage, but high rates of under and unemployment in many Third World countries and therefore less need to promote women's entry to paid employment. This analysis also ignored the unpaid productive labour, for example in rural households, already undertaken by many women.

Despite some attempts to get women into non-traditional jobs, the majority of women remained in gender segregated employment. In Cuba more emphasis was placed on achieving male full employment in the early 1960s. Attention then turned to increasing women's labour force participation. However, it soon became clear that many of those women who joined the paid workforce left soon afterwards. In 1969 76 per cent of those women who entered had left the labour force within a year (Nazzari 1989: 117). An FMC survey demonstrated that while attempts had been made to provide amenities such as nurseries to facilitate women's entry into paid employment, their insufficiency, in part due to severe material constraints, and the resulting 'double shift' combined with few means to lighten domestic labour, was responsible not only for women giving up their jobs, but rising divorce rates and a falling birthrate as well. Mozambique initially followed an agricultural development strategy which marginalized women by emphasizing state farms, which employed a mainly male workforce, over cooperatives or family farms. After its failure, the emphasis then shifted towards family farms, but women were still not included in the planning process (Urdang 1989: 24–31). In Nicaragua women's labour market participation rose from 28 per cent of the economically active population in 1977 to 45 per cent in 1989. While a traditional sexual division of labour was maintained, women also increased their share of the paid agricultural labour force, particularly within the state sector (Chuckryk 1991: 149). Despite the legal provisions for equality in employment and maternity leave, women in both Cuba and Nicaragua continued to be discriminated against in the labour market in part because organizations were unwilling to bear the costs of maternity pay and other benefits (Nazzari 1989: 121–3; Chuckryk 1991: 149).

As part of the modernizing mission of many socialist states, far reaching programmes of legislative reform were implemented to dismantle the old order. This first phase of transformation has often formed an important part of the wider transformation of pre-capitalist social relations (Molyneux 1985b). Molyneux argues that during this phase there is a coincidence between the goals of socialist development and women's emancipation. While the reforms remove some of the material and ideological bases of extreme inequalities, however, they do not secure the conditions for equality as this was not their primary aim (Molyneux 1985b). These measures range from land reform to measures specifically designed to alter existing patterns of gender relations. There are three main types of legal reforms of this latter kind (Molyneux 1985b). First, there are those which remove kin control over marriage and institute free choice unions. Second, there are measures which specifically redefine relations between men and women to put them on a more equal footing. Third, there are laws which affect women as childbearers (Molyneux 1985b: 49). The first and second types form part of the liberalization of the existing patriarchal family.

Patriarchal authority was therefore eroded by legislation. In many places this was required principally to enable the mobilization of women into political and economic activity outside the household. Family reform and land reform often went together. In China, for example, the marriage law was concerned to attack the feudal family, seen as the social base of land ownership. In Mozambique considerable emphasis was placed on ending practices such as polygamy, bride price (lobolo), child marriage, and forced marriage. Lobolo, like polygamy, was seen as stemming from an economic base. It was claimed at the second OMM conference that

This practice exists throughout the country. Its rationale is that it is compensation for the transfer of labour power from one family to another. This puts women in a situation of total dependence on men, who because they have paid for them, can use and disown them like mere objects.

(quoted in Urdang 1984b: 29)

The campaigns, however, met with mixed success. They were often more effective in the communal villages. Elsewhere, new ways of paying lobolo were found. Furthermore, Arnfred (1988: 8–9) argues that some Mozambican women defended old practices such as initiation rights and matriliny in order to protect their autonomous spaces in the face of OMM attempts, as part of the promotion of the nuclear family, to replace matriliny often found in the north with patriliny, which facilitated men taking back patriarchal power.

Once the destruction of the old order has been achieved, the second phase takes the form of the creation of a new stable social order. The new order involves the modernization of the family rather than its fundamental alteration. Outlawed family structures are replaced by the formally egalitarian heterosexual nuclear family (Molyneux 1985b: 57). The state therefore intervenes into the family and relations within it to try and secure this type of structure. In Nicaragua where the number of female headed households is high, legislation was used to try and make the nuclear family a more stable and cohesive unit (Molyneux 1985b: 56). Relations between men and women are now seen as complementary, not antagonistic. Hence the unwillingness of regimes to tackle issues of domestic and sexual violence both within the home and outside of it, except under pressure.

The enshrinement of heterosexual privilege in the new order entails restrictions on sexuality, including homosexuality. Lois Smith describes how Cuban literature on sex condemns both promiscuity and extramarital affairs and argues that 'some reformists who tried to abolish marriage could not offer better alternatives after analysing all aspects of the problem' (quoted in Smith 1992: 187). While the situation had improved by the late 1980s, in the 1970s it was too dangerous for lesbians and gay men in Cuba to talk openly about their sexuality (Randall 1992: 127). In a 1982 sex education guide, Cuban adolescents are told that homosexuals 'really don't achieve the happiness that family brings' and 'cannot develop complete sexual relations with reproductive ends' (quoted in Smith 1992: 186). More recently Cuba has also been criticized for its treatment of people with AIDs. Some similar trends have been seen in Nicaragua. A gay and lesbian network was beginning to emerge in Nicaragua by 1985, but in 1988 a number of activists were summoned to the Office of National Security and told that they were jeopardizing their membership of the FSLN by organizing and becoming more public about their sexuality (Randall 1992: 70).

Women also cease to be defined as militant revolutionary agents in this phase, particularly if the threat of counter-revolution has receded. The new socialist woman is the working mother rather than a fighter. In Nicaragua, despite the efforts of AMNLAE, women's role in the military declined. Many women were demobilized from the regular army after the 'triumph'. After pressure in the years immediately following the revolution, women's reserve battalions were created but when military service (SMP) was introduced in 1983 it was for men aged between 18 and 25 years only. The defence minister claimed that women's participation in SMP 'would be like a man breastfeeding his baby or a woman lifting weights' (quoted in Collinson 1990: 158). After protests it was agreed that women could participate in SMP on a voluntary basis but none were called up until 1986. While women played an important role in the popular militias, forming 60 per cent of their members in some urban areas, by the late 1980s they were only 20 per cent of the regular army and were not usually sent to the war front. However, following shortfalls in the numbers of soldiers in the second half of the 1980s, campaigns were launched to recruit more women into military service (Collinson 1990: 154–66).

Some of the contradictions apparent in this phase are highlighted in the ambivalent policies towards reproductive rights, particularly abortion, in Nicaragua. In the early years after the revolution, contraceptives and sex education were minimally promoted and not widely available. While abortion was available to women in Cuba, it remained illegal in Nicaragua. The FSLN did not want to alienate the Church, particularly the progressive Christians who supported them and wished to repopulate the war-torn country, encouraging women to have children for the revolution (Wessel 1991: 537). As a result, AMNLAE remained quiet in the early years on the issue of reproductive rights. However, women continued to have a high number of illegal abortions, often going to hospitals with complications resulting in high rates of mortality. While the FSLN would not contemplate the legalization or even the decriminalization of abortion, they did have a policy of not prosecuting those having or performing abortions (Collinson 1990: 118). In the mid-1980s abortion became an openly contested issue and AMNLAE moved towards a more active policy of campaigning for reproductive rights. However, amid speeches from Daniel Ortega claiming that a woman choosing not to have children 'negates her own continuity and continuity of the human species' (quoted in Collinson 1990: 119), the FSLN reiterated their position that full reproductive rights were not possible. Three main arguments were made: Nicaragua was underpopulated and had a labour shortage; the 'people' were against changes on religious grounds; and the issue was so explosive that to tackle it would lend support to the opposition (Molyneux 1988: 124). These issues became even more contested as a more autonomous women's movement began to emerge in Nicaragua.

We have seen that in all the cases under consideration attempts were made to restructure the economy and society in a modernizing project which aimed to achieve economic development and improve the well-being of its citizens as well as increasing levels of equality between men and women. Revolutionary regimes achieved mixed results with regard to their policies towards women (Molyneux 1981). Important gains for women were made in the fields of legislation and education. Mixed results were achieved in the field of political representation and very contradictory outcomes emerged in the areas of employment, sexuality and women's reproductive roles. Women's subordination within the family remained and women still bore the brunt of the reproduction of the labour force while taking on the new role of paid worker without men having to change their roles.

Women's autonomous organizing

In most revolutionary regimes women's autonomous organizing has been deemed to be unnecessary and therefore not tolerated. There is therefore little to discuss in any one of the three case studies except in Nicaragua where the roots of an autonomous movement first developed in the second half of the 1980s, as witnessed by the emergence of organizations such as CONAPRO and the establishment of independent women's centres and theatre groups (Collinson 1990: 148–50). This process speeded up after the victory of the UNO coalition in 1990. After an initially cool response from AMNLAE, a large number of different women's organizations have mushroomed, demonstrated by the 800 women who turned up at the first feminist conference held in January 1992 (Kampwirth 1992; Randall 1992: 62–9). It can be argued that the existence of AMNLAE and the policies of the FSLN, while problematic, raised the profile of gender issues. As such, it would not have been possible for a heterogeneous women's movement to emerge without the FSLN's emphasis, however partial, on equal rights for women. Autonomy, in particular what relationship women's organizations should have with the FSLN, remains a major issue for the women's movements as many activists are or have been Sandinistas and involved with AMNLAE (De Montis 1994).

Conclusion

Undoubted improvements were made, certainly initially, in many women's lives in terms of health, education and welfare in all three postrevolutionary contexts we have examined in detail. It can legitimately be asked how far this was due to the implementation of policies which improved the position of poor people in general rather than women in particular. However, it is clear that there was a genuine emancipatory agenda of sorts, but it was limited and full of contradictions. The narrow and restricted socialist analysis of the woman question together with its instrumentalism brought mixed results for many women. The relationship of many revolutionary regimes to Western style feminism has also been complex. It has had a greater influence over more recent revolutions, and increasingly the party women's organizations have taken up issues often identified with a Western feminist agenda. However, this has often happened at a time when external constraints have prevented significant changes as the continued existence of the revolution has become a priority. Despite the reluctance of revolutionary governments to allow them to exist, independent women's organizations appear a necessity so that they can act autonomously to pressurize the state.

Authoritarianism

Introduction

Authoritarian regimes have been a common occurrence in the Third World since independence. A variety of explanations have been put forward to account for this, understanding authoritarianism in terms of the historical legacies of 'traditional' society and colonialism; the weakness and permeability of the Third World state and state institutions; economic dependence and periodic economic crises (Clapham 1985; Randall and Theobald 1985; Cammack *et al.* 1993). However, throughout the vast literature on the role of the military in politics, neo-patrimonial regimes and authoritarianism in general, there is very little discussion of gender relations. While many of these analyses provide some useful insights into the causes and nature of authoritarian regimes, often couched in cultural and economic terms, none examines the gendered nature of authoritarianism. There is, however, a growing body of literature analysing the role played by Latin American women in supporting and opposing military regimes of the 1970s and 1980s as well as some material produced on women and the military in other Third World contexts such as Nigeria (Dennis 1987; Mba 1990). This chapter will attempt to provide a gendered analysis of authoritarianism, and military rule in particular, through a detailed examination of the Latin American experience, primarily the Southern Cone (particularly Argentina and Chile) in the 1970s and 1980s, supplementing this with material from other parts of the Third World.

The term authoritarianism has been used to cover a wide range of regime types. Samuel Huntington (1991: 109) defines an authoritarian regime negatively. It lacks the common institutional core present in democratic regimes, that is the principal officers of government are chosen through competitive party elections in which a majority of the population can participate. As a residual category which incorporates all other types of regime, there are tremendous variations between authoritarian regimes. The only characteristic such regimes may share is that they all, to some degree or other, suppress political participation and electoral competition along the narrow conventional and institutional lines described in Chapter 1. Huntington (1991: 110) distinguishes three major types of authoritarian regime which predominated prior to the third wave of democratization occurring since the 1970s. These are: one party states, personal dictatorships and military regimes. They often exist on a continuum, rather than as distinct entities. However, these different regime types do display significant variations in terms of their degree of institutionalization. Some military governments have exercised power on an institutional basis, often governing collegially as a junta or rotating top positions among senior generals (Huntington 1991: 110), while other military leaders have ruled in a manner verging on a personal dictatorship.

Bratton and van de Walle (1994) argue that while relatively bureaucratized military regimes, which may exhibit corporatist tendencies, are more typical of Latin America, neo-patrimonial regimes, in which the chief executive maintains state authority through personal patronage rather than through ideology or impersonal law, are more common in Africa. This happens most commonly in one party states and personal dictatorships. Bratton and van de Walle (1992b) outline three characteristics of neo-patrimonial regimes: first an extreme personalization of power; second that political power is based on clientelism, prebendalism and rent-seeking; and third the existence of an undeveloped civil society. The state tends to dominate the public realm and attempts to control political activity. The voluntary associations, such as religious or professional organizations, which are sanctioned by the state are often restricted to non-political activities. Several commentators have pointed to a withdrawal from the state, for example into informal associations, as a common response by the people to the corrupt and rapacious nature of the state (Azarya and Chazan 1987). As few women are represented within the state either in the bureaucracy or the government, they tend not to benefit from these extensive patronage networks, but building on already existing traditions of informal networks, many women withdraw from activities in the public realm and organize around more immediate issues of survival, in a variety of informal or 'voluntary' associations (Wipper 1984; Parpart 1988: 221). Some women, for example, market women in Ghana, have organized to protect themselves from the encroachments of the state, while others have become increasingly active in the illegal economy.

One party states

Looking first at one party states, we can see that one party systems gain power in a variety of ways. Some, particularly in Africa such as KANU in Kenya, gain control at independence after a nationalist anti-colonial struggle (Leys 1975). The party then, through a combination of the suppression of other parties and members of the opposition 'crossing the floor' to join the ruling party, consolidates its position in control of the state (Clapham 1985: 66). Other parties come to power as the result of a revolution. While some revolutionary parties were examined in Chapter 4, because their ideology and practices distinguish them from the majority of authoritarian regimes, there is often a blurred distinction between the two as some radical anti-colonial parties have consolidated a one party system. ZANU, an apparently left-wing guerrilla organization, took power in Zimbabwe in 1980 after a protracted national liberation struggle in the 1970s but throughout the 1980s appeared to be moving towards a one party state. The PRI in Mexico provides one of the longest standing examples of one party continuously in power in the twentieth century. One party states can therefore be on any part of the political spectrum, ranging from left-wing, for example the PNC in Guyana, to right-wing, for example the KMT in Taiwan.

Once in control, the single party effectively monopolizes power, often using patronage and clientelist networks to control access to power through the party organization, and the manipulation and rigging of elections to reinforce it (Clapham 1982). These systems can achieve a relatively high degree of political institutionalization, but they are sometimes combined with a strong president who is in effect a personal dictator, for example Hastings Banda, who relied on repression, violence and terror to consolidate his control in Malawi. Bratton and van de Walle (1994) distinguish between plebiscitary one party systems, in which a personal ruler orchestrates political rituals of mass endorsement for himself, and competitive one party systems in which voters have a restricted electoral choice among candidates from a single party. Single parties sometimes legitimate their rule through an ideology, such as African socialism, and often attempt to turn the single party into an instrument of popular mobilization by organizing and co-opting different groups through various party organizations such as for youth. Women's organizations have provided one important mechanism through which this has occurred. In Zambia, UNIP, the nationalist party which had an active women's brigade, took power at independence. While few women were among the Zambian MPs and government officials, the executive secretary of the Women's League (as it became known in 1973 when Zambia officially became a one party state) was granted formal representation on the central committee. A women's affairs subcommittee of the central committee was created in 1984 to oversee policy making on women in different government departments (Munachonga 1990). However, women's organizations have not functioned very often to represent women in the government and have frequently served to mobilize support for the ruling party, often headed by a prominent woman close to the government, such as the president's wife. The Kenyan government finally took over Maendeleo Ya Wanawake, the biggest women's organization founded in the colonial period, in the late 1980s and by 1989 it had become an extension of KANU, the ruling party (Nzomo and Staudt 1994).

Personal dictatorships

Personal dictatorships form a more diverse group of undemocratic systems, distinguished as such because the 'individual leader is the source of authority and that power depends on access to, closeness to, and support from the leader' (Huntington 1991: 111). There are many examples of personal dictators in the Third World. The Shah of Iran, Somoza in Nicaragua, Batista in Cuba, Mobutu in Zaire, Hastings Banda in Malawi and Marcos in the Philippines have been among the most notorious. Using Weber's notions of patrimonialism and sultanistic regimes, analyses of this phenomenon have focused on patronage, nepotism, cronyism and corruption. Personal dictatorships are the embodiment of neo-patrimonialism, because state authority is maintained through a network of personal patronage, rather than through ideology or impersonal law (even though a legal framework may be in place) and they do not rely on traditional forms of legitimacy (Snyder 1992). Particularly in the most sultanistic forms, personal dictatorships often display lower levels of political institutionalization than other forms of authoritarian governments because of the central role played by the dictator. Civil society is often more undeveloped under personal dictatorships and withdrawal from the state, by both men and women, more far reaching. In Malawi, all of civil society was either incorporated or suppressed and in Zaire a social space was created in a parallel economy, a religious sphere and informal association realm (Young 1994; Posner 1995). Personal dictatorships have varied in the ways in which they treated women, for example in Haiti Duvalier attempted to incorporate some women into the state as 'patriotic women' (Charles 1995). However, the demarcation between the different forms of regime is not always clear cut, as the role played by the president of a one party state or a military leader can verge on being a personal dictatorship, while a civilian dictator may often rely on the power of the army.

Military regimes

Military governments are probably the best known category of authoritarian regime in the Third World. There has been a high incidence of military intervention since independence. Three-quarters of Latin American states and around half the Asian and African states have experienced military takeovers since 1960. Only the Caribbean has seemed relatively immune from military intervention (Payne and Sutton 1993: 8–9). The nature of military coups and regimes has varied greatly over time and place such as in terms of the longevity of the intervention and the degree of institutionalization it achieves. Not surprisingly, the political role of the military has received vast attention from academics, the most sustained analyses having been produced in the Latin American context. The literature has been concerned with the reasons for military intervention and what the military does when in power.

Some explanations for intervention have concentrated on factors internal to the military itself and others on external conditions. Janowitz (1964) stressed the superior quality of the organization and shared values of the officer corps, such as patriotism and the sense that it was their duty to save the nation, as reasons for their intervention. A more negative interpretation stresses selfish corporate motives such as protecting the size of the defence budget and military salaries. Other writers have concentrated on factors external to the military. Samuel Finer (1962) argued that military intervention takes place where levels of political culture are low. In a more sophisticated analysis, Huntington links the character of the military to wider society, arguing that:

> As society changes, so does the role of the military. In the world of oligarchy, the soldier is a radical; in the middle-class world he is a participant and arbiter; as the mass society looms on the horizon, he becomes the conservative guardian of the existing order. Thus, the more backward a society is, the more progressive the role of its military; the more advanced a society becomes, the more conservative and reactionary becomes the role of its military.
>
> (Huntington 1968: 221)

Huntington outlines three different types of coup: the breakthrough, guardian and veto coup. The breakthrough coup occurs when the military wants to bring new groups, primarily the middle class, into the political process hitherto dominated by oligarchies, for example in Chile and Argentina in the 1930s and 1940s. The guardian coup often occurs when the middle class has already achieved some role in politics and the military is often concerned to implement similar policies to the preceding civilian government but to do it more effectively. The veto coup takes place when the military seeks to prevent the challenge of working-class participation in the political system. The military coup in Chile in 1973 would fall into this category. The military in this case becomes the doorkeeper of political participation, keeping the door open for the middle class and closed for the working class (Huntington 1968). Nun (1967) also stressed the links between the military and the wider society, arguing that the military represents the interests of the middle class which cannot establish itself as a hegemonic group. In many contexts the military has been content to form caretaker regimes – to remove one civilian government and oversee the installation of another civilian government more to their liking – thereby creating a role for themselves as the arbiters of politics. The military can sometimes become the mechanism by which civilian governments are changed, as occurred in Ghana in the late 1960s and early 1970s.

Despite the existence of this large literature, there has been an increasing appreciation that the circumstances are too diverse, and the reasons for intervention too varied to produce very satisfactory general theories and frameworks. The literature does provide some signposts. It highlights the necessity, when studying military regimes, of examining both the nature of the military itself and the social, economic and cultural context to which it belongs. However, for a gendered analysis of the military it is important to broaden the context even further to include not just the public sphere, but the private sphere and the often shifting boundaries between them. One starting point is an examination of the nature of militarism and militarization most authoritarian regimes have relied upon and which extends into most aspects of life under these regimes. Prior to this it is useful to discuss another aspect of the broader context, the sustenance many authoritarian regimes received from the outside as a consequence of the Cold War.

The impact of the Cold War

The support that many authoritarian regimes often received from outside was one important factor helping to sustain them until the end of the Cold War. Much of this support was the result of the desire of the West, and particularly of the United States, to prevent the spread of communism in the Third World. This support had several consequences. First, authoritarian regimes were often supported both financially and practically through arms and aid because they were anti-communist allies, enabling them to disregard the views of internal social groups. Second, Third World and particularly Latin American militaries often received special training in American influenced war colleges in the doctrine of 'national security'. These ideas formed part of particular vision of society which stressed that the war against communism and subversion was a 'total war' and, as such, action against civilians was justified. Third, it has been argued that these policies found their intellectual justification in 'order theory', the revision of modernization theory which occurred in the late 1960s when it became clear that, in much of the Third World, the expected transition to liberal democracy was not happening (O'Brien 1972). Order theorists, such as Huntington, argued that modern-ization had produced rising expectations which, in the face of economic stagnation, often turned into rising frustrations, which could easily undermine political stability. Under these new circumstances, the focus moved from how to achieve liberal democratic systems to how to preserve political order in the face of 'political decay', a reversal of the process of modernization. The emphasis shifted to finding 'effective' political institutions which could impose order on the masses from above. Alongside the bureaucracy and strong political parties, some saw the military as a group capable of imposing stability in the Third World. As such, authoritarian regimes could be viewed in a relatively positive light under some circumstances (Huntington 1968; O'Brien 1972).

The gender of militarism

Almost all authoritarian regimes rely on militarism and are often highly militarized. A sophisticated understanding of both concepts is essential. Militar-ism provides the wider social context of authoritarianism, extending into the realm of the 'private', which is necessary for a gendered understanding of authoritarianism (Enloe 1988: 205). Jacklyn Cock (1989), looking at the South African case, has argued that, although there is often slippage between them in the literature, militarism and militarization are made up of three distinct social phenomena. These are: first the military as a social institution; second, militarism as an ideology which values war and legitimates state violence as the solution to conflict; and third, militarism as a social process that involves the penetration of the military into more and more social areas until the military have a primacy in state and society (Cock 1989: 51).

Other feminists have argued for a similarly broad approach. The Chilean feminist Julieta Kirkwood has stressed the need to see authoritarianism, not just in narrow political or economic terms, but as reflecting patriarchal structures in the wider society (Kirkwood 1990). She argues that the roots of the authoritarianism lie in all social structures, not just those of the public sphere traditionally thought of as political. Authoritarianism effectively 'privatizes' and politicizes daily life through its repression of the public sphere. A consequence of this is to reveal the authoritarian relations dominant in the private sphere, particularly in the family. Therefore in order to combat authoritarianism in Latin American institutions, gender inequality must be fought against, as well as oppression along lines of race and class. Alvarez (1990a: 7) has argued that, to many Latin American feminists, authoritarianism 'represents the purist, "highest expression" of patriarchal oppression'.

However, it is overly simplistic to see authoritarianism and the militarism which frequently accompanies it as the ultimate expression of patriarchy (from which women are excluded and by which they are often victimized (Cock 1989). Militarism is not a totally male affair, as through processes of both, direct and indirect, incorporation and challenge, different groups of women play important roles within it. These linkages are obscured by two opposing perspectives: that of sexism and some variants of feminism (Cock 1989). The first excludes women from war on the grounds of their physical inferiority and the second excludes them on the grounds of their special qualities of peacefulness and nurturing. However, women have always been incorporated into war in a number of different ways: those which fit in with their designated roles, for example as the mothers of soldiers; and those which subvert those roles, such as resistance fighters and spies.

The use of opposing notions of masculinity and femininity provides an alternative approach to understanding how militarism and thus authoritarianism are gendered. It is here that the gendered division of society between the 'protectors' and the 'protected' becomes most marked (Stiehm 1982; Elshtain 1987). Indeed Cock (1989: 52) quoting Sara Ruddick argues that 'dividing the protector from the protected, defender from the defended, is the linchpin of masculinist as well as military ideology'. A rigid demarcation of gender roles exists in which the soldier is seen as the epitome of masculinity and femininity as its 'other'. In order to preserve this vision of the world, war and the male soldier are defined in such a way that

> women are categorised as peripheral, as serving safely at the 'rear', on the 'home front'. Women as women must be denied access to the 'front', to 'combat' . . . the military has to constantly define 'the front' and 'combat' as wherever 'women' are not.
>
> (Enloe 1988: 15)

However these binary divisions become problematic as the rigid demarcation between them is not always maintained in practice, leading to contradictory results. Within the military this is exemplified by the presence of female soldiers. Until recent exceptions, women soldiers have remained in 'feminine' servicing roles rather than undertaking 'masculine' combat roles. In order to sustain this binarism, definitions of femininity are widened to be able to encompass women soldiers rather than being fundamentally reworked (Cock 1989). For example the dress uniform for women soldiers worn at parades and ceremonial marches in Chile includes high heels.

More significantly, the contradictions which stem from the use of the binarism of masculinity and femininity to define combat as wherever women are not, are thrown into sharp relief when the military takes control of the state. As a result the divisions between the front and society as a whole are breached. This happens most clearly during civil wars and when militaries are operating according to the doctrine of 'national security' which turns all of society into the front in the total war against subversion and requires action against civilians. The position of women as the 'protected' away from the 'front' is less easy to sustain under these circumstances, despite the action which is often taken to sidestep this potential breach. As we will see, this separation and its breach has a number of consequences for women and gender relations.

The most sustained analyses of women and military regimes have focused on Latin America but there is some work which examines military regimes in West Africa. Nigeria has experienced a succession of military and civilian governments since independence and therefore a militarization of the state has occurred. Women have not been included on the military governments in any large numbers (Mba 1990). However, this does not mean that military regimes have ignored women. The government which took power in 1983 claimed that it was going to save Nigeria from 'indiscipline'; an important cause of this was certain groups of women neglecting their 'traditional' roles (Dennis 1987). Three groups of women were singled out: single women, working women with children and petty traders. The subsequent military government made more attempts to mobilize the élite dominated and state sponsored women's organizations to support its structural adjustment programme and its attempts to construct a new civilian order (Abdullah 1993). However, as there is far more information available on Latin America, it is more profitable to explore some of the themes raised in the first section of this chapter through an in-depth discussion of military regimes in Latin America, particularly in the Southern Cone of Argentina and Chile.

Military regimes in the Southern Cone

When analysing the military governments in the Southern Cone of Latin America, it is necessary to differentiate between 'bureaucratic authoritarian' (BA) regimes of the 1960s and the military regimes which took power in the 1970s. The military governments which seized control in Brazil in 1964 and in Argentina in 1966 had clearly defined projects and the intention of staying in power. As a result it was felt that the nature of military intervention in Latin America was changing. Guillermo O'Donnell (1977, 1979) argued that in the 1960s those countries which were originally exporters of primary products and industrialized late were experiencing economic stagnation as the easy stage of import substituting industrialization (ISI), centred around the manufacture of consumer goods, had been exhausted. This resulted in political unrest in the working and lower middle class, which was perceived as a 'threat' to the existing order. O'Donnell argues that the army intervened to remove this threat and promote industrialization by 'deepening' the economy through the production of intermediate and capital goods. Development was to be achieved through state intervention, the encouragement of direct foreign investment (DFI) and multinational corporations (MNCs), and the demobilization of the popular sectors. These aims could only be achieved through the establishment of a bureaucratic authoritarian regime based on a coalition between military and civilian technocrats overseeing a project of state-led development, which suppressed democracy and repressed and excluded the popular sectors (O'Donnell 1977, 1979). The Peruvian military regime in power between 1968–75 provides an interesting variant of bureaucratic authoritarianism. It initiated a programme of state-led economic reform coupled with a radical social ideology aimed at increasing participation, e.g. through cooperatives (Barrig 1989: 116).

While few women were high level technocrats, at the lower levels, the 'technocratization' of the Brazilian state in the 1960s and early 1970s necessitated the expansion of technical, scientific and professional education, providing opportunities for some women (Alvarez 1990a). Female participation in higher education increased by 500 per cent between 1969 and 1975, while the number of men only doubled (Alvarez 1989b: 19). Middle-class women trained to become many of the professionals and white-collar workers who staffed the growing state bureaucracy at the lower levels. This situation had important consequences, which we will discuss later.

While the formulation of the BA state seemed useful for analysing the authoritarian regimes established in Brazil and Argentina in the 1960s, it was not particularly helpful in understanding the military regimes which emerged in Argentina, Chile and Uruguay in the 1970s (Cammack 1985). While these new governments also intended to stay in power for considerable periods, they were not wedded to state-led development, preferring first a level of political repression not hitherto seen; second a more thorough-going attempt to abolish politics and restrict the activities of the public sphere; and third, New Right economic policies (O'Brien and Cammack 1985).

Political repression

Of these three distinguishing features of the military regimes of the Southern Cone, each had a contradictory impact on gender relations. One hallmark of all these regimes was the repression which accompanied the suppression of conventional political activity and formed a key part of the total war against subversion. The Chilean and Argentinian militaries intervened in the context of high levels of political polarization. In Chile, the immediate cause was the attempt of Unidad Popular, the Chilean left-wing coalition to effect a peaceful transition to socialism, while in Argentina the cause was the near collapse of the Peronist government following Perón's death and the takeover by his second wife Isobel amid guerrilla activity by the Monteneros, the left-wing Peronist guerrillas. Adherence to the doctrine of national security was used to justify a war against civilians in order to defeat the threat of communism and subversion. Pinochet made speeches on television, claiming that 'It's either me or chaos', while in 1978 the Argentinian general Videla gave an interview to British journalists in which he argued that 'a terrorist isn't just someone with a gun or a bomb, but whoever spreads ideas which are contrary to Western and Christian civilization' (quoted in Fisher 1993: 104). In Chile, a wave of repression was launched in the aftermath of the coup. Large numbers of people were arrested and taken to camps for political prisoners. The Argentinian military is infamous for escalating the 'dirty war', launched under the previous Peronist government, in which more than 10,000 suspected left-wing activists and sympathizers were kidnapped and murdered by death squads linked to the military. The same pattern was replicated in Uruguay.

Women were not immune from this repression. It is estimated that in Argentina, women formed 30 per cent of the disappeared and of these 3 per cent were pregnant (Fisher 1989: 105). Ximena Bunster–Burotto (1985) has identified two main groups of women who were singled out by the military regimes. The first comprised women targeted for their own activities. In Argentina middle-class students and activists made up many of the disappeared, a high proportion of whom were women. Children born in detention also joined the ranks of the disappeared, sometimes adopted by close associates of the military. In Chile, many women who had prominent public roles during the Allende government as union leaders, academics as well as political activists, were arrested. The second group comprised women detained because of their relationship to men: partners, sons and fathers. According to Bunster–Burotto (1985: 303), these women can be seen either as hostages in the internal war, or as possessions of men the military considered to be the enemy.

While in detention, women were brutalized and tortured in the same ways as men. But there is also evidence that women were treated in gender specific and sexualized ways. Bunster–Burotto (1985: 304–5) describes family torture, where women were tortured or raped in front of their children, or their children were beaten in front of them, in an attempt to exploit women's caring and nurturing roles. Sexual assault and rape by one or more men or by animals was commonly used. Women were raped in front of male associates in an attempt to get them to crack. There are clear parallels here with the way in which rape has been used as an instrument of war, as a means to terrorize the (male) enemy and brutalize the whole community through a violation of its 'property'. It is estimated that in the early 1970s 200,000 women were raped by Pakistani soldiers during the war which led to the creation of Bangladesh and there is evidence that American soldiers fighting in Vietnam, for example at Mai Lai in 1968, raped many women before killing them (Channel 4, *First Sex*, 20 June 1993).

The public sphere

The repression went alongside the attempts to abolish 'politics'. Trade unions and strikes were often banned or severely restricted; congresses were closed down; and political parties, particularly those on the Left, were either banned or restricted in their activities. The militaries often claimed that it was the operation of conventional politics and the actions of civilian politicians which caused the problems that led them to intervene. The conventional political arena therefore was prevented from operating in the ways it had done before. However, as we will see when we examine women's political activities, the banning of conventional politics did increase the space for women's political activities.

The military regimes of the Southern Cone (that is Chile, Argentina and Uruguay) varied in the ways in which they exercised power and the extent to which this was institutionalized. While none allowed competitive elections, the degree to which certain political parties were allowed to operate varied. The Pinochet regime in Chile attempted to institutionalize itself through the 'constitution of liberty', establishing mechanisms for plebiscites and a dominant role for the president. The Argentinean military government (1976–83) tended to be more factionalized, with power oscillating between different groupings within the ruling junta, and little political institutionalization (Philip 1984). These military governments were made up of both military personnel and civilian technocrats. The high levels of the military establishments unsurprisingly contained no women, and like other forms of political system there were few women among the ranks of the civilian technocrats. In Chile, women were excluded from membership of the legislative council as this was reserved for commanders-in-chief of the armed forces; during the 16 years that the Pinochet regime was in power only two women became ministers of state (Valenzuela 1991: 163).

While few women were found in the top echelons of military regimes, most governments had particular views on the proper roles for women. While without a detailed ideological programme, most military regimes advocated support for a version of 'traditional' values associated with the Right of the political spectrum (Tabak 1984). This generally included support for the family, god and the elevation of motherhood as women's proper role. These ideas formed part of the ideological package associated with the doctrine of national security and the espousal of 'Western Christian family values' that went with it. Women, according to Elshtain (1982), were positioned as the 'beautiful souls' while men of the military were the 'just warriors'.

Julieta Kirkwood has written that 'the [Chilean] Junta, with a very clear sense of its interests, has understood that it must reinforce the traditional family, and the dependent role of women, which is reduced to that of mother' (quoted in Chuckryk 1984: 320). Pinochet made many pronouncements on the position of women in Chilean society, stressing the important role played by women in transmitting and defending the spiritual values of the nation (quoted in Munizaga and Letelier 1988: 540, quoting from Pinochet's pronouncements in the press). He also stressed that 'the most important labour of women is motherhood' and argued that the 'Chilean woman is beautiful, an indomitable defender of her home, an unselfish, self-sacrificing loyal wife. Her nobility and dignity are not obscured by poverty and are enhanced by hardship' (quoted in Chuckryk 1984: 235). The military government therefore elevated motherhood as women's primary task and stressed women's charitable and self-sacrificing role in both the public and private sphere. In conjunction with Pinochet's military government, women were positioned as having a special role as defenders of the moral order.

The Chilean regime also attempted to incorporate women on the basis of these designated roles on a semi-formal basis. These efforts had little to do with the ideas of the New Right and are more reminiscent of a corporatist project. The autonomous right-wing women's organizations (see below) that had been active immediately prior to the coup were demobilized and incorporated. Two institutions were used to incorporate women. They were both all-women and government controlled. Because of the restriction and banning of political parties and activities, they became especially important (Bunster 1988: 487). One contradictory consequence of taking on this role, according to Bunster (1988: 488), was that some women became the 'civilian trench' and were militarized in the process.

The first organization, the National Secretariat for Women (SNM), was created in October 1973, soon after the junta took power. Pinochet's wife, Lucia Hiriart de Pinochet, was made its director for an indefinite period. It was a state organization, highly ideological and made up primarily of volunteers acting to promote Pinochet's vision of society, particularly with regard to women, and provide welfare to the poor. The volunteers were primarily from the middle and upper classes, often wives of members of the armed forces, and committed to supporting the regime, acting in keeping with the image of the 'patriotic self-sacrificing mother'. Volunteers wore uniforms, colour coded according to the activities they took part in, e.g. the Damas de Rojo (the women in red) were hospital volunteers. SNM also produced publications such as the monthly women's magazine *Revista*, and glossy booklets publicizing SNM's activities, such as 'Chilean Women and their Historical Compromise' by Lucia Hiriart de Pinochet (Munizaga and Letelier 1988). It has been estimated that between 1973 and 1983 the activities of the SNM involved two million women (Bunster 1988).

The SNM worked closely with the second type of organization, the Mothers' Centres (CEMAs). These had been established under the Christian Democrat government of Eduardo Frei in the 1960s as part of their efforts to widen participation and incorporate the marginal groups. They aimed to enable women, particularly poorer women, to meet, gain the means to generate an income and become involved in community affairs. While CEMA Chile was allegedly a private organization, after 1973 the Mothers' Centres were taken over and reorganized, Lucia Hiriat de Pinochet was appointed as its president and she appointed the executive director. The centres were mainly staffed by middle-class volunteers, again often military wives and used as a way of incorporating poorer women into a framework which supported the government. They were in competition with the more broadly oppositional organizations which were often established under the auspices of the Vicariate of the Church (Agosin 1988). In 1983 CEMA Chile had around 230,000 members, 6000 volunteers and over 10,000 centres throughout the country. Thus some women provided both material and ideological support for an authoritarian regime.

The policies specifically directed at women reflect the military's ideology. The Chilean government tried to reinforce certain public displays of masculinity and femininity, for example it tried to restrict women wearing trousers. It also tried to encourage an increase in the birthrate, facilitated by the introduction of charges for healthcare and family planning in 1986, and one of its last acts before leaving power was to further restrict reproductive rights by forbidding therapeutic abortions, the only form which had previously been permitted. The Chilean government refused to ratify the UN Convention on Women until just before the 1989 elections. However, as we will now see, the impact of other aspects of the policies of military regimes, such as their economic policies, often ran contrary to these espoused aims.

Economic policies

Many Latin American militaries seized power claiming that they were going to restore stability and order not only to the societies but also to the economies they had taken over. While the military governments of the 1960s had favoured some form of state-led development, the military regimes of the 1970s and 1980s implemented New Right economic policies with varying degrees of dedication and success. The military governments favoured freeing the market (including the labour market) by rolling back the state, privatization and deregulation. Some regimes, for example in Chile and Uruguay, promoted non-traditional export agro-industries such as forestry, fruit growing, fish farming and processing as part of the restructuring of the economy. Attempts to free the labour market were facilitated by restrictions on trade union activities, the reduction and removal of protective legislation for workers, and high levels of unemployment. The demobilization of the working class was a necessary part of neo-liberal economic policies and was helped by the repression. These measures were often combined with reductions in restrictions on the financial sectors and in tariff rates, historically maintained at high levels. As a result, the financial sectors expanded enormously and the contraction of large foreign debts was facilitated. There was, for example, an explosion of largely unregulated activity in Chile during the late 1970s as money was borrowed abroad and then re-lent within Chile at much higher rates of interest (O'Brien and Roddick 1983; Valenzuela and Valenzuela 1987). Much of the private foreign debt was used by the middle and upper classes to pay for large quantities of foreign luxury consumer goods such as Japanese electronics. The retailing sector expanded to satisfy this demand. In Chile, new shopping centres proliferated in the upmarket districts of San-tiago, and consumption became a symbol of the Pinochet regime for the rich who became better off.

At the same time recession, a reduced social wage caused by cuts in state welfare provision, inflation and falling real wages combined to increase levels of poverty and hardship for many as levels of inequality increased. Both Argentina and Chile experienced severe recessions in the early 1980s. As a consequence of the global rise in interest rates in the early 1980s, foreign debts became unsustainable and the newly formed financial empires collapsed. The reduction of tariff levels decimated the manufactured export sectors and the ISI industries. Real wages suffered further drastic falls, exacerbated by rising levels of unemployment, poverty and inflation.

The regimes did differ in the extent to which they implemented neo-liberal economic policies. In Chile Pinochet, under the guidance of the American trained 'Chicago Boys', oversaw the most thorough-going attempt to restructure the economy by freeing the market, rolling back the state and boosting non-traditional exports according to the principle of comparative advantage (O'Brien and Roddick 1983). While this resulted in two severe recessions in the mid-1970s and early 1980s, by 1985 the economic model was being heralded by some as a great success, combining low inflation and high rates of growth. Other regimes were less effective. The Argentinian military government was more half-hearted in its attempts to implement New Right economic policies, fearing the political consequences of high unemployment and unable to make great inroads into the state sector (Smith 1989). In Peru the military government implemented structural adjustment in the late 1970s (Barrig 1989).

These economic policies had a contradictory impact on different groups of women. In part they complemented the military governments' vision of a society in which women would play conventional roles as wives and mothers, and in part they conflicted with it (Waylen 1992b). Some of the effects of military regimes' social and economic policies ran contrary to their official discourses, which stressed the virtues of the family and 'traditional' woman-hood (Alvarez 1990a; Feijoó 1989: 75). In contrast to the dominant view that women should be based primarily in the household, the number of women workers grew significantly during the 1970s and 1980s. Between 1975 and 1985, in Uruguay the percentage of women either in paid work or looking for work increased from 28 to 34 per cent of the total (Fisher 1993: 44). A similar pattern was seen in Brazil and Chile. Much of this increase was a direct consequence of the economic policies introduced by military govern-ments. Two sets of factors were at work here.

Many women were drawn into the labour market by the expansion of employment opportunities in certain sectors of the restructured economy.

Women's employment was reduced in some areas, like the ISI industries such as textiles and footwear, and in the state sector, which provided employment for middle-class professional women as teachers and nurses. However, many women found employment in the newly expanded financial and retailing sectors. In Chile the dynamic agro-export industry also employed large numbers of women, who often lived in the rural shanty towns which grew up in these areas. Women were employed on a temporary basis at particular stages of the fruit growing cycle, for example thinning the blossom and young fruit, and harvesting and packing (Lago 1987). In Uruguay, women were employed in the fast-growing fish processing industry and in the new textile and leather products export industries (Fisher 1993: 49). This expansion of employment took place in the face of a reduction in the legal rights, such as maternity leave and maternity pay, accorded to women workers. As women were paid less than men, changes to the minimum wage tend to affect them disproportionately. In Chile the law concerned with maternity leave was revised in 1979 so that it became possible to sack pregnant women (Chuckryk 1989a: 153). There was also evidence of employers implementing compulsory testing to ascertain that women were not pregnant (Chuckryk 1989a: 153).

Under conditions of severe economic hardship, many women were also pushed into the labour market, forced into income generating activity as part of household survival strategies. Data from Uruguay shows that by the end of the 1970s, in around 40 per cent of those households in poverty and 68 per cent of those in absolute poverty, half the household income was contributed by women (Fisher 1993: 49). Under the dictatorship there was a significant increase in the number of female-headed households. It is estimated that in 1986 there were only 87 men for every 100 women in Montevideo, partly because men formed the majority of the large number of Uruguayans in exile (Fisher 1993: 49). Poor women in particular often moved into informal sector activities such as street selling, taking in washing and domestic service which were often insecure, illegal or only semi-legal.

The increased pressure on many poor women to generate extra income was combined with increased labour demanded by their roles as household providers and managers at the same time as there was a decline in state welfare provision. This outcome also fits with the discourse emulating the self-sacrificing role of mothers within the family by many military regimes. As we saw from the discussion of structural adjustment programmes in Chapter 2, neo-liberal economic policies rely on the elasticity of women's unpaid labour in the household. There is also evidence that, in the face of high male unemployment and economic recession, the sexual division of labour within the household is very resistant to change. As a consequence, women who are involved in income generation may pass on household tasks to other females in the household such as their daughters, often taking them out of school and thereby reducing their chances of improving their own income earning potential in the future (Brydon and Chant 1989). A further survival strategy, whose adoption has been attributed to the economic crisis in Chile, was the decline in the birthrate among the poorest women. This decline has been seen as a response to high levels of poverty (Hojman 1989). The extremely high rate of illegal abortion is seen as further evidence of this reluctance to bear children. In 1979 for every two women giving birth one was admitted into hospital in Chile with post-abortion complications (Chuchryk 1984).

While the response of many women to the policies of the military governments was to adopt individual and household survival strategies such as increasing their income generating activity in both the formal and informal sectors, large numbers of women also engaged in collective responses. Authoritarian regimes inadvertently provided many women with political space within which to organize.

Women's political activity

Before examining those activities which can be deemed to be oppositional, it is useful to look at women's organizing in support of the military regimes. There is a long history of women organizing in favour of the Right prior to military intervention in situations of political polarization and perceived threat from the Left. These mobilizations can be analysed using Kandiyoti's (1988) notion of the patriarchal bargain discussed in Chapter 1. Rather than seeing them as evidence of women's innate conservatism or naivety, it is better to interpret them as a strategy implemented by certain groups of women to hold on to a 'traditional' set up which appears to value women's roles within the private sphere, and to provide them with a degree of security within the existing system (Waylen 1992a). Prior to the 1964 coup in Brazil which ousted President Goulart, a populist reformer, massive demonstrations were organized by right-wing women's organizations, such as the Women's Campaign for Democracy. Thousands of middle- and upper-class women, using traditional symbols of femininity and motherhood, marched through the streets holding crucifixes and rosaries, demanding that the military do its 'manly duty' and intervene to restore stability to the nation (Alvarez 1990a: 6).

It is in Chile that women's activities on behalf of the Right have been most thoroughly documented. The activities of women directed against the Allende government are often seen to have played a crucial role in the downfall of Unidad Popular, the left-wing coalition attempting to follow 'a peaceful road to socialism' (Chaney 1974). Several key mobilizations are often commented on. Among the best known is the 'march of the empty pots'. This was one of the first large-scale demonstrations opposing the government. It took place on 1 December 1971 when a large number of women took to the streets to protest at the shortages and rising prices (Mattelart 1980). The major symbolic action of the protest used by the women, the majority of whom were from the middle and upper classes, was the banging of empty saucepans. Other women used the ridiculing of the masculinity of the armed forces as a tactic, for example by throwing chicken feed through the perimeter fencing of military bases and giving soldiers white feathers as a sign of their cowardice in not overthrowing the Allende government.

Women's mobilizations in support of the Right were soon coordinated by organizations like El Poder Feminino (EPF). The EPF organized across party boundaries and despite attempts to mobilize poor women, was predominantly a middle- and upper-class organization. It saw itself playing a crucial role in the fight against Unidad Popular (Crummett 1977). It used 'unfeminine', almost guerrilla-like, tactics to sabotage strike-breaking lorries and shops, which some women found empowering. One woman involved stated,

> We were important persons for the first time in our lives. We were tired of being treated like helpless, brainless individuals. We disliked being considered second class citizens . . . we felt we had acquired some independence; in this respect we can never go backwards.
>
> (quoted in Crummett 1977: 112)

Therefore while many protests had the utilization of conventional notions of masculinity and femininity and women's traditional roles as their basis, others involved the subversion of those roles.

However, it soon became clear that active and autonomously mobilized women were no longer wanted, once the military had taken power in both Brazil in 1964 and in Chile in 1973. Pinochet praised the heroic role played by women in the fight against socialism, but made it clear that the proper role for women was motherhood and that right-wing women's organizations were to be carefully controlled and incorporated into the framework of the military government in ways that have been described earlier. In Argentina, the Housewives' League, originally founded in 1956, continued to provide support for the military regime, including its attempt at introducing free market policies (Fisher 1993: 144).

Once military rule was firmly established, the repression of the conventional political arena meant that the locus of any political activity had to shift from an institutional basis, that is organization on the basis of the workplace, political party and trade union, to a community basis where women found it easier to participate. The identification of women as apolitical and therefore women's activities as not being political, allowed them certain initial room for manoeuvre, which was unavailable to men, before their activities were seen as subversive. The repression of the political arena therefore created the 'political space' which allowed women's activities to achieve a relatively high profile outside of it, while the impact of the debt crisis and the resulting structural adjustment packages pushed women into adopting collective survival strategies (Safa 1990). Despite the attempts by military regimes to depoliticize society, the late 1970s and 1980s saw the emergence of strong and heterogeneous women's movements operating outside of the conventional arena, in part a result of the combination of authoritarianism and economic recession.

Several major types of oppositional women's movements stand out, although the sometimes shifting boundaries between them makes clear delineations difficult. Two of these, human rights groups and the urban popular organizations, had women as the majority of their members and pressed primarily social and economic demands, that is practical gender interests (Molyneux 1985a). Schirmer (1993: 60) argues that, through involvement in these activities, many women have gained a gendered consciousness of political motherhood which cannot be classified in the rigid dichotomy between practical and strategic gender interests. Paradoxically attempts to abolish political activity in the public sphere increased the politicization of the private sphere. At the same time, women entered the public sphere on the basis of this politicization of their social roles, that is, as mothers and household providers.

The human rights groups grew out of the experiences of relatives trying to ascertain the whereabouts of their missing family members. They met others in similar situations as they continued their searches outside the police stations and law courts. The Madres of the Plaza de Mayo, formed in Argentina in April 1977, is the best known of the human rights groups (Femenia 1987; Fisher 1989; Navarro 1989). Similar groups, such as the Agrupaciones de Familiares de Detenidos-Desaparacidos in Chile, the Comadres in El Salvador and GAM and CONAVIGUA in Guatemala, were formed in other Latin American countries and in other parts of the world such as Sri Lanka (Schirmer 1989, 1993). The Madres engaged in one of the first open protests against the military government in Argentina, helping to bring about the 'end of fear' and achieved a high profile both nationally and internationally through their activities. Initially the Argentinian military took little notice of the Madres, dismissing them as mad, but once their activities gained a certain prominence, they too were seen as political and subject to the state's definition of subversion. However, because the demonstrators were mothers and grandmothers, the military never felt able to be as repressive towards them as it was towards others. The Madres comprised women from a variety of class backgrounds, many of whom had never before been involved in any form of political activity. The Chilean groups, because of the history of political polarization prior to the coup were more influenced by left-wing politics, and received greater support and protection from the Catholic Church than the Madres (Chuckryk 1989b).

Human rights groups such as the Madres are renowned for the innovative form as well as the content of their protests. The Madres used the military's very traditional notions of woman's proper role, that they should be at home, caring for their children, as the pivot of their protest. They argued that the disappearances prevented them from fulfilling this role and forced them to search for their children. The Madres were well-known for their weekly demonstrations on Thursday afternoons in the Plaza de Mayo, the main government square in Buenos Aires. They would march in a circle wearing white kerchiefs embroidered with the names of their missing children or grandchildren, later carrying their pictures, and demand their return. Other groups such as the Chilean Agrupaciones used similar tactics to the Madres, demonstrating every Friday afternoon outside the Moneda Palace. They engaged in civil disobedience in the Supreme Court and in 1986 published testimonies from the families of 57 missing women and children (Agrupación de los familiares detenidos-desaparacidos 1985).

Feminist academics have interpreted these protests in a variety of ways. Analysis has focused around whether these activities are regressive in that they involve women entering the public sphere on the basis of a traditional role, motherhood, or whether they are transformative. It has been argued that these activities challenge the dominant discourses of motherhood and womanhood as passive and private through their use of public space in protests (Waylen 1992a). In the face of charges of essentialism, those, influenced by notions of difference, political and revolutionary motherhood, who argue that this type of activity is transformative, see it as the foundation for a new form of politics based on an 'ethic of care' and the development of gendered political identities (Elshtain 1992: 120; Bouvard 1994). However, as we will see in the next chapter, human rights groups operating a politics of ethics found the transition from a military to a civilian government difficult.

Popular organizations also emerged in many countries under authoritarian rule. It is generally accepted that economic hardship catalysed the emergence of urban popular movements (Safa 1990). These movements grew up primarily in poor urban working-class districts and focused on the 'politics of everyday life'. Many organizations operated under the auspices of the Church and non-governmental organizations (NGOs) in the face of both recession and repression. The majority of members were women, indeed Corcoran-Nantes (1990) estimated that women formed 80 per cent of those involved in Brazilian movements. A variety of different types of organizations emerged. The focus of many of the activities of these organizations was social and economic, particularly around consumption issues, and organized on a neighbourhood basis.

Some popular organizations attempted to pressurize the state, either at a national or local level, to provide services such as water, drainage and electricity. Many examples of this type of movement can be found in Brazil, a result of the military's development strategy which led to a large increase in the urban population without a commensurate increase in public services. The favela movement, founded in 1976 to secure land titles and improved services and infrastructure to settlements, and the health movement, formed in 1973 to improve local and regional health services, are representative of the large number of popular movements which emerged in the urban areas of Brazil (Corcoran-Nantes 1993).

Other popular organizations implemented collective survival strategies either through the collective provision of necessities or through income generation. By 1982, in the face of a deep recession and cuts in welfare services, 500 popular economic organizations (OEPs) had sprung up in the poblaciones (the poor neighbourhoods) of the Chilean capital, Santiago, and by 1985 this number had grown to 1125. These OEPs have been divided into four different types (Hardy 1985). Women predominated in the two most numerous and 43 per cent of the total number were women only. The first type, organizations centred around the consumption of food, made up 48 per cent of the total. The ollas comunes (communal soup pots) dealt with the most immediate needs, through women collectively providing a large number of families' meals, often with the help of the Church (Fisher 1993). Other organizations of this type included buying committees, where women joined together to buy basic necessities in bulk and therefore more cheaply. A large number of similar organizations, such as the comedores populares (communal kitchens), also emerged somewhat later in the shanty towns of Lima in Peru. The Housewives' Movement in Buenos Aires only emerged in 1982, near to the end of the period of dictatorship in Argentina. Its formation was catalysed by the economic problems, particularly the rising cost of living, and protests took the form of buying strikes, such as the 'Don't buy on Thusdays' campaign. In contrast to other countries, the movement began in middle and lower middle-class districts, as the middle classes had been badly hit by the steep decline in real incomes and was more directly focused around protest rather than the provision of services (Feijoó 1989: 78–9).

The second major type of popular organization, concerned with collective survival strategies, were active around income generation. In Chile, organizaciones laboral-productivas, that is those producing goods and services for exchange in the market, made up around a third of the total OEPs in 1985 (Hardy 1985). Of these, 62 per cent were women only and 65 per cent of the total workers employed were women. More than 50 per cent of this type of OEP took the form of artisanal or craft workshops. Other related activities included running crèches which enabled other women to engage in income generating activity. The product best known abroad was the arpillera, or embroideries made by women, which depicted scenes from everyday life and often bore oppositional messages. Many were produced by women whose relatives had disappeared, and were sold abroad under the auspices of the Catholic Church (Agosin 1988). The government had their own non-oppositional arpilleras made through CEMA Chile which were then sold to tourists through government controlled outlets. Ten per cent of these OEPs took the form of communal bakeries.

These activities were carried out predominantly by poor and working-class women acting in their roles as mothers, household providers and managers as class and gender identities interacted. Many analysts have argued that it is a mistake to see these activities as simply economic. For a variety of reasons, they have to be seen as political. First, many women involved did not initially see their activities as political, as 'politics' was something which men did in the institutional public sphere (Caldeira 1990) but instead saw them as part of doing their 'duty' fulfilling their family responsibilities. However changes occurred both in the ways in which they saw their activities and in the ways they were seen from outside. In Chile the military, particularly at the height of the mass protests in the mid-1980s, saw most collective activities in the poblaciones as subversive. Once defined in this way by the regime, women too began to see their collective activities as 'political'. The kitchens were seen by many of the women involved as an important visible protest because their existence demonstrated the extent of hunger and unemployment (Fisher 1993).

Second, greater self-awareness and the emergence of a collective political consciousness were results of this experience of organizing in the public arena (Corcoran-Nantes 1993). With it came a sense of empowerment and a different understanding of some gender issues. Alvarez (1990b) describes this process in two neighbourhoods of São Paulo where women met at church sponsored mother's clubs which formed part of the network of the Christian base communities. The women gradually extended the range of their discussions and activities as a consequence of meeting and organizing together. Subsequently members of the women's group became active in other organizations, such as the daycare campaign, and felt that they could no longer remain a church sponsored group if their interests ranged over topics such as sexuality and reproductive rights (Alvarez 1990b). As we will see below, these experiences have helped the development of a popular feminism, and add weight to the view that to see women's involvement in urban popular movements as being solely in pursuit of practical gender interests is to impose a false dichotomy.

The period of military rule also saw the re-emergence of feminist movements comprising women organizing together as women to press gender based demands in Peru, Brazil, Chile and Argentina. Many countries had predominantly middle-class suffrage movements earlier in the century which disappeared after women gained the vote. Chile, for example, had entered what Julieta Kirkwood called a period of 'feminist silence'. In the 1970s and 1980s feminist groups began to form, engaging in a variety of activities around issues of women's inequality and subordination (Sternbach et al. 1992). Alvarez (1990a: 261) has claimed that the greatest space existed where authoritarian regimes pursued state-led development at some time, such as happened in Brazil and Peru. The resulting increase in professional and technical employment for middle-class women provided a spur for the re-emergence of feminist movements. While the radical Peruvian military government did not implement any specific policies aimed to emancipate women and the neighbourhood associations often failed to provide networks for poor women, middle-class women were increasingly incorporated into organizations such as unions and political parties, providing them with an important awareness that they were unequal partners in these ventures. As a result, the military government played an unwitting role in encouraging the development of a feminist movement in the 1970s (Vargas 1991).

Alvarez has also claimed that the least space existed where at some time authoritarian regimes implemented economic policies inspired by the New Right, e.g. in Chile and to some extent in Argentina (Alvarez 1990a). However, the evidence here is mixed. Argentina saw the emergence of relatively weak feminist movements and urban popular movements only right at the end of the dictatorship, while in Chile relatively strong women's movements, both feminist and popular, emerged particularly once political liberalization had begun. In addition, as we have seen, New Right economic policies were combined with high levels of repression, and human rights groups and urban popular movements emerged in response to these factors.

Initially many of the women who became active in the feminist movements had had links with the Left but had become disillusioned because of
the lack of attention given to gender issues. Feminists began to develop
analyses which went beyond the parameters of class and imperialism favoured
by the Left. As we have seen above, Latin American feminists made the
connections between authoritarianism and patriarchy, linking authoritarianism in the home with that in wider society, hence the slogan of the Chilean
movement: 'Democracy in the country and in the home'.

Feminist groups undertook a variety of activities. Some, for example the
Círculo de Estudios de la Mujer founded in Chile in 1977, concentrated on
the analysis of women's subordination, through discussions and seminars;
others set up women's centres such as the Flora Tristan centre in Peru, ran
workshops and courses on themes such as sexuality and health, organized
theatre groups, campaigned around issues such as sexual violence and pornography and produced feminist publications such as *Brasil Mulher* founded in
1975 and *Nos Mulheres* founded in 1976 which together became the principal
voices of the growing feminist movement in Brazil (Jaquette 1989). Umbrella organizations were also formed to help coordinate the diverse activities
of the various groups into more of a national movement, such as the Coordinating Committee formed in the late 1970s in Peru, Mujeres por la Vida
formed in Chile in 1983 and the Paulista Women's Congresses, the first one
of which was held in 1979 and drew 1000 participants (Jaquette 1989). A
number of the demonstrations around International Women's Day formed
some of the first demonstrations which occurred under military rule.

Popular feminism, which also emerged during this period, had different
roots. It grew out of the experience of working-class and poor women
organizing and campaigning self-consciously as women in the community
organizations described above. Through their experiences of organizing around
consumption issues and collective survival many women began to organize
around issues such as reproductive rights, sexuality and domestic violence,
more often identified with feminism, and set up women's centres in working-
class areas. In Chile, organizations emerged such as the Domitilas (named
after a Bolivian activist) and MOMUPO (Movimiento de Mujeres Pobladoras)
which initially refused the title 'feminist' but declared itself to be so in 1985–
6 (Schild 1992; Fisher 1993).

Its proponents consider popular feminism to be different to the feminism
of the affluent, educated professional middle classes. This latter movement is
felt to be an import from the USA, and also to have ignored the issues of
greatest concern to women of the popular classes, primarily economic survival. Middle-class feminism is seen therefore as predominantly concerned
with gender issues to the exclusion of issues around class and race. Many
popular feminists argue that they want to work with men and try to preserve
the family, which they see middle-class feminism as not doing. It is argued
that middle-class women can solve many of their problems through the
deployment of economic resources, for example by paying maids to carry out
their domestic responsibilities. Their employment of women from the popular

classes reduces the potential for common interests to exist between poor and middle-class women. Indeed many poor women feel that they have been used, for example as cannon fodder in demonstrations, by middle-class feminist organizations. However, they do believe that there can be links with middle-class feminist movements. Alliances are possible, but as they do not exist automatically they have to be constructed carefully. This concept of popular feminism is perhaps closer to Mohanty's notion of Third World feminism and its relationship to other struggles against domination discussed in Chapter 1 than the more rights orientated middle-class based feminist movements.

Conclusion

Authoritarianism and the associated phenomenon of militarism rest on gendered foundations, relying particularly on a construction of masculinity and femininity which assigns particular 'traditional' roles to women. Women have been incorporated into authoritarian regimes on this basis and supplied them with both material and ideological support. However, this designation has contradictory results as the rigid demarcation between men and women is sometimes breached. Women have not always filled their appointed roles, in part a consequence of the military's own policies. Under the authoritarian regimes of the Southern Cone in the late 1970s and 1980s, the effect of economic restructuring was to increase many women's income generating activity at the same time as increasing their labour in the household. The repression of the public sphere also allowed diverse women's movements some space for oppositional organizing, often on the basis of the politicization of their social roles. As we will see in the next chapter, different women's movements in parts of Latin America played an important role in contributing to the breakdown of authoritarian rule at a time when the political initiative lay outside the conventional arena. In contrast, the actions of neo-patrimonial regimes have resulted in a very undeveloped civil society in much of Africa. Women's organizations were either co-opted by the state or those which avoided this have either disengaged from the state or resisted its encroachments. The context of the breakdown of authoritarian regimes in Africa has therefore been different to Latin America. We can now move on to examine the relationship between democratization and gender relations, looking at the role played by different groups of women in the unfolding political process and surrounding the transition to and the consolidation of competitive electoral politics.

6

Democratization[1]

Introduction

Many authoritarian regimes find it difficult to sustain themselves in power for long periods of time. Since the 1970s the world has witnessed the so-called third wave of democratization (Huntington 1991). Beginning in the Iberian peninsula in the mid-1970s, continuing in much of Latin America in the 1980s, Eastern Europe and parts of Africa in the late 1980s and early 1990s, there has been a widespread movement towards competitive electoral politics. The reasons for these transitions have been various. Very often they are the result of internal pressure from both élite and mass movements. More recently this has been combined, particularly in the African case, with external pressure from international institutions keen to see 'good government' and accountability as a condition of aid and loans. Democratization is therefore being seen by many political scientists as one of the most significant trends of the late twentieth century.

Much of the orthodox literature on democratization produced until now concentrated on Latin America and the wider questions and issues raised in it are dominated by the Latin American experience. These tendencies are also visible in the literature on gender and democratization and, to some extent, will inevitably be replicated here. Because of the difficulties of generalizing over such a large area, this chapter will largely confine itself to examining Argentina, Brazil and Chile as the countries which have been researched in greatest depth, but will also use other examples wherever possible. A critique of the democratization literature is beginning to emerge from analysts of transitions working on sub-Saharan Africa. We will address some of the issues raised by this critique relevant to a gendered analysis of democratization in Africa before the more detailed discussion of Brazil, Argentina and Chile.

The process of democratization has recently been subdivided into three phases: the initial breakdown of authoritarian rule, the transition to and the consolidation of competitive electoral politics. The key role played by women's movements in the third wave of democratization, particularly in Latin America, while still largely neglected in much of the literature, has been increasingly recognized over the past few years (Jaquette 1989, 1994; Alvarez 1990a). The contribution of different women's activities to the initial breakdown of authoritarian rule in the Southern Cone (Chile, Argentina and Paraguay) has already been analysed in the previous chapter. We saw the extent of women's mobilization under authoritarianism with different types of women's movements directly and indirectly challenging military rule and demanding greater participation and rights as citizens. The role played by women's movements in the subsequent phases of the transition to and the process of consolidation of democratic rule has only just begun to be considered in the same depth (Jaquette 1994). This chapter will focus on the processes of transition and consolidation.

Safa (1990) has argued that, despite their prominent role under military dictatorship in Latin America, women's social movements have difficulty in converting political mobilization into institutional representation once competitive party politics has resumed. One aim of this chapter therefore is to explore how far this is the case, and consider how far the role played by the different women's movements under authoritarian rule has been sustained in the new politics. Given the heterogeneity of these movements, it is important to consider whether some movements are better able to do this than others. A second aim is to explore how far the new political conjuncture of competitive electoral politics is one of some fluidity which can allow women's movements to pressurize newly elected civilian governments into implementing policies and establishing women's bodies with the aim of improving the situation of women.

Several key themes emerge here as the reconstitution of party politics has important implications for the activities engaged in by all social movements. Once it becomes clear that conventional party politics are reconstituting, all those operating outside this arena, including feminist and other women's groups, are faced with a choice which has often been summed up as the dilemma of 'autonomy versus integration'. Should social movements carry on operating outside conventional politics, preserving their independence but risking marginalization and the loss of influence as the locus of power shifts towards the political parties, or should they throw themselves into working within the new institutions and parties and risk being co-opted and losing their autonomy (Hellman 1990)? Different women's movements have reached a variety of conclusions about the question of what role they should play in institutional politics, as did different members within groups. It is therefore important to consider which movements did or did not choose to enter the conventional political arena and why, and with what results.

This exploration will be carried out by examining three major areas. First, the newly reconstituted democratic politics will be considered, for example the impact that different women have had within the political parties. Second, the impact of state policy, both generally framed and specifically aimed at women, including some examples of women's bureaus, will be examined. Third, the various women's movements operating outside of the conventional political arena will be analysed to see how far they have been able to sustain their activities.

The conventional literature

The conventional social science literature on democracy, democratization and the role of social movements in transitions can be categorized into three types, each providing a different focus and set of explanations for the transition to democracy. This literature has had, by and large, very little to say about gender relations. Despite the lack of a gendered perspective of the majority of it, however, it is useful to consider this literature and see what it can offer a gendered analysis of democratization (Waylen 1994). The first type is the agency-led explanations, which have probably received the greatest prominence. The political development literature has long been interested in the conditions necessary for the establishment of democracies and in how they can be sustained. These concerns, particularly of American social scientists working in the 1950s and 1960s, were confounded by the trend to authoritarianism in much of the Third World, examined in the last chapter (Almond and Coleman 1962; Rustow 1970). However with the advent of the third wave of democratization, interest has once again focused on processes of transition and much of the work produced more recently demonstrates many continuities with the literature of the 1950s and 1960s (Huntington 1984; Mainwaring et al. 1992).

While this body of literature is now large, it is possible to make some general observations about its defining characteristics. The two best known works of the 1980s are the four volume study by O'Donnell, Schmitter and Whitehead (1986) and the series edited by Diamond, Linz and Lipset (1988–90). A central focus of much of the literature is unashamedly normative. O'Donnell (1986: 10), for example, writes 'Our project had from the outside a normative bias, coupled and reinforced by an empirical generalization. We have considered political democracy as desirable *per se*'.

Democracy (defined as competitive electoral politics) is seen as a good thing and therefore efforts are made to understand how to achieve and maintain it. Diamond et al. (1988) focus on the preconditions necessary for the transition to take place, examining a set of variables including political leadership and political institutions and party systems in a huge number of different cases. O'Donnell et al. (1986) concentrate more on the nature of the process itself, in particular on the actions of the political élites and the nature of the pacts which need to be made between the military and civilian groups to facilitate the transition. The emphasis is on the voluntaristic nature of the process and 'democratic outcomes are seen to depend on the choices of particular political élites and specific historical conjunctures' (Remmer 1991: 483). The need for effective leadership is stressed, as is the necessity of an opposition willing to negotiate with the authoritarian regime (Diamond 1989: 152).

These top-down approaches have a narrow view of politics which includes only the upper institutional echelons of the public sphere and concentrates on the actions of the military and the political élites. As a result many of those activities outside the conventional political arena in which women are involved are excluded. Politics appears to be a largely male activity, as women are not part of the political élites in any great numbers and therefore appear as politically inactive in this vision of the world. Indeed many analysts are wary of the activities of social movements, seeing popular pressure as a potentially destabilizing force which needs to be tamed if the process of transition is to proceed (O'Donnell and Schmitter 1986 4:48–56). Even when they do discuss human rights activists, O'Donnell and Schmitter talk of 'gestures by exemplary individuals' with no real acknowledgement that many of the human rights campaigners, as we saw in the previous chapter, were women, often active as mothers. Their restricted definitions of democracy as simply an institutional arrangement rather than focusing on the wider distribution of power in society allows them to ignore gender inequalities. Only if women were denied the vote, and perhaps not even then, would gender relations become relevant. As a result this literature makes virtually no mention of gender relations and means that it is of very little use in the study of gender relations and democratization.

The second type of literature consists of the structure-led explanations which received their classic exposition in Barrington Moore's work *The Social Origins of Dictatorship and Democracy* (1967) but more recently have received greater attention with the appearance of Rueschemeyer *et al.*'s *Capitalist Development and Democracy* (1992), following in the footsteps of Evans *et al.*'s *Bringing the State Back In* (1985). Here the focus is much more on the relationship between different social classes and the nature of the economic and social system and the ways in which this affects the political system. Rueschemeyer *et al.* (1992) play down the role of the bourgeoisie in the emergence of democracy, and focus instead on the working class in the advanced capitalist countries and the middle class in Latin America as the classes playing the key roles in the championing of democracy. They argue that because of the small size and weakness of the working class in Latin America, the middle class play the crucial role in alliance with élites in promoting a return to democracy. Indeed they argue that

> middle-class–élite alliances as decisive forces behind the breakthrough were most conducive to the stabilization of democracy. However, such alliances only emerged if at least some of the élites had representation in the party system, and in most cases they established restricted democracies only.
>
> (Rueschemeyer *et al.* 1992: 216)

They go on to say that the existence of 'significant remnants of strong parties' facilitated the creation of pro-democratic alliances and the reinstallation and consolidation of democracy (1992: 217). In contrast they argue that where these remnants were lacking but where civil society had grown in strength and new parties had been formed to express these demands, then a coordinated strategy for redemocratization was more difficult to follow. This approach therefore places greater emphasis on the role of the middle class and civil society than do the agency-led explanations. Therefore, while they too are virtually ungendered, with only a justification for using male suffrage as their indicator for democracy and a brief discussion of the importance of struggles to lessen gender inequality in their conclusion, this approach appears more helpful in offering a class-based framework which can help to explain why it is that some women and women's movements appear more successful than others in influencing the newly re-established party politics and the policy agenda.

The third body of literature has a more exclusively bottom-up focus concentrating on the activities of social movements and their role in reconstituted democracies (Mainwaring 1987; Escobar and Alvarez 1992). Interest has focused on whether popular movements begin to emerge and civil society is reconstituted prior to the transition rather than as a consequence of it. Garretón (1989) has argued that while social movements are not the source of change, they can play a critical role and that the recomposition of civil society represented by their activities forms the invisible transition to democracy. Taking a more radical view, Petras (1990) has argued that such social movements have played an important role and provided the signal that the military regimes, having failed to create an economic model with a substantial base of support, faced a crisis of legitimacy.

The vast majority of this literature, too, has displayed tendencies to remain ungendered except in remarking that the majority of participants in the social movements are women. Or, as Corcoran-Nantes (1993: 139) highlights with regard to the volume edited by David Slater (1985), the discussion on women is marginalized from the main body of the analysis in a separate section. As a result, the understanding of these movements can only be partial. This is because women often participate on the basis of the social roles which accompany their gendered identities, for example as mothers and household providers, and if this is ignored, an important aspect of popular movements cannot be fully examined. These problems do not mean that this literature has no use in the study of gender relations and democratization, as much of it has begun to focus on the key questions of the relationship between social movements and the state and social movements and political parties (Foweraker and Craig 1990). These questions are of prime importance when analysing the role of different women's movements, and the dilemmas they have experienced over the question of autonomy versus integration and, as already outlined, focusing on these questions can help to further the analysis. However, while these approaches, particularly the structure-led and bottom-up approaches, can give some clues as to useful questions to focus on, they clearly cannot be sufficient in themselves.

Transitions from neo-patrimonial regimes in Africa

Bratton and van de Walle (1994) have argued that much of the democratization literature, particularly of the first type described above, concentrates excessively on the experience of Latin America and the Iberian peninsula. It focuses primarily on transitions from relatively rule-governed and bureaucratized military regimes, ignoring the different and more chaotic transitions from other sorts of regimes such as one party states and personalistic dictatorships discussed in the previous chapter. They claim that transitions from the types of neo-patrimonial regimes often found in Africa do not take the form of élite pacted transitions frequently seen in Latin America and therefore much greater attention needs to be given to the nature of the pre-existing authoritarian regime. The mechanisms for the breakdown of authoritarian rule take a different form in this context. Neo-patrimonial regimes suffer an early crisis of legitimacy, but political transitions originate in social protest, that is in the actions of social actors not state élites. Many commentators have pointed to the upsurge in spontaneous popular protest in Africa since 1989, often begun by students and civil servants opposing structural adjustment and demonstrating about the effects of economic crisis and corruption (Bratton and van de Walle 1992a; Wiseman 1993). There is evidence from some neo-patrimonial regimes outside Africa such as the Marcos regime in the Philippines and the Duvalier regime in Haiti that women played important roles in the demonstrations which contributed to the fall of those dictators (Aquino 1994; Charles 1995). This kind of activity often pushes patrimonial regimes into political liberalization, which Bratton and van de Walle stress is not the same as democratization. One party states such as Zambia and Kenya were pushed by popular discontent towards multipartism. However, as we saw in the last chapter, neo-patrimonial regimes undercut civil society by co-opting and demobilizing it and not allowing organizations to undertake overtly political activities. This makes democratization, rather than just liberalization, difficult to achieve as it needs formal organizations such as trade unions, human rights organizations and in particular political parties, not informal organizations such as women's networks, to form a viable opposition coalition and push the transition forward (Bratton and van de Walle 1994). Once the state allows some liberalization, opposition groupings mushroom. These developments have been seen as signalling the growth of a more vibrant civil society in Africa. Heterogeneous political opposition coalitions comprising human rights groups, intellectuals and businesspeople have emerged, although the members are predominantly urban based and of the same social origins as the incumbent government (van de Walle 1994). Transitions of this type are often led by those outside the state élites and backed by the middle classes.

Transitions from different types of patrimonial regimes vary in terms of their likelihood of resulting in the consolidation of competitive electoral politics (Bratton and van de Walle 1994). Problems in transition are most likely to be extreme in personalistic dictatorships, where dictators often have to be forced to step down; these transitions are the least likely to result in the consolidation of democratic politics. Liberalization occurs in the face of the weakness of political institutions and an absence of both institutions of accommodation and civic associations, so that the opposition that does emerge is likely to be fragmented and lacking in resources. Prospects for democratic consolidation are better in one party states. Plebiscitary one party systems create enough political space for the emergence of an, albeit weak and fragmented, opposition in the early stage of the transition which then focuses around the key turning point of the national conference. Competitive one party states with their longer-standing toleration of some degree of pluralism are more likely to be pressed into allowing multiparty elections and stand the greatest chance of success. The chances of a managed transition from above are greatest in military dictatorships.

We saw in the previous chapter that, as authoritarian regimes repressed formal participatory structures, women's organizations formed an important part of the informal structures which flourished as women disengaged from the state. The long-standing prevalence of informal women's organizations operating outside the public arena combined with the co-optation of formal organizations by ruling parties and the high levels of illiteracy among many women, meant that the majority of women were not poised to play an important role in the new transition politics. However, a number of new (predominantly élite) women's organizations, with a more gender specific and feminist agenda and more directed towards the political arena than many already existing women's organizations, have been among the new groupings to emerge as a consequence of political liberalization. Usually made up of educated professional women, often lawyers, these organizations have frequently linked their demands for the improvement of women's rights to the struggle for human rights in general. Women in Nigeria (WIN) was founded in 1982, desiring more women to organize to fight for their rights and to become involved in the political arena (Mba 1990; Okonjo 1994). In Zambia, the National Women's Lobby Group was formed in 1991 (with the logo Women in Zambia for Equality and Representation or WIZER) and was made up of middle-class women, who were predominantly lawyers, advocating women's rights and a greater role for women in the public sphere (Liatto-Katundu 1993). After the change to the Kenyan constitution in late 1991 allowing multipartism, organizations of mainly élite women began to organize, culminating in the National Women's Convention held in February 1992, to coordinate a women's agenda in the democratization process (Nzomo 1993).

The new women's organizations have tended to remain aloof from the newly formed opposition political parties in part due to a desire to remain independent and politically unaffiliated. The response of the political parties to the new women's organizations has not always been positive. While the negative reaction of Zambia's ruling party UNIP to the foundation of the National Women's Lobby group was not unexpected, the hostility of MMD, the newly formed opposition party, to the lobby was more surprising (Liatto-Katundu 1993).

Despite the emergence of these women's organizations which aim to increase the participation of women in formal electoral processes, multiparty elections have not brought large numbers of women into representative assemblies. In Kenya only six women were elected as MPs out of a total of 180 in December 1992. The smallest party, the Democratic Party, had three women among its 23 MPs, while each of the other three parties had one each. KANU won 93 seats and the Forum for the Restoration of Democracy (FORD Kenya) and the breakaway FORD (Asili) won 31 each (Ajulu 1993). In Zambia only seven women members of parliament were elected in 1991 and the new MMD government contained only one woman minister and five deputy ministers (Liatto-Kantundu 1993). The development of new organizations has continued in the period after competitive elections. A new women's lobby, comprising educated urban women, has emerged in Malawi following the 1994 defeat of Hastings Banda by the United Democratic Front (Swinburne 1995).

Women's organizations proliferated in other contexts surrounding the downfall of neo-patrimonial regimes including some extreme personalistic dictatorships. In the Philippines, women's groups including the feminist organization GABRIELA joined the protests over human rights abuses, increasing militarization and the economic situation following the assassination of the opposition leader Benigno Aquino in 1983 leading up to the People's Power Revolution of 1986 which ousted Marcos (Aquino 1994). A large number of women's organizations also flourished after the fall of Duvalier in Haiti in 1986 (Charles 1995).

The other major type of transition which has taken place in Africa has been from the settler oligarchies in Zimbabwe (formerly Rhodesia), Namibia and South Africa. Bratton and van de Walle (1992b) believe that, while marked by violence, these countries have a better chance of consolidation than the transitions from neo-patrimonial regimes we have just examined. Because the minority established the institutions of pluralistic politics and competitive elections within a segregated sphere, the challenge of democratization is to extend participation in these institutions to the majority of the population. The parties, ZANU in Zimbabwe, SWAPO in Namibia and the ANC in South Africa, which took over after long struggles both inside and outside the political arena used a strategy of 'armalite and the ballot box'. They all mobilized women and as part of their radical political programmes expressed strong and far reaching commitments to women's equality. Indeed women in South Africa had a long tradition of organized resistance which predated the famous anti-pass law campaigns of the Federation of South African Women (FSAW) in the 1950s and continued in the 1970s and 1980s (Walker 1982; Seidman 1993).

In all three cases, some disappointment has been expressed either at what has already been achieved or there is anxiety for the future effectiveness of programmes to increase gender equality. Seidman (1984) argued, only four years after it had taken power, that ZANU had consistently abandoned efforts to change social institutions that reinforce gender inequality. In Namibia, despite a deliberate policy by the government to include women in the decision making process, only five of the 72 members of the constituent assembly elected in 1989 were women and only two of the 18 ministries were headed by women (Gawanas 1993; Forrest 1994). However, after the South African elections of 1994, 24 per cent of the elected representatives are women. Cheryl Walker (1994: 351) has argued that in South Africa women's rights are on the agenda, for example in the constitution, and that this is due particularly to the activities of the increasingly organized and vociferous women's lobby in the ANC as well as the National Women's Coalition and activists in some other political parties. However, she believes that there is an inherent tension between the ANC's commitment to gender equality and the engagement of the government in the 'politics of traditionalism' which is most evident in its struggle to outmanoeuvre the Inkatha Freedom Party. In the absence of a politically powerful mass women's movement and given the limitations in the way in which gender inequality is perceived by the ANC, as demonstrated in the Reconstruction and Development plan, it is likely that the ANC government will compromise and delay its commitment to gender equality (Walker 1994). The 'tradition' being negotiated is fundamentally patriarchal and according to Walker (1994) will lead to 'official' patriarchal domination, particularly in land reform, legitimized as tradition.

Given the recentness of many of these transitions and the lack of literature produced so far on gender and democratization in Africa, we have only been able to examine the gendered nature of transitions from neo-patrimonial regimes and settler oligarchies very briefly. However it is possible to explore similar issues in much more detail in the Latin American context.

Democratization in Latin America

Conventional politics

As we saw in the last chapter, authoritarian rule generally circumscribes the activity of the majority of political parties and trade unions with the exception of those supportive of or sponsored by the government. This is often accompanied by the persecution or imprisonment of politicians and political activists, predominantly men. We have seen that during periods of authoritarian rule in Latin America the repression of conventional political activity in the public sphere increased the political space available to women's activities, allowing them greater visibility and prominence. Three major trends resulted from the diminution of the conventional arena.

One effect of the supression of organizations such as trade unions and political parties was to move the locus of much political activity from institutional to community-based activities, where women had greater opportunities to participate. The focus often shifted from production to consumption issues (Corcoran-Nantes 1990). Many urban popular movements, often with a large majority of women members and aided by the Church, implemented collective survival strategies in the face of deep recession. Communal kitchens and artisanal workshops were set up and campaigns fought for the provision of better facilities for their neighbourhood from the state either locally or nationally, for example in Peru, Chile and Brazil (Hardy 1985; Caldeira 1990). Second, there is evidence that in cases where political activity was severely curtailed, for example in Chile under the Pinochet dictatorship, and many activists were either killed, imprisoned or in exile, political parties were kept going underground through the efforts of women members who were still at liberty (Angelo 1990). Third, periods of authoritarian rule also helped spawn the re-emergence of feminist movements, partly spurred by the realization that authoritarian power relations were not simply confined to the public sphere but were present in the household and the family as well (Kirkwood 1990). These, too, began by operating outside the conventional political arena, and as Vargas (1992) argues in the case of Peru were made up, in part, of women who had been active on the Left and had become disillusioned with its lack of attention to gender issues.

It is clear therefore that during the initial phase of the breakdown of authoritarian rule, the political initiative often lay outside the largely inoperative conventional political arena. Women's movements, for example campaigning for the return of their disappeared relatives, played a key role in bringing about the 'end of fear' and creating the initial opening. Military governments were often prompted by mass mobilizations to begin negotiations with civilian élites.

The second phase of democratization, the process of transition, however, was marked by the reconstitution and recreation of the conventional political arena. Political institutions and parties began to re-form, often as part of a process which was tightly controlled by the authoritarian government, restricting which parties could begin to operate and in what ways. Often left-wing and working-class parties experienced continuing restrictions, while the parties of the Centre and Right were allowed the greatest freedom of action. Social movements then faced the choice of whether or not to start working with the newly reconstituted political parties and institutions.

In some cases, the inauguration of this period of transition was marked by the decision of some political parties, often those representing the middle classes and the centre of the political spectrum, to form pacts with the military and initiate a negotiated transition. The example of Chile stands out here where the political parties of the Centre and renovated Left decided that it had become clear that Pinochet's regime would not be removed through a process of popular mobilization but through reaching agreements with the military (Petras and Leiva 1988). Obviously, any accommodation with the military will have repercussions on the type of transition that occurs and the nature of the competitive multiparty system that is set up. As the Chilean case shows, however, pressure was placed on all social movements, including women's movements, to define themselves in terms of the strategy they supported for overthrowing the dictatorship – negociación o ruptura (Serrano 1990). In general those groups, both parties of the Left and social movements, opting for 'ruptura', that is a more violent overthrow of the government based on social mobilization, found themselves increasingly outside the process of negotiated transition.

Women's movements faced the same dilemmas. Some feminists now considered it necessary to move into the orthodox structures and try to change those from within (Sternbach *et al.* 1992). During this period, women already active within the opposition political parties, the so-called 'políticas' – political activists (primarily left-wing) who often did not see themselves as feminists – were joined by avowed feminists who now believed that the way forward could not lie simply in maintaining an autonomous feminist movement as this alone was not enough in the changed circumstances. There is some evidence that the old antagonism often reported between 'feministas' and 'políticas' was reduced in this period, and indeed the distinctions between the two became increasingly blurred as políticas became increasingly sympathetic to ideas associated with feminism (Serrano 1990). This migration resulted in overtly feminist women's organizations being set up in some political parties which tried to raise feminist questions in both the parties and national politics generally (Alvarez 1990; Valenzuela 1992). The Federación de Mujeres Socialistas (FMS), set up in one part of the Chilean socialist party in 1986, is a good example of this phenomenon, as was the women's division of the opposition PMDB in Brazil (Alvarez 1989a: 50). However, Alvarez (1990a: 150) has argued that in Brazil some feminists abandoned activism for party work, and that the autonomous parts of the feminist movement were initially weakened by the 1982 electoral conjuncture, and feminist party activists lost touch with women's movements.

Despite these developments, there is evidence that women organizing in political parties active during transition politics face many of the problems common to women active in political parties during more 'normal' periods of competitive party politics. It has been reported that women's organizations were often marginalized within the party structures without any meaningful power and influence, and were even used as a device whereby women were kept out of the important bodies where important decisions are taken (Alvarez 1990a: 268). There are other examples where quota systems instituted to increase the representation of women on party bodies have been ignored at key times, such as happened in the reformed left party, the PPD, in Chile (Saa 1990).

However, there is also evidence that women activists find it easier to make headway in the newly formed parties. The Chilean Partido Humanista (PH) adopted a feminist, Laura Rodriguez, as its presidential candidate for the first election and measures such as positive discrimination and the implementation of special training in political action to help women rise within the party (Molina 1989). As a result, over half the members of the PH are women with an average age of between 25 and 28 (Rodriguez 1991). However many of these parties do not, as yet, attract a mass following. The most notable exception is the Workers' Party (PT) in Brazil. The PT, formed in 1979, emerged not just from the 'new unionism' but also from the social movements active in and around São Paulo and therefore has been heralded as a way in which the popular sectors can have some representation in institutional politics, overcoming the dilemmas of autonomy and integration (Keck 1992). In 1981–2 many feminists also saw the PT as the potential expression of the social movements in institutional politics and became active within the

party. However, both Alvarez (1990a: 157) and Caldeira (1986) have analysed PT activities in particular neighbourhoods and found that the core
organizers were men and that women were reluctant to be involved as they
felt that the party was inhospitable to them. Alvarez (1990a: 259) also argues
that the responsiveness of the PT to women's issues is greatly conditioned by
the pressure that feminists exert on the party, and to some extent is coun-
terbalanced by the Christian Left, and she is left wondering what would
happen if the PT women's committee became marginal.

The trends evident during the period of transition have continued during
the third phase of the consolidation of multiparty politics. Despite a commitment to equality on the part of many Latin American political parties, there
are few examples of women being chosen as candidates by political parties
in the first competitive elections to be held, and a lack of women chosen as
ministers and for other high offices once newly elected governments take
power. At the beginning of the 1990s women formed only 5 per cent of the
parliament in Chile and 6.7 per cent in Argentina. There has also been a
singular lack of women appointed to top government posts: in 1987 there
were no women in ministerial positions in Peru and Argentina and only one
in Brazil, and in 1993 in Chile the only woman at cabinet level was the
director of the women's bureau SERNAM (Servicio Nacional de la Mujer),
while only three out of the 27 vice ministers were women. However, many
parties have tried to appeal to women voters specifically as women to increase their support, and some have gone so far as to set up specific ministries
and organizations for women, for example Alfonsín and the UCR in Argentina, the PMDB in Brazil and the Concertación in Chile. These groups will
be discussed in the section on state policy and its impact.

While there has been heightened awareness of the importance of women's
votes among the parties of the Right, Centre and Left, the right-wing parties
tend to hold fairly traditional views about women's roles, talking of the need
to maintain the family. Feminists have therefore made greater headway in the
parties of the Centre and the Left, particularly the 'renovated' Left, for
example the Christian Democrats and Socialists in Chile and new parties such
as the PT in Brazil. There has been a reluctance on the part of some of the
more orthodox Left, such as the Chilean communist party, to relinquish its
view of feminism as a 'bourgeois deviation'. There is also widespread evidence that, on the whole, women still find it hard to permeate political parties
and reach positions of power and influence rather than getting sidelined in
separate and powerless women's organizations. Indeed there is some evidence
from the Chilean context that once political parties can act freely again and
the exiled male leaders return from abroad, some women lose their positions,
as they were seen as caretakers until better days returned.

Clearly the relationship between democratization and the role of women
in conventional politics is complex. In the Latin American context, some
women activists appear to have made the greatest headway within the political parties in those countries experiencing a relatively long drawn out and
negotiated transition such as Brazil and Chile in which the middle classes

have reached an accommodation with the military (Alvarez 1990a). These transitions have been based on the establishment of a restricted democracy, and in the Chilean case on the resurrection of a strong party system. As such, these restrictions have provided more political space for some women's movements to operate, and enabled them to campaign relatively effectively to influence the newly re-emerged political parties. But the majority of women advocating some form of 'integration', both feminists and those not declaring themselves as such, active in party politics, are middle-class professional women who are in a better position to play a role in the negotiated middle-class transition, which Rueschemeyer et al. (1992) claim stands the greatest chance of consolidating democracies.

State policy

This section will only deal with the policies implemented by the newly elected civilian governments. These can be divided into two: those general policies which have an impact on particular groups of women; and those policies which are particularly targeted at women. One major question to consider is the degree of manoeuvrability possessed by the new governments. Negotiated transitions, comprising pacts and deals with the military, frequently circumscribe the actions of the civilian governments, particularly if the military has played a major role in designing the electoral system in such a way as to guarantee its own role and limit the ability of the new government radically to change anything. The electoral system and constitution imposed by the Chilean military provides a good example of a system biased in favour of the Right which gives the military continuing influence (Angell and Pollock 1990; Garretón 1990/1). Where the transition has been swifter, involving the more wholesale discrediting of the military, such as happened in Argentina in the aftermath of the military's defeat in the Falklands/Malvinas conflict with the United Kingdom or a patrimonial dictator has fled, then it is possible to argue that a new civilian government has greater freedom of action. This freedom is only relative, however, as virtually all civilian governments have had severe limits, from both internal and external sources, placed on the sorts of policies they can pursue, and have, to some extent, maintained the status quo.

The area of general policy where this accommodation with the military to safeguard its position and interests can be seen most clearly in is the field of human rights. Women played prominent roles in the campaigns against the human rights abuses committed by military governments, demanding the return of their disappeared relatives and the prosecution of those involved. In Chile and Argentina, civilian governments have distanced themselves from the demands of the human rights activists and either decided not to prosecute members of the military or even issued an amnesty to all but the most senior members, for example Menem's 'Indulto' which caused such protest. The populace have been exhorted to forgive and forget the atrocities which took place. As will be seen below, the rejection of their demands has left human rights campaigners such as the Madres in Argentina and the Agrupaciones in Chile increasingly marginalized from the mainstream of political life (Loveman 1991). The lack of willingness and ability of civilian governments once in office to exert power and authority over the military to reduce its influence and punish previous abuses has been seen not just in Latin America but in other parts of the Third World, for example in the Philippines and more recently in South Africa.

With regard to economic policy, economic liberalization has frequently accompanied political liberalization. Many civilian governments have maintained continuity with the previous government in terms of social and economic policies. These have on the whole been fairly orthodox, mainly conforming to the structural adjustment packages demanded by international institutions such as the IMF and World Bank. In some Latin American states, after the failure of more heterodox measures, civilian governments, such as Menem's in Argentina and Fujimori's in Peru (although his commitment to democracy seems very fragile), have implemented much harsher policies than the military regimes ever did (Anglade and Fortin 1990). As we have seen in Chapters 2 and 5, economic liberalization in general and more specifically structural adjustment packages have particular implications for different groups of women, even relying on the elasticity of women's labour both paid and unpaid. Evidence from Brazil shows that female headed households were hardest hit by recession in the 1980s (Caldeira 1992). Increased economic burdens may provide yet another factor which impedes poor women from participating in the activities associated with competitive electoral politics, further contributing to its 'remasculinization'.

Many of the newly democratic governments have adopted policies particularly aimed at women and indeed realize the importance of trying to woo women voters. It is impossible to make generalizations about patterns over such a wide area, particularly as there has been more than one civilian government in office in many countries, for example in Argentina, Brazil and Peru, often with very different attitudes and policies. There is evidence, however, that 'gender has become politicized' as Alvarez has described it. It is clear that many political parties have tried to gain women's support by placing 'women's issues' on the political and electoral agenda. In Argentina, Alfonsín ended his campaign with a speech criticizing machismo and all the way through the election campaign the UCR used slogans reminiscent of the Madres (Feijoó 1989: 89). During the long drawn out transition in Brazil, all the political parties, particularly the opposition, influenced by the feminists working in their ranks, adopted policies which it was felt would appeal to women voters. The daycare campaign, for example, was adopted by politicians even to the extent of exaggerating hugely the number of centres which had been built (Alvarez 1989b). In Chile all major parties now pay lip-service to women's equality, but the renovated Right places it in the context of woman's special role at the centre of the family and as the bearer of moral values (Valenzuela 1992: 179). There have been widespread discussions, for example in Chile and Argentina, about changing the civil codes which affect women's rights. These discussions have involved issues such as mothers' lack of control over children, especially patria potestad (literally 'power of the father' and the name given to the laws surrounding aspects of marriage and the family, particularly the control of children), and the introduction of improved maternity leave, for example in Brazil, and even divorce.

There have also been a number of policy initiatives aimed specifically at women, reflecting the influence of a feminist agenda. Most notable among these were the creation of Women's Councils at state and national level in Brazil and the creation in Chile of SERNAM, a national governmental body directly responsible to the president and partly staffed by feminists from the Christian Democrats and Socialists, coordinating, evaluating and executing government policies on women. Other initiatives have included special units to combat sexual violence directed at women on the streets of São Paulo. All these programmes are in part a result of the decisions of feminists to move into the political parties and influence from within as well as from without. Both Chilean and Brazilian feminists saw the state as a potential agent of empowerment for women. It is unlikely that the Concertación government in Chile would have established SERNAM without the pressure from women's organizations, like the Concertación de Mujeres por la Democracia which will be discussed in the next section.

The establishment of SERNAM in Chile was opposed by the right-wing political parties who saw it as a threat to the family. The Catholic Church has also opposed some of its proposals, reflecting both the Church's transformation from playing an oppositional role under military rule to a more traditionally conservative one, retrenching on its social programmes to concentrate on 'evangelización', and its long-standing antipathy to reproductive rights and divorce (Schild 1992). The Concertación government has also been divided over what role SERNAM should play with the Christian Democrats, favouring a greater emphasis on preserving the family. These divisions have been reflected within SERNAM itself, with those associated with the Christian Democrats holding more conservative views compared to those associated with the Socialists who tend to be more influenced by feminism. As a result SERNAM has steered clear of divisive issues such as abortion.

It is too early to judge what long term impact these kinds of bodies will have, or indeed how long lasting they will be. SERNAM's effectiveness has been impeded by its limited budget, unclear brief, and a lack of formal machinery to oversee the operations of other government departments. It has also been constrained because the Concertación government, while prepared to give some support to measures furthering practical gender interests, is far more reluctant to contemplate measures which further strategic gender interests, discussed in Chapter 1.[2] It has found it easier to establish pilot projects and advocate policy around issues which focus on poverty alleviation such as employment training for women and are seen as less controversial, rather than measures which would directly challenge existing gender relations such as divorce and reproductive rights (Waylen 1995).

Commentators have also disagreed over whether these initiatives constitute an advance for feminists or whether they are evidence of the co-optation of some of the more acceptable demands of the women's movements. Have feminists been confined to small and relatively powerless organizations like SERNAM while those involved lose touch with the grassroots movements? Can these organizations be used by governments to impose their own aims on the 'women's issues' policy agenda without any real change occurring in the power structures outside? Alvarez (1990a: 201) has shown that in 1983 the São Paulo Women's Council was accused by some feminists of being a partisan body, filled entirely with PMDB members.

Women's political activity

A complex picture has emerged in the period since the return to competitive electoral politics. It is impossible to reach a single general conclusion on whether the role played by women mobilized under military rule has been sustained and extended, since the diversity and heterogeneity of the women's movements has become, if anything, more apparent with the return to civilian rule. Some women's movements, often those organizing around practical gender interests, appear to have become increasingly marginalized as the processes of transition have continued. This appears particularly marked in the Chilean case, in part as a consequence of the nature of the transition which has seen the renewed dominance of rather conventional party and institutional politics and the exclusion and demobilization of social movements (Angell and Pollack 1995). This is particularly true of those popular organizations which are organized around social and economic demands, typically directed at the state, perhaps the type of organization considered the archetypal Latin American social movement. The orthodox structural adjustment policies described above, which have typically been pursued by civilian governments, do not allow them to do much to satisfy the demands of popular sectors – particularly poor women – and to incorporate them into wider society. In addition, many of the popular organizations are ambivalent and wary about connections with the political parties, fearing manipulation and control through clientalistic structures, while the parties, particularly of the Centre, fear the mobilization and radicalization of the popular sectors and do not want too much participation by them, treating them with a degree of paternalism (Oxhorn 1989).

Barrig (1992) outlines many of these processes in the Peruvian case, describing how, at their inception, the leaders of the popular women's organizations defended their autonomy from political parties and even rejected coordination with male leaders from other neighbourhoods and municipal authorities. In the mid-1980s, however, a centralized pyramidal structure was introduced which could facilitate negotiation with the government and NGOs, for example over the provision of cheap food. Barrig argues that two strengths of the women's popular organizations became their weaknesses. First, the centralization of the movement created a distance between the leadership and the base. Second, in rejecting contact with political parties and other neigh-bourhood leaders, autonomy became isolation, particularly important in the context of the Sendero's campaign in the poor areas of Lima (Barrig 1992).

The human rights campaigners, such as the Madres of the Plaza de Mayo in Argentina and the Agrupaciones in Chile, have often found themselves increasingly outside the processes of transition and consolidation. They have remained active, campaigning for justice, but the President of Agrupaciones de familiares de detenidos-desaparacidos (AFDD) in Chile has claimed that it is 'prudence' that is on offer as the civilian governments are anxious to remain on good terms with the military and therefore take very little con-crete action over human rights abuses. It has been claimed that groups such as the Madres have found the transition difficult, as their role has changed from very effectively pressurizing a military government to attempting to influence a civilian one. They have even split over the issues of appropriate tactics and strategy in the new democratic context (Bouvard 1994). The breakaway group, the Linea Fundadora, increasingly unhappy with the Madres's continued demand for the return of their children alive and opposition to exhumations, opted for greater compromise with the civilian government, for example, presenting proposals to parliament (Fisher 1993: 122).

The feminist movements which re-emerged and came out into the open during the period of the breakdown of authoritarian rule have continued to be active during the period of transition and after. It is these groups contain-ing women organizing as women and pressing gender based political de-mands on the state which can be seen as conforming more closely to the Western European model of modern social movements. While some feminist organizations, often termed radical feminist, have opted to remain outside of the state, other groups of women (many of whom are middle-class feminist professionals, academics and party activists, also pressing gender based demands of a more strategic nature) have also achieved a limited role as members of the political élite. Matear (1993) describes how the women influential in SERNAM are part of the Chilean political class not only on their own account but also in terms of their connections to other members of that élite. They have, however, had some success in placing 'women's issues' in the policy agenda within the political parties.

The establishment of bodies like SERNAM and the Women's Councils in Brazil has also had an effect on women's movements. Since the return to competitive electoral politics, international NGOs frequently channel re-sources through the state rather than directly to grassroots organizations. As a result bodies like SERNAM receive money which might previously have gone to autonomous women's groups which now have to engage in a clientalistic relationship with SERNAM to get funding. Schild (1994b) has claimed that the establishment of SERNAM has beheaded the feminist movement as feminists have migrated into the state. SERNAM is not effect-ively responsive to the women's movements even though it has replaced the women's movements as the interlocutor in the public discourse on women (Chuchryk 1994: 88). However, women's bodies within the state like

SERNAM lose some of their power and influence if the women's movements outside of the state are weakened.

The return to competitive party politics can also lead to a fracturing of women's movements along party lines, as sectarianism and attempts by parties to control women's organizations become widespread. As Alvarez (1990a: 150) has noted, two rival International Women's Day events were held in Brazil in 1981. She argues that single issue campaigns were better able to resist these pressures than the broad umbrella organizations. Jaquette (1994: 231) has described attempts by the state to incorporate women's groups, for example through the provision of emergency aid which should be available to all but is in fact provided in exchange for political support. While women's organizations in Chile have tried to remain united in the face of a divided political opposition, this has not always been possible. Many centrist and feminist organizations left MEMCH 83, an umbrella group named after a suffrage campaign active earlier in the century, as it became increasingly identified with the more radical strategy of popular mobilization to overthrow the dictatorship associated with the Left (Molina 1989: 143–5).

There have been several examples of women's organizations set up to try and maintain the unity of the women's movement and mobilize women in a non-sectarian manner. The Chilean feminist organization, Mujeres por la Vida, is a good example of this. Attracting 10,000 to its first meeting in 1983, this organization continued to have an impact within other umbrella groups (Valenzuela 1990). Indeed the experience of marginalization and the difficulties of articulating women's demands within party politics have prompted feminists to set up wide umbrella organizations which are better placed to articulate the demands of feminist groups on the national political scene, as happened in Uruguay in 1984 (Fisher 1993: 56). In Chile the perception of many feminists of lack of influence of women on political processes in the run-up to the plebiscite, and the selection of very few women candidates, provided the major impetus for the creation of the autonomous Concertación de Mujeres por la Democracia by women from a wide range of parties in the Concertación and independent feminists (Montecino and Rossetti 1990). This group had three aims: to raise women's issues on the national political scene; to formulate a programme on women for the future democratic government; and to work in the presidential and parliamentary campaign. Many of their proposals were incorporated into the Concertación programme, including the proposal to set up a women's ministry which became SERNAM under the new civilian government (Valenzuela 1992: 181).

Feminist organizations have therefore continued their activities both inside and outside the arena of institutional politics. However there seems to be unanimity among many activists and commentators that engagement in the conventional political system can only occur within the context of an autonomous movement. Chilean feminists interviewed by Gloria Angelo (1990) argued that an autonomous feminist movement is needed as a resource for those women who have moved into party politics to fall back on. Caldeira (1992), looking at the more recent Brazilian experience, argues that the

maintenance of a feminist agenda and the achievement of policy transformations depend less on the existence of institutional space per se than
on the organic relation of this space with autonomous feminist and
women's organizations.

Alvarez (1994: 49–50) points to the multifaceted developments in the
Brazilian feminist movements in the face of shrinking political spaces which
were open in the immediate aftermath of the return to civilian government.
The emergence of feminist policy-orientated NGOs pressurizing the state has
been accompanied by the growth of wider feminist and lesbian social and
cultural movements, popular feminism and black feminism outside the realm
of the state.

It appears, therefore, that feminist organizations can often have a greater
influence over transition politics than popular women's movements. One
explanation is that in a negotiated transition of pacts intent on maintaining
much of the status quo, the more middle-class based organizations can participate more meaningfully. The Chilean organization Mujeres por la Vida
represented women in the Asamblea de la Civilidad, a broad (and moderate)
opposition front set up in 1986 to focus opposition to the dictatorship. This
occurred amid feelings that middle-class women's organizations were participating in the Asamblea who did not represent the popular based women's
organizations, marginalizing their interests as a consequence (Valenzuela 1990).
Similar reservations have been voiced about the representativeness of the
Concertación de Mujeres por la Democracia.

Conclusion

It is too early to answer one of Safa's (1990) questions and decide whether
women's movements in Latin America have formed a short term sporadic
protest movement or can be seen as part of a longer term transformation.
While it is difficult to generalize about the impact of democratization on
women and women's movements, it is clear that some women's movements,
often campaigning around practical gender interests, have become more
marginal to the processes of transition, as popular and social movements have
been demobilized. This marginalization has occurred while other groups of
women, who are often middle-class and pressing more strategic gender based
political demands on the state, have had an impact (however limited) on the
newly reconstituted competitive party politics and policy agendas.

Some political space has existed during this conjuncture for women's
movements to pressurize the state and achieve some gains. But the experiences of women's movements highlight the importance of several issues
which have dominated wider discussions of the relationship between social
movements and political parties and social movements and the state. First is
the importance of autonomy: how far any engagement in conventional politics,
whether through political parties or the state, must be done on the basis of
autonomous movements. The issue is now seen by many women not as a

choice between either autonomy or integration, but as the necessity of both. Second is the question of whether there is a need for greater coordination between women's movements, so that demands can be put more coherently to the state. It may be, given the diversity of the different movements, that this would be a difficult task to realize. The experiences of women's bodies such as SERNAM in the state have shown many feminists that engagement with the state is a complex and contradictory process. The state is not a neutral tool and some outcomes are much easier to achieve than others, causing less opposition both inside and outside the state.

Finally, while Rueschemeyer *et al.* (1992) may be correct in arguing that a negotiated transition involving the middle-class offers the greatest likelihood of consolidating (an albeit restricted) democracy, and while it may also allow some middle-class feminists a role as part of the political élite, this is likely to be a type of transition that will marginalize the popular sectors, including poor women, from the conventional political arena. The resurrection of a strong party system can also present obstacles to women seeking access to power, as old clientelistic practices which act to exclude women are resumed. Some of the new political parties appear to offer many women, including women of the popular sectors, a greater opportunity, however limited, for participation and representation in the formal arena. However, the emphasis in this type of negotiated transition on procedural democracy, rather than on social and economic change, has important implications for many groups of women, further marginalizing the wider demands of human rights groups, popular sectors and the Left.

Preliminary evidence from the very different transitions which have taken place in Africa suggest that some similar trends may be at work. While popular protest may be important in provoking political liberalization, political parties play a key role in subsequent phases of transition. Women's informal associations, which played an important role in eroding the legitimacy of authoritarian rule, have not become involved in multiparty politics. However, new women's organizations, made up of predominantly élite women have emerged to press gender specific agendas to reduce inequality and to increase women's participation in electoral politics. These groups have had a mixed reception from the political parties and perhaps with the exception of South Africa, few women have formed part of the new governments.

Notes

1 An earlier version of this chapter has appeared as 'Women's Movements and Democratisation in Latin America', *Third World Quarterly*, 14 (3), 573–87.
2 This point was made by M. Valenzuela at the Conference on Women and the Transition from Authoritarian Rule in Latin America and Eastern Europe, Berkeley, CA, December 1992.

7 Conclusion

This book has not set out to provide a definitive analysis of gender in Third World politics. Instead it has attempted to give some insight into the complex nature of the relationship between gender relations and politics in the Third World, and the variety of different perspectives which can be used to analyse that relationship. It has analysed some of the issues, such as democratization, which currently predominate in the study of comparative politics and challenged many of the existing approaches. Some of the problems which are currently being debated by feminists have also been discussed, and, as such, this book is both an attempt to help to gender the discipline of politics and a contribution to the development of feminist approaches to the study of politics.

In addition to using some of the important insights of feminist political scientists and theorists, for example in deconstructing the public–private divide and widening the definitions of the 'political', I have tried to utilize elements of wider feminist theorizing from a range of disciplines. For example, I have taken what I see as some of the useful elements of the structural analyses of socialist feminists developed in the 1970s and early 1980s, which highlight the importance of the development of capitalism in the construction of gender relations in different parts of the Third World. I have tried to link this kind of approach with some of the more exciting theoretical developments of the 1980s, such as the emphasis on difference and the construction of gendered subjectivities, emerging both from the First World and the Third World. Some may think that this approach is overly eclectic. However, I believe that it offers a useful way forward as the structural approaches of the 1970s often overlooked questions of agency, while some of the developments of the 1980s downplay the importance of wider social and economic structures.

Work emanating from the frameworks which reached some prominence in the 1980s and which looks at gender and Third World politics is at a very early stage in its development, but is moving the study of politics in some interesting directions. These kinds of insights have important implications for the analysis of political identities which form the basis for a wide range of political actions. I have tried to draw all these sometimes diverse threads together to form a coherent approach which can provide an adequate analysis of both 'high' and 'low' politics.

This approach has been used to explore the ways in which some of the most important political processes, not just competitive electoral politics, are gendered in the Third World. Women are largely absent from the higher echelons of formal politics, whether it is a revolutionary, authoritarian or democratizing system. However, political projects such as colonialism and authoritarianism are fundamentally constructed around particular notions of gender and particular forms of gender relations as well as other factors such as race and class. This gender element has so often been ignored in the past.

This approach has also been used to analyse the impact of state policies on women and gender relations. Colonial policies, for example, had a very different effect on different groups of men and women and both colonial and 'traditional' authorities wanted to control the changes in gender relations to which the new policies were contributing. We saw the attempts of revolutionary regimes to implement a narrow and instrumentalist vision of an emancipatory agenda for women, with mixed and contradictory results. In several formations, we have seen how economic crisis has interacted with political factors. Economic liberalization, primarily in the form of structural adjustment programmes (SAPs), has been introduced by authoritarian regimes and frequently accompanied political liberalization. SAPs have particular implications for different groups of women, often increasing both their paid and unpaid labour with implications for the collective activities they can undertake.

In addition to looking at formal politics and the impact of state policies, we used the widened definition of the political to consider the activities of different groups of women, their interaction with the conventional political arena and their autonomous activities.

Several themes have emerged throughout the analysis of the very different formations. First is the importance of incorporating specificity and difference into the analysis of gender and politics. It is rarely, if ever, possible to generalize about all women and their interests. We saw the very different roles played in formal politics by middle-class and élite women as well as women of different races in different contexts. Different groups of women undertake a variety of activities outside the conventional political arena. Feminism, for example, does not have the same meanings for all women.

Second, the importance of developing a sophisticated feminist analysis of the state emerged from the analysis of all the formations. In a variety of different contexts we have seen the ways in which the state can be a site of struggle. We saw that, during moments of greater fluidity at times of political change and flux, some groups of women were better placed to use whatever limited spaces had opened up to try to influence the state and improve their situation. For a number of years during the colonial period in Africa, some women used the colonial courts to try to free themselves of certain restrictions such as those surrounding marriage. In some countries in Latin America, democratization has enabled some feminists to pressurize political parties of the Centre and Left to take up gender issues and implement a version of state feminism. Engagement with the state, however, has brought complex and contradictory outcomes, often not the ones that were intended.

Third, we saw how women's movements in a variety of contexts were more successful in their efforts to influence the state if they were operating from the background of autonomous movements. Several commentators have pointed to ways in which the absence of strong autonomous women's movements can contribute to the limited effectiveness of programmes to increase gender equality. The nature of the relationship between women's movements and the state is another key area for investigation in the future, enabling a better understanding of the strategies which can be employed to enter the state and the opportunities which exist in different political formations.

Bibliography

Abdullah, H. (1993) 'Transition politics' and the challenge of gender in Nigeria, *Review of African Political Economy*, 56: 27–41.

Ackelsberg, M. (1992) Feminist analyses of public policy, *Comparative Politics*, 24 (4): 477–93.

Afshar, H. and Dennis, C. (eds) (1992) *Women and Adjustment Policies in the Third World*, Basingstoke, Macmillan.

Agarwal, B. (1984) Rural women and the high yielding variety rice technology in India, *Economic and Political Weekly*, 19 (13): 39–52.

Agarwal, B. (1986) Women, poverty and agricultural growth in India, *Journal of Peasant Studies*, 13 (4): 165–220.

Agosin, M. (1988) *Scraps of Life*, London, Zed Press.

Agrupación de los familiares detenidos-desaparacidos (1985) ¿*Dónde Estan?* Santiago, Agrupación de los familiares detenidos-desaparacidos.

Ajulu, R. (1993) The 1992 Kenya general elections: a preliminary assessment, *Review of African Political Economy*, 56: 98–102.

Alavi, H. (1972) The state in post-colonial societies: Pakistan and Bangladesh, *New Left Review*, 74: 59–81.

Allman, J. (1991) Of 'spinsters', 'concubines' and 'wicked women': reflections on gender and social change in colonial Asante, *Gender and History*, 3 (2): 176–89.

Almond, G. and Coleman, J. (eds) (1962) *The Politics of Developing Areas*, Princeton, NJ, Princeton University Press.

Alvarez, S. (1989a) Contradictions of a 'women's space' in a male-dominant state: the political role of the commissions on the status of women in postauthoritarian Brazil, in K. Staudt (ed.) *Women, International Development and Politics*, Philadelphia, PA, Temple University Press.

Alvarez, S. (1989b) Women's movements and gender politics in the Brazilian transition, in J. Jaquette (ed.) *The Women's Movement in Latin America: Feminism and the Transition to Democracy*, London, Unwin Hyman.

Alvarez, S. (1990a) *Engendering Democracy in Brazil: Women's Movements in Transition Politics*, Princeton, NJ, Princeton University Press.

Alvarez, S. (1990b) Women's participation in the Brazilian People's Church: a critical appraisal, *Feminist Studies*, 16 (2): 381–408.

Alvarez, S. (1994) The (trans)formation of the feminism(s) and gender politics in democratizing Brazil, in J. Jaquette (ed.) *The Women's Movements in Latin America: Participation and Democracy*, 2nd edn, Boulder, CO, Westview Press.

Angell, A. and Pollack, B. (1990) The Chilean elections of 1989 and the politics of the transition to democracy, *Bulletin of Latin American Research*, 9 (1): 1–23.

Angell, A. and Pollack, B. (1995) The Chilean elections of 1993: from polarisation to consensus, *Bulletin of Latin American Research*, 14 (2): 105–26.

Angelo, G. (1990) Nuevos espacios y nuevas practicas de mujeres en una situación de crisis: hacia le surgiemiento y consolidación de un movimiento de mujeres. El caso de Chile, *Cuadernos de la Morada*, Santiago, La Morada.

Anglade, C. and Fortin, C. (1990) Accumulation, adjustment and the autonomy of the state in Latin America, in C. Anglade and C. Fortin (eds) *The State and Capital Accumulation in Latin America*, vol. 2, London, Macmillan.

Aquino, B. (1994) Philippine feminism in historical perspective, in J. Nelson and J. Chowdhury (eds) *Women and Politics Worldwide*, New Haven, CT, Yale University Press.

Arnfred, S. (1988) Women in Mozambique: gender struggle and gender politics, *Review of African Political Economy*, 41: 5–16.

Ayubi, N. (1991) *Political Islam: Religion and Politics in the Arab World*, London, Routledge.

Azarya, V. and Chazan, N. (1987) Disengagement from the state in Africa: reflections on the experience of Ghana and Guinea, *Comparative Studies in Society and History*, 29 (1): 106–31.

Azicri, M. (1987) Women's development through revolutionary mobilization, in I. Horowitz (ed.) *Cuban Communism*, 6th edn, New Brunswick, NJ, Transaction Books.

Barnes, T. (1992) The fight for the control of African women's mobility in colonial Zimbabwe, *Signs: Journal of Women in Culture and Society*, 17 (3): 586–608.

Barratt Brown, M. (1963) *After Imperialism*, London, Heinemann.

Barrett, M. (1981) *Women's Oppression Today*, London, Verso.

Barrett, M. (1991) *The Politics of Truth: From Marx to Foucault*, Cambridge, Polity Press.

Barrett, M. (1992) Words and things: materialism and method in contemporary feminist analysis, in M. Barrett and A. Phillips (eds) *Destabilising Theory: Contemporary Feminist Debates*, Cambridge, Polity Press.

Barrett, M. and Phillips, A. (eds) (1992) *Destabilising Theory: Contemporary Feminist Debates*, Cambridge, Polity Press.

Barrig, M. (1989) The difficult equilibrium between bread and roses: women's organizations and the transition from dictatorship in Peru, in J. Jaquette (ed.) *The Women's Movement in Latin America: Feminism and the Transition to Democracy*, London, Unwin Hyman.

Barrig, M. (1992) Violence and economic crisis: the challenges of the women's movement in Peru, paper presented to the Conference on Women and the Transition from Authoritarian Rule, Berkeley, CA, December.

Beckles, H. (1989) *Natural Rebels: A Social History of Enslaved Women in Barbados*, London, Zed Press.

Beneria, L. (ed.) (1982) *Women and Development: The Sexual Division of Labour in Rural Societies*, New York, Praeger.

Beneria, L. and Sen, G. (1981) Accumulation, reproduction, and women's role in economic development: Boserup revisited, *Signs*, 7 (2): 279–98.

Bergman, A. (1974) *Women of Vietnam*, San Francisco, CA, People's Press.

Bernstein, H. (1979) The sociology of underdevelopment versus the sociology of development, in D. Lehmann (ed.) *Development Theory. Four Critical Studies*, London, Frank Cass.

Bernstein, H. and Crow, B. (1988) The expansion of Europe, in B. Crow, M. Thorpe *et al.* (eds) *Survival and Change in the Third World*, Cambridge, Polity Press.

Bhabha, H. (1993) *The Location of Culture*, London, Routledge.

Birkett, D. (1992) The 'white women's burden' in the 'white man's grave': the introduction of British nurses in colonial West Africa, in N. Chaudhuri and M. Strobel (eds) *Western Women and Imperialism: Complicity and Resistance*, Bloomington, IN, Indiana University Press.

Bock, G. and James, S. (eds) (1992) *Beyond Equality and Difference: Citizenship, Feminist Politics and Female Subjectivity*, London, Routledge.

Booth, A. (1992) European courts protect women and witches: colonial law courts as redistributors of power in Swaziland 1920–1950, *Journal of Southern African Studies*, 18 (2): 253–75.

Boserup, E. (1970) *Women's Role in Economic Development*, New York, St Martin's Press.

Bourque, S. and Warren, C. (1990) Access is not enough: gender perspectives on technology and education, in I. Tinker (ed.) *Persistent Inequalities: Women and World Development*, Oxford, Oxford University Press.

Bouvard, M. (1994) *Revolutionizing Motherhood: The Mothers of the Plaza de Mayo*, Wilmington, Scholarly Resources Books.

Bratton, M. and van de Walle, N. (1992a) Popular protest and political reform in Africa, *Comparative Politics*, 24 (4): 419–42.

Bratton, M. and van de Walle, N. (1992b) Regime type and political transition in Africa, paper presented to APSA annual conference, Chicago, September.

Bratton, M. and van de Walle, N. (1994) Neopatrimonial regimes and political transitions in Africa, *World Politics*, 46 (4): 453–89.

Brett, E.A. (1985) *The World Economy Since the War: The Politics of Uneven Development*, London, Macmillan.

Brownfoot, J. (1984) Memsahibs in colonial Malaya: a study of European wives in a British colony and protectorate 1900–1940, in H. Callan and S. Ardener (eds) *The Incorporated Wife*, London, Croom Helm.

Brownmiller, S. (1975) *Against Our Will: Men, Women and Rape*, London, Secker and Warburg.

Brydon, L. and Chant, S. (1989) *Women in the Third World: Gender Issues in Rural and Urban Areas*, Aldershot, Edward Elgar.

Bunster, X. (1988) Watch out for the little Naziman that all of us have inside: the mobilization and demobilization of women in militarized Chile, *Women's Studies International Forum*, 11 (5): 485–91.

Bunster-Burotto, X. (1985) Surviving beyond fear: women and torture in Latin America, in J. Nash and H. Safa (eds) *Women and Change in Latin America*, South Hadley, MA, Bergin and Garvey.

Burbach, R. (1994) Roots of the postmodern rebellion in Chiapas, *New Left Review*, 205: 113–24.

Burton, A. (1992) The white women's burden: British feminists and the 'Indian woman', 1865–1915, in N. Chaudhuri and M. Strobel (eds) *Western Women and Imperialism: Complicity and Resistance*, Bloomington, IN, Indiana University Press.

Bush, B. (1990) *Slave Women in Caribbean Society 1650–1838*, London, James Currey.

Bush-Slimani, B. (1993) Hard labour: women, childbirth and resistance in British Caribbean slave societies, *History Workshop Journal*, 36: 83–99.

Butler, J. (1989) *Gender Trouble: Feminism and the Subversion of Identity*, London, Routledge.

Butler, J. and Scott, J. (eds) (1992) *Feminists Theorize the Political*, London, Routledge.

Buvinic, M. (1983) Women's issues in Third World poverty: a policy analysis, in M. Buvinic, M. Lycette and W.P. McGreevey (eds) *Women and Poverty in the Third World*, Baltimore, MD, Johns Hopkins University Press.

Caldeira, T. (1986) Electoral struggles in a neighbourhood in the periphery of São Paulo, *Politics and Society*, 15 (1): 43–66.

Caldeira, T. (1990) Women, daily life and politics, in E. Jelin (ed.) *Women and Social Change in Latin America*, London, Zed Press.

Caldeira, T. (1992) Justice and individual rights: challenges for women's movements and democratization in Brazil, paper presented to the Conference on Women and the Transition from Authoritarian Rule in Latin America and Eastern Europe, Berkeley, CA, December.

Callan, H. (1984) Introduction, in H. Callan and S. Ardener (eds) *The Incorporated Wife*, London, Croom Helm.

Callaway, H. (1987) *Gender, Culture and Empire: European Women in Colonial Nigeria*, Urbana, IL, University of Illinois Press.

Callaway, H. and Helly, D. (1992) Crusader for empire: Flora Shaw/Lady Lugard, in N. Chaudhuri and M. Strobel (eds) *Western Women and Imperialism: Complicity and Resistance*, Bloomington, IN, Indiana University Press.

Cammack, P. (1985) The political economy of contemporary military regimes in Latin America: from bureaucratic authoritarianism to restructuring, in P. O'Brien and P. Cammack (eds) *Generals in Retreat: The Crisis of Military Rule in Latin America*, Manchester, Manchester University Press.

Cammack, P. (1996) *Capitalism and Democracy in the Developing World: The Doctrine for Political Development*, London, Francis Pinter.

Cammack, P., Pool, D. and Tordoff, W. (1993) *Third World Politics: A Comparative Introduction*, 2nd edn, Basingstoke: Macmillan.

Cardoso, F.H. (1973) Associated dependent development: theoretical and practical implications, in A. Stepan (ed.) *Authoritarian Brazil*, New Haven, CT, Yale University Press.

Cardoso, F.H. and Faletto, E. (1979) *Dependency and Development in Latin America*, Berkeley, CA, University of California Press.

Chaliand, G. (1977) *Revolution in the Third World*, Hassocks, Sussex, Harvester Press.

Chaney, E. (1974) The mobilization of women in Allende's Chile, in J. Jaquette (ed.) *Women in Politics*, New York, John Wiley.

Chaney, E. (1979) *Supermadre: Women in Politics in Latin America*, Austin, TX, University of Texas Press.

Channock, M. (1982) Making customary law: men, women and courts in colonial Northern Rhodesia, in M. Hay and M. Wright (eds) *African Women and the Law: Historical Perspectives*, Boston University Papers on Africa, 7.

Channock, M. (1985) *Law, Custom and Social Order: The Colonial Experience in Malawi and Zambia*, Cambridge, Cambridge University Press.

Charles, C. (1995) Gender and politics in contemporary Haiti: the Duvalierist state, transnationalism and the emergence of a new feminism 1980–90, *Feminist Studies*, 21 (1): 135–64.

Charlton, S., Everett, J. and Staudt, K. (eds) (1989) *Women, State and Development*, Albany, NY, SUNY Press.

Chatterjee, P. (1990) The nationalist resolution of the women question', in K. Sangari and S. Vaid (eds) *Recasting Women: Essays in Indian Colonial History*, New Brunswick, NJ, Rutgers University Press.

Chaudhuri, N. and Strobel, M. (eds) (1992) *Western Women and Imperialism: Complicity and Resistance*, Bloomington, IN, Indiana University Press.

Chinchilla, N. (1977) Mobilizing women: revolution in the revolution, *Latin American Perspectives* (4): 83–102.

Chinchilla, N. (1990) Revolutionary popular feminism in Nicaragua: articulating class, gender and national Sovereignty, *Gender and Society*, 4 (3): 370–97.

Chinchilla, N. (1994) Feminism, revolution and democratic transitions in Latin America, in J. Jaquette (ed.) *The Women's Movements in Latin America: Participation and Democracy*, 2nd edn, Boulder, CO, Westview Press.

Chuchryk, P. (1984) Protest politics and personal life: the emergence of feminism in a military dictatorship, unpublished PhD thesis, University of York (Canada).

Chuchryk, P. (1989a) Feminist anti-authoritarian politics: the role of women's organizations in the Chilean transition to democracy, in J. Jaquette (ed.) *The Women's Movement in Latin America: Feminism and the Transition to Democracy*, London, Unwin Hyman.

Chuchryk (1989b) Subversive mothers: women's opposition to the military regime in Chile, in S. Charlton, J. Everett and K. Staudt (eds) *Women, State and Development*, Albany, NY, SUNY Press.

Chuchryk, P. (1991) Women in the revolution, in T. Walker (ed.) *Revolution and Counterrevolution in Nicaragua*, Boulder, CO, Westview Press.

Chuchryk, P. (1994) From dictatorship to democracy: the women's movement in Chile, in J. Jaquette (ed.) *The Women's Movements in Latin America: Participation and Democracy*, 2nd edn, Boulder, CO, Westview Press.

Clapham, C. (ed.) (1982) *Private Patronage and Public Power: Clientelism in the Modern State*, London, Pinter.

Clapham, C. (1985) *Third World Politics: An Introduction*, London, Croom Helm.

Cock, J. (1989) Keep the fires burning: militarisation and the politics of gender in South Africa, *Review of African Political Economy*, 45/46: 50–64.

Collinson, H. (ed.) (1990) *Women and Revolution in Nicaragua*, London, Zed Press.

Cooper, F. and Stoler, A. (1989) Introduction: tensions of empire: colonial control and visions of rule, *American Ethnologist*, 16 (4): 609–21.

Corcoran-Nantes, Y. (1990) Women and popular urban social movements in São Paulo, *Bulletin of Latin American Research*, 9 (2): 249–64.

Corcoran-Nantes, Y. (1993) Female consciousness or feminist consciousness?: women's consciousness raising in community-based struggles in Brazil, in S. Radcliffe and S. Westwood (eds) *Viva: Women and Popular Protest in Latin America*, London, Routledge.

Crummett, M. (1977) El poder feminino: the mobilization of women against socialism in Chile, *Latin American Perspectives*, 4 (4): 103–13.

Das, V. (1986) Gender studies, cross-cultural comparison and the colonial organization of knowledge, *Berkshire Review*, 21: 58–76.

Deere, C.D. (1977) Changing social relations of production and Peruvian peasant women's work, *Latin American Perspectives*, 4 (1–2): 48–69.

De Groot, J. (1989) Sex and 'race': the construction of language and image in the nineteenth century, in S. Mendus and J. Rendell (eds) *Sexuality and Subordination*, London, Routledge.

Deighton, J., Horsley, R., Stewart, S. and Cain, C. (1983) *Sweet Ramparts: Women in Revolutionary Nicaragua*, London, War on Want/Nicaragua Solidarity Campaign.

De Montis, M. (1994) Genero, participación política y poder alternativo de las mujeres en Nicaragua, paper presented at Cross Currents in Latin American Gender Theory, Portsmouth, July.

Dennis, C. (1987) Women and the state in Nigeria: the case of the federal military government 1984–5, in H. Afshar (ed.) *Women State and Ideology*, London, Macmillan.

Denzer, L. (1976) Towards a study of West African women's participation in nationalist politics: the early phase, 1935–1950, *Africana Research Bulletin*, VI (4): 65–86.

Diamond, L. (1989) Beyond authoritarianism and totalitarianism: strategies for democratization, *Washington Quarterly*, 12: 141–63.

Diamond, L., Linz, J. and Lipset, S. (eds) (1988) *Democracy in Developing Areas*, Boulder, CO, Lynne Rienner.

Dix, R. (1984) Why revolutions succeed and fail, *Polity*, 16: 423–46.

Edholm, F., Harris, O. and Young, K. (1977) Conceptualising women, *Critique of Anthropology*, 3, 9 and 10: 101–30.

Elshtain, J. (1982) On beautiful souls, just warriors and feminist consciousness, *Women's Studies International Forum*, 5 (3/4): 341–8.

Elshtain, J. (1987) *Women and War*, New York, Basic Books.

Elshtain, J. (1992) The power and powerlessness of women, in G. Bock and S. James (eds) *Beyond Equality and Difference: Citizenship, Feminist Politics and Female Subjectivity*, London, Routledge.

Elson, D. (1991) Male bias in the development process: an overview, in D. Elson (ed.) *Male Bias in the Development Process*, Manchester, Manchester University Press.

Elson, D. (1992) Male bias in structural adjustment, in H. Afshar and C. Dennis (eds) *Women and Adjustment Policies in the Third World*, Basingstoke, Macmillan.

Elson, D. (1993) Gender aware analysis and development economics, *Journal of International Development*, 5 (2): 237–47.

Elson, D. and Pearson, R. (1981) The subordination of women and the internationalization of factory production, in K. Young, C. Wolkowitz, and R. McCullagh (eds) *Of Marriage and the Market: Women's Subordination in International Perspective*, London, CSE Books.

Enloe, C. (1988) *Does Khaki Become You?: The Militarization of Women's Lives*, London, Pandora Press.

Enloe, C. (1989) *Bananas, Beaches and Bases: Making Feminist Sense of International Politics*, London, Pandora Press.

Enloe, C. (1993) *The Morning After: Sexual Politics at the End of the Cold War*, Berkeley, CA, University of California Press.

Escobar, A. and Alvarez, A. (eds) (1992) *The Making of Social Movements in Latin America: Identity, Strategy and Democracy*, Boulder, CO, Westview Press.

Etienne, M. (1980) Women and men, cloth and colonization: the transformation of production–distribution relations among the Baule (Ivory Coast), in M. Etienne and E. Leacock (eds) *Women and Colonization: Anthropological Perspectives*, New York, Praeger.

Etienne, M. and Leacock, E. (eds) (1980) *Women and Colonization: Anthropological Perspectives*, New York, Praeger.

Evans, P., Rueschemeyer, D. and Skocpol, T. (eds) (1985) *Bringing the State Back in*, Cambridge, Cambridge University Press.

Everett, J. (1989) Incorporation versus conflict, in S. Charlton, J. Everett and K. Staudt (eds) *Women, State and Development*, Albany, NY, SUNY Press.

Feijoó, M. (1989) The challenge of constructing civilian peace: women and democracy in Argentina, in J. Jaquette (ed.) *The Women's Movement in Latin America: Feminism and the Transition to Democracy*, London, Unwin Hyman.

Femenia, N.A. (1987) Argentina's Mothers of the Plaza de Mayo: the mourning process from junta to democracy, *Feminist Studies*, 13 (1): 9–18.

Ferguson, K. (1984) *The Feminist Case Against Bureaucracy*, Philadelphia, PA, Temple University Press.

Fieldhouse, D.K. (1981) *Colonialism: 1870–1945*, London, Weidenfeld and Nicolson.

Finer, S. (1962) *The Man on Horseback*, London, Pall Mall.

Firestone, S. (1970) *The Dialectic of Sex*, London, Paladin.

Fisher, J. (1989) *Mothers of the Disappeared*, London, Zed Press.

Fisher, J. (1993) *Out of the Shadows: Women, Resistance and Politics in South America*, London, Latin American Bureau.

Flax, J. (1987) Postmodernism and gender relations in feminist theory, *Signs: Journal of Women in Culture and Society*, 12 (4): 621–43.

Foot, R. (1990) Where are the women?, *Diplomatic History*, 14 (4): 615–22.

Forrest, J. (1988) The quest for state 'Hardness' in Africa, *Comparative Politics*, 20 (4): 423–42.

Forrest, J. (1994) Namibia – the first post apartheid democracy, *Journal of Democracy*, 5 (3): 88–100.

Foweraker, J. and Craig, A. (eds) (1990) *Popular Movements and Political Change in Mexico*, Boulder, CO, Lynne Rienner.

Franco, J. (1994) Crossed wires: gender theory North and South, paper presented to Conference on Latin American Cross Currents in Gender Theory, Portsmouth, July.

Frank, A.G. (1969) *Capitalism and Underdevelopment in Latin America: Historical Studies of Brazil and Chile*, New York, Monthly Review Press.

Franzway, S., Court, D. and Connell, R.W. (1989) *Staking a Claim: Feminism, Bureaucracy and the State*, Cambridge, Polity Press.

Fraser, N. (1989) *Unruly Practices: Power, Discourse and Gender in Contemporary Social Theory*, Cambridge, Polity.

Garretón, M.A. (1989) Popular mobilisation and the military regime in Chile: the complexities of the invisible transition, in S. Eckstein (ed.) *Power and Popular Protest: Latin American Social Movements*, Berkeley, CA, University of California Press.

Garretón, M.A. (1990/1) Democratic inauguration in Chile: from Pinochet to Aylwin, *Third World Quarterly*, 12 (3/4): 64–80.

Gartrell, B. (1984) Colonial wives: villains or victims, in H. Callan and S. Ardener (eds) *The Incorporated Wife*, London, Croom Helm.

Gawanas, B. (1993) Legal rights of Namibian women and affirmative action: the eradication of gender inequalities, *Review of African Political Economy*, 56: 116–22.

Geiger, S. (1987) Women in nationalist struggle: TANU activists in Dar es Salaam, *International Journal of African Historical Studies*, 20 (1): 1–26.

Genovese, M. (ed.) (1993) *Women as National Leaders*, London, Sage.

Gill, S. and Law, D. (1988) *The Global Political Economy: Perspectives, Problems and Policies*, Hemel Hempstead, Harvester Wheatsheaf.

Gilligan, C. (1983) *In a Different Voice*, Cambridge, MA, Harvard University Press.

Gilpin, R. (1987) *The Political Economy of International Relations*, Princeton, NJ, Princeton University Press.

Goodwin, J. and Skocpol, T. (1989) Explaining revolutions in the contemporary Third World, *Politics and Society*, 17 (4): 489–509.

Grant, R. (1991) The sources of gender bias in international relations theory, in R. Grant and K. Newland (eds) *Gender and International Relations*, Milton Keynes, Open University Press.

Grier, B. (1992) Pawns, porters and petty traders: women in the transition to cash crop agriculture in colonial Ghana, *Signs*, 17 (2): 304–28.

Guevara, E. (1963) *Guerrilla Warfare*, New York, Monthly Review Press.

Hafkin, N.J. and Bay, E.G. (eds) (1976) *Women in Africa: Studies in Social and Economic Change*, Stanford, CA, Stanford University Press.

Halliday, F. (1986) *The Making of the Second Cold War*, 2nd edn, London, Verso.

Halliday, F. (1990) *Cold War, Third World*, London, Hutchinson.

Hansen, K.T. (1992) White women in a changing world: employment, voluntary work and sex in post World War Two Northern Rhodesia, in N. Chaudhuri and M. Strobel (eds) *Western Women and Imperialism: Complicity and Resistance*, Bloomington, IN, Indiana University Press.

Hardy, C. (1985) Estragias orginazadas de subsistencia: los sectores sociales frente a sus necessidades en Chile, Santiago: PET Working Paper 45.

Harris, H. (1983) Women in struggle: Nicaragua, *Third World Quarterly*, 5 (4): 899–904.

Harris, L. (1988) The IMF and mechanisms of integration, in B. Crow, M. Thorpe *et al. Survival and Change in the Third World*, Cambridge, Polity Press.

Harris, N. (1987) *The End of the Third World*, Harmondsworth, Penguin.

Hartmann, H. (1981) The unhappy marriage of Marxism and feminism: towards a more progressive union, in L. Sargeant (ed.) *Women and Revolution: The Unhappy Marriage of Marxism and Feminism*, New York, Monthly Review Press.

Hay, M. (1976) Luo women and economic change during the colonial period, in N.J. Hafkin and E.G. Bay (eds) *Women in Africa: Studies in Social and Economic Change*, Stanford, CA, Stanford University Press.

Hay, M. (1982) Women as owners, occupants, and managers of property in colonial western Kenya, in M. Hay and M. Wright (eds) *African Women and the Law: Historical Perspectives*, Boston University Papers on Africa, no. VII.

Hay, M. and Stichter, S. (eds) (1984) *African Women South of the Sahara*, London, Longman.

Hellman, J.A. (1990) The study of new social movements in Latin America and the question of autonomy, *LASA Forum*, 21: 7–12.

Henn, J. (1984) Women in the rural economy: past, present and future, in M. Hay and S. Stichter (eds) *African Women South of the Sahara*, London, Longman.

Hernes, H. (1987) Women and the welfare state: the transition from the private to public dependence, in A. Showstack (ed.) *Women and the State*, London, Hutchinson.

Hewitt, T. (1992) Developing countries – 1945 to 1990, in R. Allen and A. Thomas (eds) *Poverty and Development in the 1990s*, Oxford, Oxford University Press.

Higgott, R. (1983) *Political Development Theory*, London, Croom Helm.

Hojman, D. (1989) Neo-liberal economic policies and infant and child mortality: a simulation of a Chilean paradox, *World Development*, 17 (1): 93–108.

hooks, b. (1984) *Feminist Theory: From Margin to Center*, Boston, MA, Southend Press.

Hunt, N. (1990) Domesticity and colonialism in Belgian Africa: Usumbara's foyer social, 1946–1960, *Signs*, 15 (3): 447–74.

Huntington, S. (1968) *Political Order in Changing Societies*, New Haven, CT, Yale University Press.

Huntington, S. (1984) Will more countries become democratic? *Political Science Quarterly*, 99, summer: 193–218.

Huntington, S. (1991) *The Third Wave: Democratization in the Late Twentieth Century*, Norman, OK, The University of Oklahoma Press.

Hyam, R. (1990) *Empire and Sexuality: The British Experience*, Manchester, Manchester University Press.

Jackson, C. (1993) Women/nature or gender/history: a critique of ecofeminist development, *Journal of Peasant Studies*, 20 (3): 389–419.

Janowitz, M. (1964) *The Military in the Political Development of New Nations: An Essay in Comparative Analysis*, Chicago, IL, University of Chicago Press.

Jaquette, J. (1973) Women in revolutionary movements in Latin America, *Journal of Marriage and the Family*, 35: 344–54.

Jaquette, J. (1982) Women and modernization theory: a decade of feminist criticism, *World Politics*, XXXIV (2): 267–84.

Jaquette, J. (ed.) (1989) *The Women's Movement in Latin America: Feminism and the Transition to Democracy*, London, Unwin Hyman.

Jaquette, J. (ed.) (1994) *The Women's Movement in Latin America: Participation and Democracy*, 2nd edn, Boulder, CO, Westview Press.

Jayawardena, K. (1986) *Feminism and Nationalism in the Third World*, London, Zed Press.

Joekes, S. (1987) *Women in the World Economy*, Oxford, Oxford University Press.

Johnson, C. (1982) Grassroots organising: women in anticolonial activity in southwestern Nigeria, *African Studies Review*, XXV (2 and 3): 137–57.

Johnson, C. (1986) Class and gender: a consideration of Yoruba women during the colonial period, in C. Robertson and I. Berger (eds) *Women and Class in Africa*, New York, Holmes and Meier.

Kabeer, N. (1994) *Reversed Realities: Gender Hierarchies in Development Thought*, London, Verso.

Kampwirth, K. (1992) The revolution continues: Nicaraguan women's organizations under the UNO, paper presented to APSA annual meeting, Chicago, IL, September.

Kandiyoti, D. (1988) Bargaining with patriarchy, *Gender and Society*, 2 (3): 271–90.

Kandiyoti, D. (1991) Identity and its discontents: women and the nation, *Millennium: Journal of International Studies*, 20 (3): 429–43.

Kaplan, T. (1982) Female consciousness and collective action: the case of Barcelona 1910–1918, *Signs: Journal of Women in Culture and Society*, 7: 546–66.

Katzenstein, M.F. (1978) Towards equality: cause and consequence of the political prominence of women in India, *Asian Survey*, 18 (5): 473–86.

Keck, M. (1992) *The Worker's Party and Democratization in Brazil*, New Haven, CT, Yale University Press.

Kirkwood, D. (1984) Settler wives in Southern Rhodesia, in H. Callan and S. Ardener (eds) *The Incorporated Wife*, London, Croom Helm.

Kirkwood, J. (1990) *Ser Política en Chile. Los Nudos de la Sabiduría Feminista*, Santiago, Editorial Cuarto Propio.

Kruks, S. and Wisner, B. (1989) Ambiguous transformations: women, politics and production in Mozambique, in S. Kruks, R. Rapp and M. Young (eds) *Promissory Notes: Women in the Transition to Socialism*, New York, Monthly Review Press.

Lago, M. (1987) Rural women and the neo-liberal model in Chile, in C. Deere and M. de Leon (eds) *Rural Women and State Policy*, Boulder, CO, Westview Press.

Larguia, I. and Dumoulin, J. (1985) Women's Equality and the Cuban Revolution, in J. Nash and H. Safa (eds) *Women and Change in Latin America*, South Hadley, MA, Bergin and Garvey.

Lazreg, M. (1988) Feminism and difference: the perils of writing as a woman on women in Algeria, *Feminist Studies*, 14 (1): 81–107.

Leftwich, A. (1993) Governance, democracy and development in the Third World, *Third World Quarterly*, 14 (3): 605–24.

Lever, H. and Huhne, C. (1985) *Debt and Danger: The World Financial Crisis*, Harmondsworth, Penguin.

Leys, C. (1975) *Underdevelopment in Kenya: The Political Economy of Neo-Colonialism*, London, Heinemann.

Liatto-Katundu, B. (1993) The women's lobby and gender relations in Zambia, *Review of African Political Economy*, 56: 79–83.

Liddle, J. (1992) Women and nationalism under the British Raj, paper delivered at the Gender and Colonialism Conference, Galway, May.

Liddle, J. and Joshi, R. (1986) *Daughters of Independence: Gender, Caste and Class in India*, London, Zed.

Lim, L. (1990) Women's work in export factories: the politics of a cause, in I. Tinker (ed.) *Persistent Inequalities: Women and World Development*, Oxford, Oxford University Press.

Lonsdale, J. and Berman, B. (1979) Coping with the contradictions: the development of the colonial state in Kenya 1895–1914, *Journal of African History*, 20: 487–505.

Loomba, A. (1993) Dead women tell no tales: issues of female subjectivity, subaltern agency and tradition in colonial and post-colonial writings in widow immolation in India, *History Workshop Journal*, 36: 209–27.

Loveman, B. (1991) Mision cumplida? Civil military relations and the Chilean political transition, *Journal of Inter-American Studies and World Affairs*, 33 (3): 35–74.

Lovett, M. (1990) Gender relations, class formation and the colonial state in Africa, in J. Parpart and K. Staudt (eds) *Women and the State in Africa*, Boulder, CO, Lynne Rienner.

McClintock, A. (1993) Family feuds: gender, nationalism and the family, *Feminist Review*, 44: 61–80.

McGrew, A. (1992) The Third World in the new global order, in R. Allen and A. Thomas (eds) *Poverty and Development in the 1990s*, Oxford, Oxford University Press.

Mackinnon, C. (1983) Feminism, Marxism, method and the state: toward a feminist jurisprudence, *Signs*, 8: 635–58.

Mainwaring, S. (1987) Urban popular movements, identity and democratization in Brazil, *Comparative Political Studies*, 20 (2): 131–59.

Mainwaring, S., O'Donnell, G. and Valenzuela, J.S. (eds) (1992) *Issues in Democratic Consolidation: The New South American Democracies in Comparative Perspective*, Notre Dame, IN, University of Notre Dame Press.

Mani, L. (1987) Contentious traditions: the debate on sati in colonial India, *Cultural Critique*, fall: 119–56.

Manicom, L. (1992) Ruling relations: rethinking state and gender in South African history, *Journal of African History*, 33: 441–65.

Matear, A. (1993) SERNAM: women and the process of democratic transition in Chile 1990–93, paper presented at Society of Latin American Studies Annual Conference, Manchester, April.

Mattelart, M. (1980) Chile: the feminine version of the coup d'etat, in H. Nash and J. Safa (eds) *Sex and Class in Latin America*, South Hadley, MA, Bergin and Garvey.

Mba, N. (1990) Kaba and khaki: women and the militarized state in Nigeria, in J. Parpart and K. Staudt (eds) *Women and the State in Africa*, Boulder, CO, Lynne Rienner.

Mies, M. (1982) *Lacemakers of Narsapur*, London, Zed Press.

Mies, M. (1986) *Patriarchy and Accumulation on a World Scale: Women in the International Division of Labour*, London, Zed Press.

Migdal, J. (1988) *Strong Societies and Weak States: State-Society Relations and State Capabilities in the Third World*, Princeton, NJ, Princeton University Press.

Miller, F. (1991) *Latin American Women and the Search for Social Justice*, Hanover, NE, University Press of New England.

Mitter, S. (1986) *Common Fate, Common Bond: Women in the Global Economy*, London, Pluto Press.

Moghadam, V. (1994) Introduction: Women and Identity Politics in Theoretical and Comparative Perspective, in V. Moghadam (ed.) *Identity Politics and Women: Cultural Reassertions and Feminisms in International Perspective*, Boulder, CO, Westview Press.

Mohanty, C. (1988) Under Western eyes: feminist scholarship and colonial discourses, *Feminist Review*, 30: 61–88.

Mohanty, C. (1991) Introduction: cartographies of struggle: Third World women and the politics of feminism, in C. Mohánty, A. Russo and L. Torres (eds) *Third World Women and the Politics of Feminism*, Bloomington, IN, Indiana University Press.

Mohanty, C. and Mohanty, S.P. (1990) Contradictions of colonialism, *Women's Review of Books*, 7 (6): 19–20.

Molina, N. (1989) Propuestas políticas y orientaciones de cambio en la situación de la mujer, in M.A. Garretón (ed.) *Propuestas Políticas y Demandas Sociales*, vol. 3, Santiago, FLACSO.

Molyneux, M. (1981) Socialist societies old and new: progress towards women's emancipation, *Feminist Review*, 8: 1–34.

Molyneux, M. (1985a) Mobilization without emancipation? Women's interest, the state and revolution in Nicaragua, *Feminist Studies*, 11 (2): 227–54.

Molyneux, M. (1985b) Family reform in socialist states: the hidden agenda, *Feminist Review*, 21: 47–66.

Molyneux, M. (1985c) Women, in T. Walker (ed.) *Nicaragua: the First Five Years*, New York, Praeger.

Molyneux, M. (1988) The politics of abortion in Nicaragua: revolutionary pragmatism or feminism in the realm of necessity? *Feminist Review*, 29: 114–32.

Molyneux, M. (1989) Women's role in the Nicaraguan revolutionary process, the early years, in S. Kruks, R. Rapp and M. Young (eds) *Promissory Notes: Women in the Transition to Socialism*, New York, Monthly Review Press.

Montecino, S. and Rossetti, J. (eds) (1990) *Tramas para un Nuevo Destino: Propuestas de la Concertación de Mujeres por la Democracia*, Santiago, Chile.

Moore, B. (1967) *The Social Origins of Dictatorship and Democracy*, London, Allen Lane.

Moraga, C. and Anzaldua, G. (eds) (1983) *This Bridge Called My Back: Writings by Radical Women of Color*, New York, Kitchen Table Women of Color Press.

Moser, C.O.N. (1991) Gender planning in the Third World: meeting practical and strategic needs, in R. Grant and K. Newland (eds) *Gender and International Relations*, Milton Keynes, Open University Press.

Moser, C.O.N. (1993) *Gender Planning and Development: Theory, Practice and Training*, London, Routledge.

Munachonga, M. (1990) Women and the state: Zambia's development policies and their impact on women, in J. Parpart and K. Staudt (eds) *Women and the State in Africa*, Boulder, CO, Lynne Rienner.

Munizaga, G. and Letelier, L. (1988) Mujer y regimen militar, in Centro de Estudios de la Mujer (ed.) *Mundo de Mujer: Continuidad y Cambio*, Santiago, CEM.

Nash, J. (1980) Aztec women: the transition from status to class in empire and colony, in M. Etienne and E. Leacock (eds) *Women and Colonization: Anthropological Perspectives*, New York, Praeger.

Nasimiyu, R. (1993) The History of Maendeleo ya Wanawake movement in Kenya, in S.A. Khasiani and E.I. Njiro (eds) *The Women's Movement in Kenya*, Nairobi, AAWORD.

National Union of Eritrean Women (1983) Women and revolution in Eritrea, in M. Davies (ed.) *Third World, Second Sex*, London, Zed Press.

Navarro, M. (1989) The personal is political: Las Madres de Plaza de Mayo, in S. Eckstein (ed.) *Power and Popular Protest: Latin American Social Movements*, Berkeley, CA, University of California Press.

Nazzari, M. (1989) The 'woman question' in Cuba: an analysis of material constraints on its resolution, in S. Kruks, R. Rapp and M. Young (eds) *Promissory Notes: Women in the Transition to Socialism*, New York, Monthly Review Press.

Nelson, B. and Chowdhury, N. (eds) (1994) *Women and Politics Worldwide*, New Haven, CT, Yale University Press.

Nicholson, L. (ed.) (1990) *Feminism/Postmodernism*, London, Routledge.

Nun, J. (1967) The middle class military coup, in C. Veliz (ed.) *The Politics of Conformity in Latin America*, Oxford, Oxford University Press.

Nzomo, M. (1993) The Kenya women's movement in a changing political context, in S.A. Khasiani and E.I. Njiro (eds) *The Women's Movement in Kenya*, Nairobi, AAWORD.

Nzomo, M. and Staudt, K. (1994) Man-made political machinery in Kenya: political space for women? in B. Nelson and N. Chowdhury (eds) *Women and Politics Worldwide*, New Haven, CT, Yale University Press.

O'Barr, J. (1984) African women in politics, in M. Hay and S. Stichter (eds) *African Women South of the Sahara*, London, Longman.

O'Brien, D. (1972) Modernisation, order and the erosion of a democratic ideal: American political science 1960–1970, *Journal of Development Studies*, 8 (2): 351–78.

O'Brien, P. and Cammack, P. (eds) (1985) *Generals in Retreat: The Crisis of Military Rule in Latin America*, Manchester, Manchester University Press.

O'Brien, P. and Roddick, J. (1983) *Chile: The Pinochet Decade*, London, Latin America Bureau.

O'Donnell, G. (1977) Corporatism and the question of the state, in J. Malloy (ed.) *Authoritarianism and Corporatism in Latin America*, Pittsburgh, PA, University of Pittsburgh Press.

O'Donnell, G. (1979) Tensions in the bureaucratic authoritarian state and the question of democracy, in D. Collier (ed.) *The New Authoritarianism in Latin America*, Princeton, NJ, Princeton University Press.

O'Donnell, G. (1986) Introduction to the Latin American cases, in G. O'Donnell, P. Schmitter and L. Whitehead (eds) *Transitions from Authoritarian Rule*, vol. 2, Baltimore, MD, Johns Hopkins University Press.

O'Donnell, G. and Schmitter, P. (1986) Tentative conclusions and uncertain democracies, in G. O'Donnell, P. Schmitter and L. Whitehead (eds) *Transitions from Authoritarian Rule*, vol. 4, Baltimore, MD, Johns Hopkins University Press.

O'Donnell, G., Schmitter, P. and Whitehead, L. (eds) (1986) *Transitions from Authoritarian Rule*, 4 vols. Baltimore, MD, Johns Hopkins University Press.

Okeyo, A. (1980) Daughters of the lakes and rivers: colonization and the land rights of Luo women, in M. Etienne and E. Leacock (eds) *Women and Colonization: Anthropological Perspectives*, New York, Praeger.

Okonjo, K. (1976) The dual sex political system in operation: Igbo women and community politics in midwestern Nigeria, in N.J. Hafkin and E.G. Bay (eds) *Women in Africa: Studies in Social and Economic Change*, Stanford, CA, Stanford University Press.

Okonjo, K. (1994) Reversing the marginalization of the invisible and silent majority: women in politics in Nigeria, in B. Nelson and N. Chowdhury (eds) *Women and Politics Worldwide*, New Haven, CT, Yale University Press.

Ong, A. (1988) Colonialism and modernity: feminist representations of women in non-Western societies, *Inscriptions*, 3/4: 79–93.

Ostergaard, L. (ed.) (1992) *Gender and Development: A Practical Guide*, London, Routledge.

Oxhorn, P. (1989) Democratic transitions and the democratization process in Chile, unpublished PhD thesis, Cambridge, MA, Harvard University.

Padula, A. and Smith, L. (1985) Women in socialist Cuba 1959–1984, in S. Halebsky and J. Kirk (eds) *Cuba: Twenty Five Years of Revolution 1959–1984*, New York, Praeger.

Palmer, I. (1992) Gender equity and economic efficiency in adjustment programmes, in H. Afshar and C. Dennis (eds) *Women and Adjustment Policies in the Third World*, Basingstoke, Macmillan.

Park, K.A. (1993) Women and development: the case of South Korea, *Comparative Politics*, 25 (2): 127–45.

Parker, A., Russo, M., Sommer, D. and Yaeger, P. (eds) (1992) Introduction, *Nationalisms and Sexualities*, London, Routledge.

Parpart, J. (1986) Class and gender on the Copperbelt: women in Northern Rhodesian copper mining communities, 1926–1964, in C. Robertson and I. Berger (eds) *Women and Class in Africa*, New York, Holmes and Meier.

Parpart, J. (1988) Women and the state, in D. Rothchild and N. Chazan (eds) *The Precarious Balance: State and Society in Africa*, Boulder, CO, Westview Press.

Parpart, J. (1993) Who is the Other?: A postmodern feminist critique of women and development theory and practice, *Development and Change*, 24: 439–64.

Parpart, J. and Staudt, K. (eds) (1990) *Women and the State in Africa*, Boulder, CO, Lynne Rienner.

Pateman, C. (1983a) Feminist critiques of the public/private dichotomy, in S. Benn and G. Gaus (eds) *The Public and Private in Social Life*, London, Croom Helm.

Pateman, C. (1983b) Feminism and democracy, in G. Duncan (ed.) *Democratic Theory and Practice*, Cambridge, Cambridge University Press.

Pateman, C. (1989) *The Disorder of Women: Democracy, Feminism and Political Theory*, Cambridge, Polity Press.

Payne, A. and Sutton, P. (eds) (1993) Introduction, *Modern Caribbean Politics*, Baltimore, MD, Johns Hopkins University Press.

Peake, L. (1993) The development and role of women's political organizations in Guyana, in J. Momsen (ed.) *Women and Change in the Caribbean*, London, James Currey.

Peterson, V. and Runyan, A. (1993) *Global Gender Issues*, Boulder, CO, Westview Press.

Peterson, V.S. (ed.) (1992) *Gendered States: Feminist (Re)Visions of International Relations Theory*, Boulder, CO, Lynne Rienner.

Petras, J. (1990) The redemocratization process, in S. Jonas and N. Stein (eds) *Democracy in Latin America: Visions and Realities*, New York, Bergin and Garvey.

Petras, J. and Leiva, F. (1988) Chile: the authoritarian transition to electoral politics, *Latin American Perspectives*, 15 (3): 97–114.

Philip, G. (1984) The fall of the Argentine military, *Third World Quarterly*, 6 (3): 624–37.

Posner, D. (1995) Malawi's new dawn, *Journal of Democracy*, 6 (1): 134–45.

Potter, D. (1992) Superpower rivalry in South Asia and southern Africa, in A.G. McGrew and P.G. Lewis (eds) *Global Politics*, Oxford, Polity Press.

Presley, C. (1986) Labor unrest among Kikuyu women in colonial Kenya, in C. Robertson and I. Berger (eds) *Women and Class in Africa*, New York, Holmes and Meier.

Presley, C. (1992) *Kikuyu Women, the Mau Mau Rebellion and Social Change in Kenya*, Boulder, CO, Westview Press.

Pringle, R. and Watson, S. (1992) Women's interests and the post-structuralist state, in M. Barrett and A. Phillips (eds) *Destabilizing Theory: Contemporary Feminist Debates*, Cambridge, Polity Press.

Radcliffe, S. and Westwood, S. (eds) (1993) *Viva: Women and Popular Protest in Latin America*, London, Routledge.

Rai, S. (1995) Women and public power: women in the Indian parliament, *IDS Bulletin*, 26 (3): 110–16.

Ramos, C. (1994) Genero e historia: la histiografia sobre la mujer, paper presented at Latin American Cross Currents on Gender Theory, Portsmouth, July.

Ramusack, B. (1992) Cultural missionaries, maternal imperialists, feminist allies: British women activists in India, in N. Chaudhuri and M. Strobel (eds) *Western Women and Imperialism: Complicity and Resistance*, Bloomington, IN, Indiana University Press.

Randall, M. (1992) *Gathering Rage: The Failure of Twentieth Century Revolutions to Develop a Feminist Agenda*, New York, Monthly Review Press.

Randall, V. and Theobald, R. (1985) *Political Change and Underdevelopment: A Critical Introduction to Third World Politics*, London, Macmillan.

Randall, V. (1987) *Women and Politics*, 2nd edn, London, Macmillan.

Ranger, T. (1983) The invention of tradition in colonial Africa, in E. Hobsbawm and T. Ranger (eds) *The Invention of Tradition*, Cambridge, Cambridge University Press.

Ravenhill, J. (1990) The North–South balance of power, *International Affairs*, 66 (4): 732–48.

Reddock, R. (1985) Women and slavery in the Caribbean: a feminist perspective, *Latin American Perspectives*, 12 (1): 63–80.

Reddock, R. (1993) Transformation in the needle trades: women in garment and textile production in early twentieth century Trinidad, in J. Momsen (ed.) *Women and Change in the Caribbean*, London, James Currey.

Reif, L. (1986) Women in Latin American guerrilla movements: a comparative perspective, *Comparative Politics*, 18 (2): 147–69.

Remmer, K. (1991) New wine or old bottlenecks, *Comparative Politics*, 23: 479–95.

Richter, L. (1990–1) Exploring theories of female leadership in south and south east Asia, *Pacific Affairs*, 63 (4): 524–40.

Riley, D. (1988) *Am I That Name: Feminism and the Category of 'Women' in History*, London, Macmillan.

Roberts, P. (1987) The state and the regulation of marriage: Sefwi Wiawso (Ghana), 1900–40, in H. Afshar (ed.) *Women, State and Ideology*, Basingstoke, Macmillan.

Robertson, C. (1976) Women and socio-economic change in Accra, Ghana, in N.J. Hafkin and E.G. Bay (eds) *Women in Africa: Studies in Social and Economic Change*, Stanford, CA, Stanford University Press.

Robertson, C. and Berger, I. (eds) (1986) *Women and Class in Africa*, New York, Holmes and Meier.

Roddick, J. (1988) *The Dance of the Millions*, London, Latin America Bureau.

Roddick, J. and O'Brien, P. (1983) *The Pinochet Decade*, London, Latin America Bureau.

Rodney, W. (1972) *How Europe Underdeveloped Africa*, London/Dar es Salaam, Bogle L'Ouverture Publications/Tanzania Publishing House.

Rodriguez, L. (1991) The old politics are obsolete: an interview with Laura Rodriguez, *Report on the Americas*, XXV (1): 6–7.

Rogers, B. (1980) *The Domestication of Women: Discrimination in Developing Societies*, London, Kogan Page.

Rothchild, D. and Chazan, N. (eds) (1988) *The Precarious Balance: State and Society in Africa*, Boulder, CO, Westview Press.

Ruddick, S. (1989) *Maternal Thinking: Towards a Politics of Peace*, London, The Women's Press.

Rueschemeyer, D., Stephens, E. and Stephens, J. (1992) *Capitalist Development and Democracy*, Cambridge, Polity Press.

Rustow, D. (1970) Transitions to democracy: towards a dynamic model, *Comparative Politics*, 2 (3): 337–63.

Saa, M.A. (1990) Interview, *Crítica Social*, May: 32–8.

Safa, H. (1990) Women's social movements in Latin America, *Gender and Society*, 4 (3): 354–69.

Said, E. (1978) *Orientalism*, London, Routledge and Kegan Paul.

Sangari, K. and Vaid, S. (eds) (1990) *Recasting Women: Essays in Indian Colonial History*, New Brunswick, NJ, Rutgers University Press.

Saporta, N., Navarro, M., Chuckryk, P. and Alvarez, S. (1992) Feminisms in Latin America: from Bogota to San Bernardo, *Signs*, 17 (2): 393–434.

Schild, V. (1991) The hidden politics of neighbourhood organizations: women and local level participation in the poblaciones of Chile, *North/South*, 30: 137–58.

Schild, V. (1992) Struggling for citizenship in Chile: a 'Resurrection' of civil society, paper presented to Latin American Studies Association Congress, Los Angeles, September.

Schild, V. (1994) 'Becoming subjects of rights': citizenship, political learning and identity formation among Latin American women, paper for XVIth IPSA Congress, Berlin, August.

Schirmer, J. (1989) Those who die for life cannot be called dead: women and human rights protest in Latin America, *Feminist Review*, 32: 3–29.

Schirmer, J. (1993) The seeking of truth and the gendering of consciousness: the

Comadres of El Salvador and the CONAVIGUA widows of Guatemala, in S. Radcliffe and S. Westwood (eds) *Viva: Women and Popular Protest in Latin America*, London, Routledge.

Scott, J. (1986) Gender: a useful category of historical analysis, *American Historical Review*, 91 (5): 1053–75.

Scott, J. (1988) Deconstructing equality versus difference, *Feminist Studies*, 14 (1): 33–50.

Scott, J. (1992) Experience, in J. Butler and J. Scott (eds) *Feminists Theorize the Political*, London, Routledge.

Seager, J. and Olson, A. (1986) *Women in the World: An International Atlas*, London, Pan Books.

Seers, D. (1979) The meaning of development, in D. Lehmann (ed.) *Development Theory: Four Critical Studies*, London, Frank Cass.

Seidman, G. (1984) Women in Zimbabwe: post independence struggles, *Feminist Studies*, 10 (3): 419–40.

Seidman, G. (1993) 'No freedom without the women': mobilization and gender in South Africa, 1970–1972, *Signs*, 18 (2): 291–320.

Sen, A.K. (1990) Gender and cooperative conflicts, in I. Tinker (ed.) *Persistent Inequalities: Women and World Development*, Oxford, Oxford University Press.

Sen, S. (1993) Motherhood and mothercraft: gender and nationalism in Bengal, *Gender and History*, 5 (2): 231–43.

Sen, G. and Grown, C. (1987) *Development, Crises and Alternative Visions: Third World Women's Perspectives*, London, Earthscan Publications.

Serrano, C. (1990) Chile: entre la autonomia y la integración, in *Transiciones: Mujeres en los Procesos Democraticos*, Santiago, Isis Internacional.

Showstack-Sassoon, A. (ed.) (1987) *Women and the State*, London, Hutchinson.

Silkin, T. (1983) Eritrea: women in struggle, *Third World Quarterly*, 5 (4): 909–15.

Silverberg, H. (1990) What happened to the feminist revolution in political science? *Western Political Quarterly*, 43 (4): 887–903.

Sinha, M. (1992) Chathams, Pitts and Gladstones in petticoats: the politics of gender and race in the Ilbert Bill Controversy, 1883–1884, in N. Chaudhuri and M. Strobel (eds) *Western Women and Imperialism: Complicity and Resistance*, Bloomington, IN, Indiana University Press.

Skocpol, T. (1979) *States and Social Revolutions*, Cambridge, Cambridge University Press.

Skocpol, T. (1985) Bringing the state back in: strategies of analysis in current research, in P. Evans, D. Rueschemeyer and T. Skocpol (eds) *Bringing the State Back in*, Cambridge, Cambridge University Press.

Slater, D. (ed.) (1985) *New Social Movements and the State*, Amsterdam, CEDLA.

Smelser, N.J. (1968) Toward a theory of modernization, in N.J. Smelser (ed.) *Essays in Sociological Explanation*, Englewood Cliffs, NJ, Prentice Hall.

Smith, L. (1992) Sexuality and socialism in Cuba, in S. Halebsky and J. Kirk (eds) *Cuba in Transition: Crisis and Transformation*, Boulder, CO, Westview Press.

Smith, W. (1989) *Authoritarianism and the Crisis of Argentine Political Economy*, Stanford, CA, Stanford University Press.

Snyder, R. (1992) Explaining transitions from neopatrimonial dictatorships, *Comparative Politics*, 24 (4): 401–17.

Spero, J.E. (1990) *The Politics of International Economic Relations*, 4th edn, London, Routledge.

Spivak, G. (1987) *In Other Worlds: Essays in Cultural Politics*, London, Routledge.

Staudt, K. (1986) Stratification: implications for women's politics, in C. Robertson and I. Berger (eds) *Women and Class in Africa*, New York, Holmes and Meier.

Staudt, K. (1989a) Gender politics in the bureaucracy: theoretical issues in comparative perspective, in K. Staudt (ed.) *Women, International Development and Politics*, Philadelphia, PA, Temple University Press.

Staudt, K. (1989b) The state and gender in colonial Africa, in S. Charlton, J. Everett and K. Staudt (eds) *Women, State and Development*, Albany, NY, SUNY Press.

Sternbach, N.S., Navarro-Aranguen, M., Chuchryk, P. and Alvarez, S. (1992) Feminisms in Latin America: from Bogota to San Bernardo, *Signs*, 17 (2): 393–434.

Stewart, F. (1992) Can adjustment programmes incorporate the interests of women? in H. Afshar and C. Dennis (eds) *Women and Adjustment Policies in the Third World*, Basingstoke, Macmillan.

Stiehm, J. (1982) The protected, the protector, the defender, *Women's Studies International Forum*, 5 (3/4): 367–76.

Stoler, A. (1989) Making empire respectable: the politics of race and sexual morality in 20th-century colonial cultures, *American Ethnologist*, 16 (4): 634–60.

Strobel, M. (1991) *European Women and the Second British Empire*, Bloomington, IN, Indiana University Press.

Stubbs, J. (1994) Cuba: revolutionizing women, family and power, in B. Nelson and N. Chowdhury (eds) *Women and Politics Worldwide*, New Haven, CT, Yale University Press.

Swinburne, C. (1995) Waving not drowning, *Everywoman*, March: 21.

Sylvester, C. (1990) The emperor's theories and transformations: looking at the field through feminist lenses, in D. Pirages and C. Sylvester (eds), *Transformations in Global Political Economy*, London, Macmillan.

Sylvester, C. (1994) *Feminist Theory and International Relations in the Post Modern Era*, Cambridge, Cambridge University Press.

Tabak, F. (1984) Women and authoritarian regimes, in J. Hicks Stiehm (ed.) *Women's Views of the Political World of Men*, Dobbs Ferry, NY, Transaction Publishers.

Thapar, S. (1993) Women as activists, women as symbols: a study of the Indian nationalist movement, *Feminist Review*, 44, summer: 81–96.

Tickner, J.A. (1992) *Gender in International Relations: Feminist Perspectives on Achieving Global Security*, New York, Columbia University Press.

Tinker, I. (1976) The adverse effect of development on women, in I. Tinker and M. Bramsen (eds) *Women and World Development*, Washington DC, Overseas Development Council.

Tinker, I. (ed.) (1990) *Persistent Inequalities: Women and World Development*, Oxford, Oxford University Press.

Toye, J. (1987) *The Dilemmas of Development: Reflections on the Counter Revolution in Development Theory*, Oxford, Basil Blackwell.

United Nations (1991) *The World's Women 1970–90: Trends and Statistics, Social Statistics and Indicators*, series K, no. 8, New York, United Nations.

Urdang, S. (1979) *Fighting Two Colonialisms, Women in Guinea-Bissau*, New York, Monthly Review Press.

Urdang, S. (1984a) Women in national liberation movements, in M. Hay and S. Stichter (eds) *African Women South of the Sahara*, London, Longman.

Urdang, S. (1984b) The last transition? Women and development in Mozambique, *Review of African Political Economy*, 27/28: 8–32.

Urdang, S. (1989) *And still they dance: Women, war and the struggle for change in Mozambique*, London, Earthscan Publications.

Valenzuela, M.E. (1992) Women and the democratization process in Chile, paper presented at the *Conference on Women and the Transition from Authoritarian Rule in Latin America and Eastern Europe*, Berkeley, CA, December.

Valenzuela, J. and Valenzuela, A. (eds) (1987) *Military Rule in Chile: Dictatorship and Oppositions*, Baltimore, MD, Johns Hopkins University Press.

Valenzuela, M.E. (1990) Mujeres y política: logros y tensiones en el proceso de redemocratización, *Proposiciones*, 18: 210–32.

Valenzuela, M.E. (1991) The evolving roles of women under military rule, in P. Drake and I. Jaksic (eds) *The Struggle for Democracy in Chile*, Lincoln, NB, University of Nebraska Press.

Van Allen, J. (1972) Sitting on a man: colonialism and the lost political institutions of Igbo women, *Canadian Journal of African Studies*, 6 (2): 165–82.

Van Allen, J. (1976) 'Aba Riots' or Igbo 'Women's War'? ideology, stratification, and the invisibility of women, in N.J. Hafkin and E.G. Bay (eds) *Women in Africa: Studies in Social and Economic Change*, Stanford, CA, Stanford University Press.

van de Walle, N. (1994) Political liberalization and economic policy reform in Africa, *World Development*, 22 (4): 483–500.

Vargas, V. (1991) The women's movement in Peru: streams, spaces and knots, *European Review of Latin American and Caribbean Studies*, 50: 7–50.

Vargas, V. (1992) Women: tragic encounters with the Left, *Report on the Americas*, XXV (5): 30–5.

Walker, C. (1982) *Women and Resistance in South Africa*, London, Onyx Press.

Walker, C. (1990) Gender and the development of the migrant labour system c.1850–1930, in C. Walker (ed.) *Women and Gender in Southern Africa to 1945*, Cape Town, David Philip.

Walker, C. (1994) Women, 'tradition' and reconstruction, *Review of African Political Economy*, 61: 347–58.

Warren, B. (1980) *Imperialism: Pioneer of Capitalism*, London, Verso.

Watson, S. (1990) *Playing the State*, London, Verso.

Waylen, G. (1986) Women and neoliberalism, in J. Evans et al. (eds) *Feminism and Political Theory*, London, Sage.

Waylen, G. (1992a) Rethinking women's political participation and protest: Chile 1970–90, *Political Studies*, 40 (2): 299–314.

Waylen, G. (1992b) Women, authoritarianism and market liberalization in Chile 1973–1989, in H. Afshar and C. Dennis (eds) *Women and Adjustment Policies in the Third World*, Basingstoke, Macmillan.

Waylen, G. (1993) Women's movements and democratisation in Latin America, *Third World Quarterly*, 14 (3): 573–88.

Waylen, G. (1994) Women and democratization: conceptualising gender relations in transition politics, *World Politics*, 46 (3): 327–54.

Waylen, G. (1995) Women's movements, the state and democratization in Chile, *IDS Bulletin*, 26 (3): 86–93.

Weiner, M. (ed.) (1966) *Modernization*, New York, Basic Books.

Wessel, L. (1991) Reproductive rights in Nicaragua: from the Sandinistas to the government of Violeta Chamorro, *Feminist Studies*, 17 (3): 537–49.

Wheelwright, J. (1993) Winning the peace, paper presented to the PSA/DSA Day School on Women and Politics, York, May.

White, C. (1989) Vietnam: war, socialism and the politics of gender relations, in S. Kruks, R. Rapp and M. Young (eds) *Promissory Notes: Women in the Transition to Socialism*, New York, Monthly Review Press.

Whitehead, A. (1990) Food crisis and gender conflict in the African countryside, in H. Bernstein, B. Crow, M. Mackintosh and C. Martin (eds) *The Food Question: Profits versus People?* London, Earthscan Publications.

Williams, M. (1994) *International Economic Organisations and the Third World*, Hemel Hempstead, Harvester Wheatsheaf.

Wilson, E. (1977) *Women and the Welfare State*, London, Tavistock.

Wipper, A. (1984) Women's voluntary associations, in M. Hay and S. Stichter (eds) *African Women South of the Sahara*, London, Longman.

Wiseman, J. (1993) Democracy and the new political pluralism in Africa: causes, consequences and significance, *Third World Quarterly*, 14 (3): 439–49.

Wolf, E. (1982) *Europe and the People Without History*, Berkeley, CA, University of California Press.

Wolkowitz, C. (1987) Controlling women's access to political power: a case study in Andhra Pradesh, India, in H. Afshar (ed.) *Women State and Ideology*, London, Macmillan.

Worsley, P. (1979) How many worlds? *Third World Quarterly*, 1 (2): 100–7.

Young, C. (1994) Zaire: the shattered illusion of the integral state, *Journal of Modern African Studies*, 32 (2): 247–63.

Young, K. (1978) Modes of appropriation and the sexual division of labour: A casestudy from Oaxaca, Mexico, in A. Kuhn and A.M. Wolpe (eds) *Feminism and Materialism*, London, Routledge and Kegan Paul.

Young, K. (1982) The creation of a relative surplus population: a casestudy from Mexico, in L. Beneria (ed.) *Women and Development: The Sexual Division of Labour in Rural Societies*, New York, Praeger.

Young, K. (1992) Household resource management, in L. Ostergaard (ed.) *Gender and Development: A Practical Guide*, London, Routledge.

Young, K., Wolkowitz, C. and McCullagh, R. (eds) (1981) *Of Marriage and the Market: Women's Subordination in International Perspective*, London, CSE Books.

Yuval-Davis, N. and Anthias, F. (eds) (1989) *Women–Nation–State*, London, Macmillan.

Index